Words of the Huron

Words of the Huron

John L. Steckley

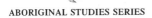

ABORIGINAL STUDIES SERIES

Wilfrid Laurier University Press

WLU

We acknowledge the financial support of the Government of Canada through the Book Publishing Industry Development Program for our publishing activities.

Library and Archives Canada Cataloguing in Publication

Steckley, John L., 1949–
    Words of the Huron / John L. Steckley.

(Aboriginal studies)
Includes bibliographical references and index.
ISBN-13: 978-0-88920-516-1
ISBN-10: 0-88920-516-7

    1. Wyandot Indians—Languages—History—17th century. 2. Wyandot Indians—Intellectual life—17th century. 3. Wyandot Indians—Social life and customs—17th century. 4. Wyandot Indians—Material culture—History—17th century. I. Title. II. Series: Aboriginal studies series (Waterloo, Ont.)

PM1366.S68 2007   497'.555   C2006-906951-4

Cover design by P.J. Woodland. Text design by Catharine Bonas-Taylor.

∞

This book is printed on Ancient Forest Friendly paper (100% post-consumer recycled).

Printed in Canada

Every reasonable effort has been made to acquire permission for copyright material used in this text, and to acknowledge all such indebtedness accurately. Any errors and omissions called to the publisher's attention will be corrected in future printings.

Contents

Jesuit Symbols and Their Function

SYMBOL	NAME	SOUND
ι	iota subscriptum	-y-
θ	theta	-t- plus post-aspiration
χ	chi	-k- plus post-aspiration
8	-ou-	-w- before vowels and -u- before consonants
ʼ	pre-aspiration	like an -h-
on	nasal -o-	like in French word 'bon'
en	nasal -e-	like in French word 'bien'
an	nasal -a-	like in French word 'chanter'
in	nasal -i-	like in French word 'vin'

OTHER SYMBOLS

* indicates a word or word part that is hypothesized by linguists but not supported by direct evidence

Introduction

The Huron: A Familiar People

The Huron are a familiar people to Canadian readers. Many of us studied them in grade six, where we learned that they grew corn, beans, and squash, lived in longhouses, and used canoes as transportation. From the maps we saw in our classrooms, we may be forgiven for having thought that the Huron still had communities in Ontario (they don't). In grade eight, we may have learned their key role in the fur trade. From the way the story was told, we may be forgiven for thinking that the Huron became extinct, as a number of textbooks still say, rather than continuing on and thriving in contemporary communities in Quebec, Kansas, and Oklahoma. Read the following from a recently published anthropology textbook as an example:

> As the fur trade moved westward, competition between France and England for fur increased. This, in turn, led to rivalries in which some indigenous groups, such as *the Huron, were wiped out*. (Schultz and Lavenda 2005:68; emphasis mine)

At a loftier college and university level, many people have read the stellar works of Bruce Trigger, who has done more than anyone else to advance our knowledge of the Huron. A classic bestseller in the ethnographic case study literature is his *Huron: Farmers of the North*, first published in the Holt, Rinehart and Winston series of anthropological case studies in 1969 and then in a revised version in 1990. Trigger's two-volume study *The Children of Aataentsic*, which appeared in 1976, outlined the Huron story from pre-contact to the dispersal of the Huron midway through the seventeenth century. He told their story in such a comprehensive way that the work has become a must-read for all later scholars and other students of the Huron.

In another mode of learning, we "know" the Huron from the "Huron Carol," written during this missionary period (probably around 1640), most likely by Father Jean de Brébeuf, the first Jesuit to learn the language, then completely reworded in English into the form familiar to us by J. E. Middleton in the 1920s. The "Huron Carol" forms a distinct part of North American Christmas culture, especially in Canada. It is possibly the most often recorded Canadian song.

Further, each year, thousands of schoolchildren, tourists, and Catholic pilgrims learn of the Huron in Ontario at the popular historic site of Sainte-Marie-Among-the-Hurons in Midland, where the Jesuits had their mission community from 1639 to 1649, and at the related sites of the Huron Village and the Martyr's Shrine, also in Midland.

There are two primary forms of evidence that have been used in constructing our knowledge of the Huron: archaeological evidence[1] and missionary literature.

The most important literary source is the *Jesuit Relations and Allied Documents* (1899 and 1959), a seventy-three-volume collection composed. mainly of annual reports compiled and edited by the Superior of the Jesuit order in New France. A good number of those volumes (numbers ten, thirteen, seventeen and twenty-one come immediately to my mind) are dedicated exclusively to discussing the Huron mission. The other main mission document is Récollet Brother Gabriel Sagard's *Long Journey to the Country of the Hurons* (1939), based on Sagard's life with the Huron from 1623 to 1624. Scholars such as historical geographer Conrad Heidenreich and anthropologists Elisabeth Tooker and Bruce Trigger have mined these sources well. Contemporary Huron scholar Georges E. Sioui[2] has shed new interpretive light on the lives of their ancestors.

Learning the Huron Language

It is now more than thirty years since I decided to learn the Huron language. I began when I was a graduate student in linguistic anthropology at the University of Toronto in the academic year 1973–74. My exposure to Aboriginal languages prior to that had been taking a one-year informal course in Ojibwe (a language unrelated to Huron) at what was then called the Indian Friendship Centre in downtown Toronto, not far from the university. I learned from elder Fred Wheatley, then working as a janitor for the University of Toronto. (Later, when his encyclopedic knowledge of what he referred to as "Oxford Ojibwe" became recognized, he would teach the language to Native studies students at Trent University.) I was working as a teaching assistant for Roy Wright, a brilliant and eccentric linguist who was working on, among many other projects, a computerized dictionary based on the Wyandot-language fieldnotes of Marius Barbeau. In the early twentieth century Barbeau had done fieldwork with the last speakers of Wyandot, a dialect of Huron, in Oklahoma. The people had been driven a long way since they had lived by the shores of Georgian Bay, Ontario.

Roy hired me to help him with the dictionary. As I entered the words on the old data entry cards, and with a mind that often wanders, I began to learn the language. I discovered that, although the language was dead, there were many documents discussing and recording the language, and I was hooked. I obtained a copy of the 1920 Ontario Archive Report that contained a Huron dictionary, grammar, and collection of missionary texts put together by eighteenth-century Jesuit missionary linguist Father Pierre Potier. Throughout the 1970s, I collected a series of seventeenth-century manuscript dictionaries that, fortunately for me, had been put on microfilm by Victor Hanzelli as part of a project on missionary linguistics.

Recognition for my early work came easily. Within two years I had presented a paper on the language twice and received a great deal of respect, not necessarily for the quality of my work (it was flawed) but for the novelty of my project. That paper became my first academic article, published in 1978. Learning the Huron language did not come so easily. I struggled with the seventeenth- and eighteenth-century French into which the Huron words were translated as well as the Latin. My Latin—often used in the dictionaries to explain grammatical points (as well as translating dirty words)—was non-existent. I had no elders to consult for points of clarification. I needed to teach myself Huron. I remember that one critical reader of an early article of mine referred to me, somewhat disdainfully, as an "autodidact," as opposed to someone who studied the language with the guidance of a university teacher. I had to look the word up. But when I read Ivan Illich's *De-Schooling Society* (1976), in which he praised autodidacts for the originality they had compared with that of "merely schooled" scholars, I felt more comfortable with my learning strategy.

Linguistic Sources

By concentrating on archaeological evidence and missionary literature, scholars have largely overlooked a major source of information about the

Huron: linguistic material. Of course that is not wholly their fault. The fact that the language lost its last speaker in Oklahoma midway through the twentieth century has something to do with that, of course. And there have been only isolated studies done on the language. These include the already mentioned French Canadian folklorist and government anthropologist Marius Barbeau, whose records of Huron and Wyandot myths were published in 1915 and 1960.[3] Pierrette Lagarde (1980) published, in French, a study of the Huron verb. There are my own scattered and admittedly fairly obscure works (see References).[4] Clearly, there was a need for a scholar to pursue a systematic investigation of the insights that can be gleaned from the broad fields of linguistic evidence, and this book is an attempt to fill that need.

Published Sources

The linguistic sources are both published and unpublished. Published linguistic sources include not only the scattered terms in the standard Huron ethnohistorical works of the Jesuit Relations (hereafter (JR) and Récollet Brother Gabriel Sagard's *Long Journey to the Country of the Hurons* (1939), but two others that are both more obscure and more fruitful ethnolinguistic material. The earlier of the two comes from Sagard. He put together a French–Huron phrase book, the first dictionary of any Canadian Aboriginal language, published first in 1632 and then in 1866, and now available online. Unfortunately, when the Champlain Society published Sagard's *Long Journey* in 1939, they neglected to publish the phrase book, cutting scholars off from a very valuable historical source. This work is the product of his time with the Huron in 1623–24, combined with the linguistic labours of at least one earlier visitor or a group, possibly Fathers Nicholas Viel, Joseph Le Caron, or Joseph de la Roche Daillon, or even the layman Estienne Brulé. The source contains linguistic diversity. Sagard lived with the Southern Bear, an ethnic division of the Bear nation of the Huron (see next chapter), while the earlier contributor or contributors must have spent time with the Rock nation, the first Huron people to have contact with the French. Sagard's phrase book is often difficult to interpret, because his spelling is inconsistent, and the Huron words are sometimes missing one or more of their syllables (see Steckley 1987a:14 and 15).

The second major overlooked published source is the *Fifteenth Report of the Bureau of Archives for the Province of Ontario, 1918–1919* (Potier 1920). This contains a Huron grammar, a Huron–French dictionary organized according to the five Iroquoian conjugations, and an extensive collection of religious works written in Huron, all copied by Jesuit Father Pierre Potier, who lived with the Wyandot from 1744 to 1781. It is from that collection that I chose and translated *De Religione* (2004), written by a relatively obscure Jesuit, Father Phillipe Pierson. *De Religione* appears to be the longest of the surviving texts in the Huron language.

New Jesuit missionaries would learn Huron by copying out the work of those who preceded them. In time they would add newly acquired knowledge to the model they were copying. Potier's dictionary of 1751 was produced by copying from seventeenth-century manuscripts associated with Jesuit Father Etienne de Carheil (Potier 1920:xvii), who, in turn, had built upon the base of linguistic pioneers such as Fathers Jean de Brébeuf, Antoine Daniel, and Pierre Chaumonot. As with other copyists before him, Potier added what he heard to the work—in his case the additions are from the Wyandot dialect of Huron.

Unpublished Sources

The unpublished material in Huron is unparalleled in any other Canadian Aboriginal language. It is hard to describe adequately their extent and thorough nature to someone who has not seen them or hasn't waded deep into their pages, fishing for information and usually pulling out a prize catch. You could say with no fear of contradiction that, in terms of grammar and dictionary development, these works are superior to any comparable material in and about the English language (though not the French language) during the same period. The Jesuits, particularly the early missionaries, dedicated their considerable scholarly skills to learning the language, and both their dedication and skill show up well. You would not find their equal in Canadian Aboriginal languages until well into the twentieth century.

In the collection of unpublished dictionaries that are being drawn upon here, the earliest is a French–Huron–Onondaga manuscript (hereafter FHO), probably written by Jesuit Fathers Pierre Chaumonot and Claude Dablon during the mid-1650s (Steckley 1982a:29). The second is the French–Huron section (hereafter FH62) of a dictionary most likely of the same period. Both FHO and FH62 contain some Northern Bear dialect forms that are not found in the Huron–French section (hereafter HF62). An example is the following, in which virtually the same word (different only in aspect[5]) occurs with a -ı8- sequence in HF62 but not in FH62, an absence characteristic of Northern Bear dialect:

| Northern Bear | *Soneiachasenni* | il s'est mis en colere contre nous (FH62) [he has become angry at us] |
| Other Dialect | *Son₁8eiachasennik* | il se fasche contre nous (HF62:142) [he gets angry at us] |

Three other French–Huron dictionaries (FH67, FH1693, and FH1697) were evidently written at later dates. With FH67, this conclusion depends less on the content than on the style of entry, which is more complete than the earlier sources. FH1693 can be said to have been completed no later than 1693 because, in the dictionary's list of missionary names, Chaumonot's (or rather his Huron name, *Hechon*) is conspicuously not mentioned. It seems likely that only Chaumonot, who died in 1693, would have left himself out—monkish modesty. Later writers would not have neglected to mention the missionary who had spent some fifty years with the people. The manuscript here labelled FH1697 is given that date because it includes a reference to "L'ancienne Lorette" (FH1697:250), a Huron settlement that would not have received that name until the Huron moved to the second or "Jeune Lorette" in 1697.

There are five conjugations in Huron, based on the pronominal prefixes that go with the noun or verb. Huron–French dictionaries are structured according to conjugation, with entries in each conjugation arranged alphabetically. The earliest is HF62, which seems to be transitional, as it contains both the Northern Bear–influenced French–Huron entries and the Huron–French entries. Following this dictionary are the Huron–French dictionaries HF59 and HF65, which bear no distinguishing evidence for dating yet determined.

Huron Ethnolinguistics

Anthropological linguistics, or ethnolinguistics, is a hybrid field. It involves, like linguistics, the study of languages. However, there is ideally another component: the connection of language to an understanding of the culture of the people. As such, it has great potential for aiding the work of scholars and teachers in other fields. The disciplines of archaeology, cultural anthropology, history, and psychology come immediately to mind. This is especially true in the study of the Huron, because the linguistic source material touches on so many areas of life.

Huron ethnolinguistics is not without substantial difficulties. No native speakers exist to act as knowledgeable informants. The tangled web of

dialects took me years to unravel. Almost all of the source material was written by French Jesuit missionaries, people who, despite their obvious language experience and skills, only learned the Huron language as adults.
They acquired their linguistic experience with Indo-European languages
(such as French, Latin, Greek, Italian, and English) and Semitic languages
(such as Hebrew), which could have left them with expectations that hin-
dered their progress in understanding Huron.

How different were the language experiences of Huron and Jesuits?
Addressing this question helps to provide a context for understanding both
the source material and some of the linguistic difficulties experienced by
the Huron and the Jesuits. Of course, there were similarities. French and
Huron both contain nouns and verbs, although in distinctively different
percentages; the former is dominated by nouns, the latter by verbs (see
Steckley 2004:12–13). Huron, like other Aboriginal languages such as Inuktitut, has no adjectives. Both languages make a distinction in their pronouns between male and female. In this respect, Huron resembles French
more than does the neighbouring but unrelated language of Ojibwe, or
any other Algonquian languages, which do not have this pronominal distinction. Further, as with French, Huron can be divided into conjugations.
However, the five Huron conjugations are not based on verb endings but
on the pronominal prefixes that appear at the beginning of nouns and
verbs.

The Jesuits were more interested in the spiritual than the material
world, so the vocabulary collected reflects that. This is particularly unfor-
tunate when it comes to that most familiar (to archaeologists) item of
Huron material culture: pots. While there are terms in the dictionaries
that show how the noun 'pot' was used (see chapter 6), especially as a
metaphor, the material aspects of pots (i.e., necks, lips, and decorative patterns) so beloved of archaeological analysis are absent. The Jesuits did,
however, spend a lot of time in Huron longhouses, and so can provide us
with many Huron words useful in understanding the structure of those
buildings (see chapter 6 on material culture).

Because of this otherworldly focus, and because of the patriarchal European culture they came from, and partly because of their general lack of
knowledge or comfort regarding women, the Jesuits under-represented
vocabulary relating to women's activities. This leaves us with sadly inade-
quate collections of words to do with such important features of seventeenth-century Huron culture as botany and the culture of corn. Only the
beads that women wore are described well in the dictionaries, as these
items were traded and therefore of great interest to the French.

More interpretive difficulties flow from the Jesuits' use of European languages. Translations of Huron words, phrases, and longer passages are either in seventeenth- or eighteenth-century French, which contains pitfalls for researchers more familiar with the twenty-first-century variety. A further challenge is the idiomatically abbreviated Latin of the Jesuits, part of their day-to-day language culture, that presents difficulties for the non-Jesuit scholar.

Purpose and Nature of this Book

This study is intended to be read more by non-linguists than by linguists. It is not a grammar, nor does grammar feature prominently, except in the first chapter. Yet it should not be disparaged as a source of understanding of a people. The section on the dualic prefix of the Huron language should illustrate that. This book is not an ethnography. All areas of culture are not touched on—limitations result from the interests and sets of competence of the Jesuits and of myself. If anyone were to write a comprehensive ethnography of the Huron,[6] the material contained in this work would be necessary.

The main purpose of this book is to give some kind of voice to the people. The Huron noun root -8end- means both 'word' and 'voice,' which is rather suitable for a non-literate culture. Each chapter aims to draw out how the Huron saw and spoke of life and of the nature of their contact—social, material, and spiritual—with the new people in their country.

Summary

Despite our familiarity with the topic of the Huron people, we have not yet given their language a fair opportunity to tell us of their lives and how they experienced Europeans at the time of early contact. The primary sources that are brought to bear in this work have until now been relatively silent in the academic record. The dictionaries, both French–Huron and Huron–French, that the Jesuit missionaries produced during more than a century spent listening to the words of the Huron have a lot to say. They add more of the Huron perspective than we have been able to hear before.

Notes

1 Notably the work of Wilfred Jury, Kenneth Kidd, and Norman Emerson, and more recently Dean Knight, Marti Latta, and Gary Warwick.

2 See his *For an Amerindian Autohistory: An Essay on the Foundations of a Social Ethic* (1992) and his *Huron–Wendat: The Heritage of the Circle* (1999).

3 Barbeau's Wyandot linguistic work, both published and unpublished, has recently been tapped for study by linguists Bruce Pearson and Craig Kopris.

4 The most comprehensive and available of these studies are Steckley 1992, 1997, and 2004.

5 The Northern Bear word takes the stative aspect, which is somewhat like the present perfect tense. The other dialect form (with the -k- added) takes the habitual aspect.

6 The 1990 version of Bruce Trigger's *Huron: Farmers of the North* is the most comprehensive Huron ethnography to date.

1 The Wendat Language

Some Points of Clarification

In this chapter, and in a number of references in later chapters, we use the word "Wendat" as more or less interchangeable with "Huron." Wendat is the word that the Huron used to name themselves. "Huron" came from the French (as we will see later). I find it useful to call the language by the name Wendat because a dialect, or dialects, of that language was also spoken by their neighbours to the west, called by the French "Petun." Further confusion springs from the fact that the name "Wyandot," which is derived from "Wendat," refers to a specific people that were made up primarily of the Petun.

Wendat is a Northern Iroquoian language. That makes it related to the living languages of the Six Nations of the Iroquois—Mohawk, Oneida, Onondaga, Cayuga, Seneca, and Tuscarora—as well as to the Southern Iroquoian language of Cherokee. The language(s) of the St. Lawrence Iroquoians that Jacques Cartier encountered during the 1530s (which gave us the word *Canada* 'village') and those of the Andaste or Susquehannock, the Erie, and the Neutral are dead relatives, also Northern Iroquoian. (The languages of the diverse groups known as the Neutral and the Erie cannot be more accurately placed, as we have only a few words from each by which to judge.)

The Iroquoian languages are conventionally divided up in the following way:

Northern Iroquoian

A. Tuscarora–Nottaway
   1) Tuscarora
   2) Nottaway (an extinct language of Virginia)

B. Proto-Lake Iroquoian
   i) Huron–Wyandot (Wendat)
   3) Huron
   4) Wyandot
   5) St. Lawrence Iroquoian (languages or dialects)
   6) Onondaga
   7) Susquehannock

   ii) Seneca–Cayuga
   8) Seneca
   9) Cayuga

   iii) Mohawk–Oneida
   10) Mohawk
   11) Oneida

Southern Iroquoian
   12) Cherokee

Wendat Grammar

The following is a brief look at the structure of the Wendat verb. It is not meant in any way to be exhaustive (or exhausting), just to be an introduction. I would like to issue something of a warning here to the non-linguist. This chapter can be hard going for readers who do not have a background in linguistics. You might want to skip over most of the rest of the chapter to get to the more accessible section on the dualic prefix.

Most of Wendat grammar entails the morphology or structure of the verb. An over-whelming majority of the words in the language are verbs, and they carry within them by far the greater part of the grammatical work. In having word morphology dominate grammar, the Wendat language is following the general pattern found in the Aboriginal languages of Canada, as opposed to English and other Indo-European languages, which depend more on syntax or word order. Syntax tells you such things as subject and object in sentences like "The dog chased the cat." Nothing in the structure of the nouns 'dog' or 'cat' tells you anything in that regard.

The Wendat verb can be broken up into eight different structural positions, most of which can only be filled by one morpheme—or meaningful word part—at a time. All come in a fixed structural order, something that an early twentieth-century scholar, A. E. Jones (1908), neglected to learn (see chapter 2 and the section on Huron village names in chapter 5). The eight positions are as follows:

PREFIXES
1. pre-pronominal
2. pronouns
3. voice

ROOTS
4. noun root
5. verb root

SUFFIXES
6. root suffix
7. aspect
8. expanded aspect

Position One: Prepronominal Prefixes

The morphemes that fit into this position can be divided into two categories: (a) non-modal prefixes; and (b) modal prefixes. The former typically come before the latter, but there are exceptions. The Jesuits separated some of the non-modal prefixes (the ones indicating the negative, subjunctive, coincident, and the dualic) from the rest of the word. In this discussion, we will be reuniting them.

Non-Modal Prefixes
(1) Partitive (-*i*-)
The partitive typically refers to a particular quantity or other physical characteristic. It is often translated as 'such,' with another word specifying what the characteristic is:

itionnhetsi	(it is) for the length of our lives
ihennonha	they are (such a number) together
iotindi,onr8ten	their minds, thoughts are of such a nature

(2) Translocative (-*e*- or -*a*-)
The translocative performs three functions. The first is to give the sense of 'going or being away from the speaker.' The second is to give the meaning

of 'forever, perpetually' to the verb. The third is to give the meaning of 'every,' when the translocative occurs in combination with the dualic prefix (discussed below).

eha8e'tinnen	he went there (i.e., to a place away from the speaker)
eohahontie'ti	path goes there (i.e., to a place away from the speaker)
akonkontak	they have entered a state forever
eha8enda₁ont	his word is forever, he is a man of his word
ate₁entron	it dwells everywhere
atetsa₁8achitonten	every one of us has feet

(3) Cislocative (*-(e)ti-* or *-a-*)

The cislocative typically refers to a particular location in time or space. When the verb is one of motion, it implies moving or coming towards the speaker at a specific location.

etion₁8atonnhonti	since we were given life
etioteχa	where it burns
aset	come here from such a place

(4) Repetitive (*-(e)(t)s(i)-*)

The repetitive typically adds the meaning of 'again' or 'returning to a state' to a verb. With the negative prefix (*-te-* discussed below) it gives the meaning of 'no longer.' It also is used with reference to oneness, either concrete (i.e., with the verb root *-t-*, signifying 'to be one') or through a more abstract Wendat notion of returning to the oneness of peace, health, freedom, or generally any kind of balance.

tseata8e₁i	they are together again
etsik8atonnhont	we will be revived, returned to a state of living [notice the future prefix *-e-*]
etsesaerista'k8en	they will make recompense for you or with you [notice the future prefix *-e-*]
tetsa₁oata₁etsi	they are no longer diminishing, wasting away [notice the negative prefix *-te-*]

(5) Dualic (*-t(e)-* or *-k8-*)

The dualic refers either to a concrete twoness—e.g., something done with two eyes (looking, staring) or two legs (running, jumping)—or to a more abstract twoness with negative implications of conflict, danger, uncertainty, or emotional disturbance (see discussion below).

tesandijas	it cuts your fingers/hands in two
taiesaeraten	they would make a mixture for you
titsakannren	look at it!
tesaskenheaten	it will astonish you [notice the future prefix -e- here]

(6) Coincident (-chi(a)-)

The coincident usually makes reference to relationships of time. Typically it can be translated as '(at the time) when,' 'earlier,' 'before,' or 'immediately afterwards.' When it is followed by the dualic prefix, it indicates equality or sameness, usually of time.

chieχeationt	when I will introduce them
chiaιotetsirati	earlier they suffered [the first -a- is part of the pronominal prefix]
chiaiaihej	before they would die [the first -a- is part of the pronominal prefix]
chiatees'ontonnhont	at the same time they will be revived [notice the dualic -te-]

(7) Subjunctive (-t(e)-)

The subjunctive puts the verb into a hypothetical situation and is usually translated with 'if' and the English subjunctive:

tek8aatetsi	if the body were our length, our extent (i.e., the sum total of what we are)
tek8aatontak8i	if we were attached to our body
taιonaronhiaenton	if I put you in the sky, flattered you

(8) Negative (-t(e)-)

The negative prefix has the obvious meaning of negation. Usually it is found after the independent word *stan* (which the Jesuits often join with the negative in one word). It occurs most often with the future prefix and the dislocative and purposive suffixes (see below) to give a sense of negative intention or prediction of the future. As noted above, when it is used with the repetitive prefix, we get the meaning of 'no longer.'

stante aonι8atiatara8andik	they do not separate from us
te8entrache	day will not arrive
tesk8atieronχ8a	it is no longer strong

Modal Prefixes

There are three modal prefixes in Wendat, and they are usually found with the punctual aspect (a verb part explained below). Not discussed here is the imperative prefix, which alters the pronominal prefix but does not take an independent sound. It will be discussed with respect to the imperative suffix, the second part of the formation of the imperative.

(9) Optative (*-a-*, *-a8-*, *-ai-*, or *-ae-*)
The optative prefix usually adds the sense of 'would' (more rarely 'should') to a verb.

aₗatonnhia8ist	my life would be extended
a8ennonnhek8ik	they would have provided life
teaek8aₗennionhend	we would not have surpassed it [notice the negative prefix]

(10) Factual (*-a(8)-*)
The factual prefix typically refers to something that has just happened, or happened close to the period being discussed in the narrative, or, more rarely, is just about to happen. I usually translate these more rare forms with 'at the point of.'

ahona8endrak8at	they followed his word
a8echiaχe	one is at the point of searching for it
aherhonska	he was at the point of wishing for it

(11) Future (*-e-*)
The future is used with the purposive or the punctual aspect. It can be translated either as 'will' or, with the past suffix, as 'would.'

eₗonesat	I will mistreat you
eski8eₗik	they (two) will be together, or will have been together
tetsetsi8andihe	you will not take it from them (by force)
techiesk8ahenchend	you would not have hated it

Position Two: Pronominal Prefixes

This is probably the most difficult structural position of Wendat verb morphology for the English or French speaker to learn. Pronominal prefixes exist in many forms, belong to five conjugations, and make grammatical distinctions that are distinctly "foreign" to such a person.

The following is a basic introduction to Wendat pronominal prefixes. We will begin with the grammatical roles of agent and patient. The agent is relatively straightforward. It is much like the subject of a verb:

| *onta₍araska* | when I left [first person singular agent] |
| *e₍onesat* | I will mistreat you [first person singular agent combines with second person singular patient] |

Dealing with the patient is not so straightforward. As the last example illustrates, it is similar to an object when used with an agent. However, when it occurs on its own, without an agent, it acts like a subject. This most often happens with the stative aspect (i.e., when the verb describes the state or condition of something). It is difficult to explain this. There seems frequently to be some sense of the patient being a negative or positive beneficiary (or victim) of what is existing or happening, without being the initiator. It would be easy and probably misleading to make too much of this philosophically (e.g., to conclude that the Wendat saw external forces as grammatically unspecified agents of what we do or of the situations we find ourselves in). It is probably a creature more of grammatical logic or regularity, like the designation of masculine or feminine in French. Further investigation into the elusive realm of Wendat philosophy is necessary before anything close to definitive could be said. The following are examples of the patient alone.

| *hoteienda₍aate* | he has ability in abundance (i.e., he is the beneficiary of abundant skill or ability) |
| *ennonnhe* | they [feminine] live (i.e., they benefit from their life existing) |

More distinctions are made with agent than with patient forms. One reason for this concerns grammatical number. Wendat distinguishes between dual (two) and plural (more than two), but only for agents, not patients.

The first person dual and plural features another difference: with the agent, but not the patient, the language distinguishes between first person inclusive (i.e., including the listener in the 'we') and exclusive (i.e., excluding the listener from the 'we'). For example, if I were speaking to someone and said to her, *ti8e₍i* 'we [inclusive dual] are together,' I would be saying that the two of us are together, she and I. If, I said to her, *a₍i8e₍i* 'we [exclusive dual] are together,' I would be reporting about myself and someone other than her. Thus, for first person agent there would be five forms—singular, dual inclusive, dual exclusive, plural inclusive, and plural exclusive—while for first person patient there would be two: singular and plural.

Another pronominal form that an English or French speaker might find foreign is the indefinite third person, usually translated as 'they,' 'them,' or 'people.' It seems to occur whenever the gender or even specific identification of the persons referred to is not known or not considered significant. The form appears with both agent and patient, but never simultaneously, i.e., an indefinite agent with an indefinite patient.

Wendat, like other Northern Iroquoian languages, possesses five conjugations of verbs (and nouns) based on the forms of pronominal prefixes they take. The conjugations are generally referred to as: -*a*- stem, consonant stem, -*e*- stem, -*i*- or -*ιen*- stem, and -*o*- stem.

Position Three: Voice Prefixes

(1) Semi-reflexive Voice (-*(a)t(e/i)*- or -*k*-)
The main jobs of the semi-reflexive voice prefix are to make an active verb passive or a transitive verb intransitive. It typically makes the pronominal prefix take the -*a*- stem conjugation forms.

aιotiesti	they have been assembled
tetsonk8endieraχon	their many voices are again mixed
hatetsens	he is a doctor

(2) Reflexive Voice (-*(a)tat(e/i)*- / -*(a)tak*-)
The reflexive voice prefix can make an action mutual, giving a meaning of 'to, among, or between each other.' French translations typically add 'des uns des autres' or 'entre' to the French verb. Sometimes the reflexive prefix makes the verb passive. Other times it adds the reflexive notion of action upon oneself, with the French translation for the verb form beginning with 'se' or ending with 'soi meme.' This prefix causes the pronominal prefix to take an -*a*- conjugation form.

teontakonchiok	they will look at themselves, at their reflections in the water
aiontatienteha	they would know each other
ontatetsentak8a	it is used to cure them, they are cured by it
aontatiatingenk	they are put outside

Position Four: Noun Stems

Noun stems are often added to verbs, always immediately before the verb roots. Nouns occur incorporated into verbs in this way much more frequently than they stand on their own. Most noun stems are simply noun roots. However, sometimes they are formed by adding a nominalizer or 'nounmaker' -*ch(r)*-, and rarely the instrumental root suffix -*k8*- (see below for examples) to a verb root. Usually an -*a*- appears between the noun

stem and the verb root. By far the most commonly found noun roots in
the Jesuit documents are *-at-* 'body, living being' and *-rih8-* 'matter (of
importance), affair, news.' The following are examples of incorporated
noun stems:

aierih8io	they would make the matter great (i.e., be believers)
shaatat	he is one
e8atondechaten	a country, the world will end [with the nominalizer]
ₗandaₗenchaₗn	it is inside the pit (i.e., place of sowing) [with the nominalizer]

Position Five: Verb Roots

The verb root, of course, is the heart of the Wendat verb. There are approximately one thousand different verb roots in the language, most of which
can take more than one thousand forms. This tells us something about the
productive capacity of Wendat verbs; they are capable, at least hypotheti-
cally, of producing over one million words. In *De Religione,* the longest (at
fifty-three pages) surviving text in the language (see Steckley 2004), the
frequently occurring verb roots *-8ten-* 'to be (of) such (a nature)' and *-er-*
'to wish,' took sixty-one and forty-nine different forms respectively.

Position Six: Root Suffixes

One reason why each Wendat verb can generate so many words is that the
root suffix position is very productive. There are eleven different root suffixes, most of which occur commonly. More than one root suffix can occur
at a time—in the first example given below, for instance, there are three.
Usually, however, only one appears.

(1) Dislocative (*-h-* or *-ch-* or *-n(d)-*)
The dislocative root suffix has the same meaning and function in Wendat
as the cognate form in the related language of Oneida, described in a classic, ground-breaking study of that language by Floyd Lounsbury, who stated
that this root suffix had meanings "which correspond exactly to those of
going to when used as auxiliary verbs in English, and, as in English, can be
taken in the literal sense of *being on the way to do something,* or in the
future-tense sense of *being about to,* or *intending to do something*" (Lounsbury 1953:83). The dislocative is the usual root suffix used with the purposive aspect (see below). The only other root suffix occurring with the
purposive is the progressive:

teherhonde	he is not going to wish it, he does not intend to wish it
aχirih8aienstandihe	we go about teaching them
tsirih8aienstandiha	go teach them!
aiaχirih8aienstandiha	we would go to teach them

(2) Inchoative

The inchoative is a root suffix that adds the meaning or sense of 'coming into being' to a verb root. In the Jesuit Wendat dictionaries, we find it translated into French as 'devenir,' 'se trouver,' 'tomber' and 'commencer a.' Typically, it does not so much take an independent form as it affects the aspect form that follows it in position seven. You usually detect its presence by the aspect form used (e.g., *-ha-* for punctual, *-ndi-* for stative):

esk8arih8ateha	we will again come to know it
onχiondiₗonrhendi	they have come to forget us
aₗaata8iha	it became rotten

(3) Transitive (*-(ra)(h)8/o(i)-*)

The transitive makes the semantic content of the verb transitive, enabling it to take an object. Often this entails putting something in or on something else.

aonsa8atennontrak	it would again be put inside (with the verb root *-nnont-* to be inside)
haₗeaₗenh8indi	he is putting it outside for me (with the verb root *-aₗen-* to go outside)
ahaarohose	he is at the point of going to put a net in the water (with the verb root *-o-* to be water, fluid, wet)

(4) Undoer (*-(aska)8a-*)

The undoer adds the sense of undoing or opposing the semantic content of the verb root. It usually takes *-8a-*, which is sometimes preceded by an *-(a)ska-*, an addition that does not appear (to me) to change the meaning:

ateₗiatendasonta8a	they two are separated (with the verb root *-ndasont-* 'to join')
tate8atiataχaska8a	it is not divided (with the negative prefix and the verb root *-χ-* 'to join, unite')
a8atiatora8a	it has detached (with the verb root *-ora-* 'to affix')

(5) Causative (*-(a)(')t-*)

The causative is a commonly used root suffix, which typically introduces to the verb the notion of causality.

techiakenrentak	you were not made unimportant, diminished
k8atonietha	we breathe by such a means[1]
aχeationt	I cause them to enter

(6) Causative-Instrumental (-*st*-)

The causative-instrumental can add one of two basic meanings. One is similar to that of the causative, giving the sense of 'to cause something to be or happen.' The second is similar to the instrumental, meaning 'to serve as something for performing some action.'

etsesaerista'k8en	they will make recompense for you, cause you to be complete in something (i.e., emotionally)
esk8atatiat8tenst	you will be made such, be caused to be such
a₁8arih8aiensten	I taught you it, caused you to have skill in it
aiesandek8aest	we would strike you, cause you to be struck with water (i.e., baptized)

(7) Instrumental (-*(a)k(8)*-)

The instrumental is a root suffix that typically adds a 'by such a means' or 'to or at such a place.' When the translocative prefix occurs with it, we get the meaning of 'forever,' with the instrumental perhaps adding the meaning of 'at such a time' to the translocative sense of 'going away.' With a very few roots, the instrumental acts as a nominalizer or noun-maker, transforming a verb root into a noun stem:

k8atoioannonχ8a	we were moved by such a means
aion₁8atientak	we would be put in such a place
atek8akontak	we will enter a state forever
eonditiok8ichien	they will be formed into a group [as noun-maker with -₁*entio*- 'to be a matrilineal clan']
etserak8a₁en	they will see the sun again [as noun-maker with -*ra*- 'to rise']

(8) Distributive (-*an/on)on*- or -*(ai)on*-)

The distributive root suffix adds the meaning of 'many' to the verb, in the sense of 'many objects, places, or times.' Sometimes, a second distributive suffix, -*nion*-, is added. It seems to reinforce the meaning, making it 'very many,' but the evidence is not clear in every case.

taiesannonronk8annonhonj	they would oil your scalp many times, greet you with respect
hontieronnonnionk	they do many damaging things

| *tesk8atonnhontaion8a* | you will have your life withdrawn from many place (i.e., be tortured) |
| *chrih8anderaχonnionhonk* | you make many mistakes [with two distributive suffixes] |

(9) Dative (-*(a/en)(d)*- or -*senni*-)

The dative root suffix adds the notion that the meaning of the verb root is for the advantage or disadvantage of someone or some people, that it is for the benefit of, or has an effect on the person(s) specified. It often makes a verb transitive, usually appearing with both an agent and a patient.

ιaonι8atiechandik	they envy us
chionχisk8ahendi	at the same time they hate us
teι8rih8ensennihe	I will not let fall or forget, your matter or affair
esk8atonk8en	you will desire it

(10) Progressive (-*(h)ati(e)*-)

The progressive adds the meaning of 'go about,' 'go along,' or 'continue' to the verb root. An unusual feature of this suffix is that the stative aspect (see below) always appears directly before it, regardless of which other aspect comes afterward. (As with the dislocative suffix, the progressive can appear with the purposive aspect.)

aιi8eιihatia	they two would go about together
ek8aιeiheration	I went about going straight there
haaιotenrihatiend	he went about continuing to have pity on them
teιaonι8ennontraties	they go about following us

(11) Frequentative (-*skon*-)

The frequentative is, ironically, a relatively uncommon root suffix, and it appears only in the stative aspect. It is translated as 'frequently.'

aιorih8anderaskon	they frequently made mistakes
otieronnonskon	it frequently did damage in many places
tsonι8aron8askon	we frequently took it back

Position Seven: Aspects

Aspect is a grammatical feature that differs from tense in that it deals not with the time something happened (i.e., past, present, and future), but what can be called temporal flow. Aspect typically involves contrasts such as completed (sometimes called perfective) versus incomplete (imperfective), single versus repeated action, and action versus state. Along with the pronominal prefixes and the verb roots, the aspects are necessary parts of virtually every Wendat verb. Usually there is only one aspect in a particular verb form, but, sometimes, there can be two (or even more rarely, three).

(1) Stative (-(ı)i-/-on-)

The stative aspect typically provides one of two types of meaning. One entails being in a particular state (hence the name); the other is the sense of completed action typically associated with the perfective form in other languages (e.g., the verbs taking 'to have' or *'avoir'* as auxiliaries in English and French respectively. The stative aspect commonly appears with a patient rather than an agent, particularly when the verb involves just one grammatical player. A number of verb roots take only the stative aspect. In such cases, when there is a need to communicate the sense of a different aspect, Wendat relies on a separate auxiliary verb, -ıen- to which the other aspect attaches. When the stative form occurs with another aspect, it always appears first.

ıannonchia8asti	it is a beautiful house
*oh8ichaıenhe***on**	one's life force has died
ek8a8eıik	we will be, will have been together
aionderatik	it would have been a mistake

(2) Habitual (-ch- or -s- or -ha-)

The habitual aspect is generally used for repeated or continuing action. It can express the idea that some action or state is characteristic or typical. When occurring with other aspects, it goes after the stative and before the punctual.

tsontatiatichiach	they search, are searching for each other again
ieak8astis	they are (characteristically) beautiful
aiaonnhiska	it would ignore, overlook something (repeatedly)
aiesaronhiatentatiesk8a	they would have gone about putting you in the sky, praising you

(3) Punctual (-j-, -k-, -en-, or -(h)a-)

The punctual occurs with the modal prefixes (i.e., the optative, future, and factual) and tends to refer to a single action, rather than a state or repeated action. When sharing a verb form with other aspects, it comes after them. Often when the Jesuits wrote verbs taking this aspect, they indicated that it had no particular sound (see third example below). You know that it is the punctual, as there is no other aspect form following the verb stem, and as the verb is preceded by a modal prefix.

aion₁etsistorej	they would cover me with fire
aha₁onatonnia	he made them
echeatorast	you will take them (living beings) out of the fire
aontaion₁8atondorek	we would be or would have been worthless, useless

(4) Imperative (*-j-* or *-k-* or *-en-* or *-(h)a-*)

The imperative exists both as a prefix and as an aspect suffix identical to the punctual. The subject can be either second person (singular, dual, or plural) or first person (dual or plural; e.g., as "let's"). The imperative prefix typically alters the form of the pronominal prefix, rather than taking a distinct form of its own.

seatonastatha	preserve them! [the *-che-* pronominal prefix is changed to *-se-*]
satharat	do good! [the *-chi-* pronominal prefix is changed to *-s-*]
titsiatoret	examine it! [the *-etsi-* pronominal prefix is changed to *-tsi-*]

(5) Purposive (*-e-*)

The purposive aspect appears to add the notion of intention or probability, both negative and positive. It typically follows the dislocative root suffix, but also sometimes follows the progressive. The most frequent form the purposive takes is with the negative and future prefixes.

on₁8atiatannondande	it is going to take care of us
ek8a8e₁ihatie	we will go about together
tesk8atindia₁aenche	they will not get their fingers out (i.e., they will not escape)
teonk8ennonχ8achend	they would not have put wood in the fire

Position Eight: Expanded Aspect Suffixes

As the name implies, expanded aspect suffixes follow aspects. There are two clear members of this group: the past and the diminutive.

(1) Past (*-nnen-* or *-k(8a)-* or *-n(n/d)-*)

The past takes various forms, depending on which aspect it follows. It does not appear with the punctual, because the punctual combined with the factual prefix already signifies the past.

aₗoataₗastinnen	they were consumed
ichiatierhak	you did it, used to do it
techieski8ahenchend	you would not have hated it

(2) Diminutive (*-(i)a-*)
The diminutive adds the sense of 'little' to the verb, and seems always to follow the stative aspect. In the chapter on kinship, I identify what I feel is a particular social use of the diminutive as a possessive form, used with certain kinship terms, as well as with domesticated animals, axes, pipes, pots, and nets (see also Steckley 1993a:56–7).

i8aia	it is little, small
onₗiena	they have me as child

The Dualic

One of the longest debates in linguistic anthropology, although it has quietened down recently, concerns the validity of something called the Sapir–Whorf hypothesis. In its strongest form, put forward by Benjamin Whorf, it argues for linguistic determinism: language determines or causes how people in a certain culture perceive reality. In a weaker form, in line with the writing of the more conservative Edward Sapir, it argues for a kind of linguistic relativity, a dialogic relationship between language and culture in which each speaks and each listens to the other.

I will suggest here that such a relationship existed between the dualic prefix (*-t(e)-* or *-k8-*) and Wendat culture. The grammatical logic of the dualic's use was influenced by the nature of twoness in Wendat thought. The grammar repeated this message back to the speaker. Of course, this is highly speculative, since there are no speakers on whom to test this theory. Still, I believe that the idea helps us understand the language and culture of the Wendat people in the early seventeenth century.

There are a good number of ways in which the cultural world of the seventeenth-century Huron was divided into twos. They believed that people had two souls (JR39:18–19; and Steckley 1978). One was sometimes referred to with the noun root *-ndiₗonr-*, translatable as 'mind, thought, spirit of thoughts'(Potier 1920:449). Based on its use in verbs, we can also see that it was associated with happiness, calm, peace, love and the wisdom of the elders. The other soul was referred to with the noun root *-eiachi-* 'heart' (Potier 1920:454). Its use in verbs reveals it as a soul of strong emotions such as anger, vengeance, sadness, and courage. The two souls existed

in a kind of conflict, not unlike that of the Freudian opposition of super-
ego and id.

As with other Aboriginal groups, the Huron were divided into (on the
one side) chiefs, councils, and council houses of peace and (on the other)
chiefs, councils, and council houses of war. The former were associated
with the mind spirit. The council houses of peace were termed *endionrra
ondaon* 'one's mind spirit, its place' (JR13:59) while the council houses of
war were called *otinnontsishiaj ondaon* 'their cut-off heads, its place.' The
following Jesuit missionary statement shows both the contrast and the association of the mind spirit with the peace chief:

> *ennonchien ond8ta₁e'te eskarihontak; ₁andi₁onra iθochien ta₁8arihontak*
>
> Do not give me the office of one who bears the war mat [see warfare chap-
> ter]; give me the position of the mind spirit.
>
> French translation: *ne me faites pas chef de guerre, mais seulement chef de
> conseil.*
>
> Do not make me the war chief, but only the council chief. (Potier 1920:420)

There is a distinct possibility that the Huron had two clan-lumping moieties (Steckley 1982). The term "moiety" (based on the French word for
half) refers to a social unit that for ceremonial purposes (e.g., for funerals)
encompasses one half of society. In addition, one of their clans, the Loon/
Sturgeon clan, was dual (for no reason that I can figure); it was represented
by two animals rather than the usual one. As we will see later, perhaps
seven of the thirty-three known village names, possess the dualic prefix,
indicating some concept of duality.

Finally, the culture heroes of the Huron origin myth are twins that
entered into conflict. One is *Iouskeha*, the so-called good twin; the other
is *Tawiscaron,* the bad twin whose blood gave the Huron *ata8iskara,* or
'flint' (Potier 1920: 445).

In chapter 8 I will argue that there was a duality as well of mats of war
and mats of peace. Did all this twoness in the culture have a listener in the
language that spoke back with similar views? I suggest it did.

Uses of the Dualic

Obvious Twoness

The most common use of the dualic was what can easily be termed obvious twoness. This includes such meanings as the number two, *tendi,* and
verbs relating to division into two (*'k8-a'ti* ... diviser en deux' (Potier
1920:161)), two objects rubbing together (*'k8-achiendie'ti* ... faire du feu

avec du bois' (162)), being beside each other ('*k8ateχen* ... avoir les champs proches' (185)), and being joined to each other ('*k8-atonti* ... se joindre, se mettre 2 ensemble' 197)).

Anatomical Twoness

Anatomical twoness occurs when something is done with two eyes or two legs. There are verbs that incorporate the noun root -*ₗak*- 'the whites of the eyes' (446), an example of which is *k8-akaken* 'to open the eyes' (164), and those that have the noun root -*ₗar*- 'eye' (446), which includes *k8-akaringenh8i* 'to give a look of anger at someone' (literally to have one's eyes go out (165)) and *k8-akanditi* 'to fix one's sight on someone, some object' (literally, to strengthen one's eyes (165)). There is also the verb root -*ₗannr*- 'to look' (233), which also takes a dualic prefix, even though it does not incorporate a noun meaning 'eyes.'

As for the legs, the dualic can occur without any nouns specifying legs. Examples include *k8-aratati* 'to run' (171), *k8-arate* 'to go on snowshoes' (172), and *k8-atsingenron* 'faire la reverence pliant le genou. Com: les fem.' [to make reverence bending the knee, as females [do]] (205). This also works with references to shoes, as in '*k8-arakora* ... prendre les souliers, se chausser (quasi dicas) ficher les souliers au bout des les pieds [to put on shoes ... (as if to say) to attach the shoes to the end of the feet]' (426).

Cultural Twoness

Beyond this physical twoness, we have more cultural twoness, one that I believe shares in the negativity and conflict between two souls, two councils, and two cultural heroes with opposing purposes.

We see this in the appearance of the dualic prefix in words communicating sudden loud sounds and violent actions. These are essentially negative in nature. No term for singing, however (even loud singing), or for talking, uses the dualic. If these words followed a pattern of anatomical twoness (i.e., two lips), then we would not find such a difference. It is intriguing, therefore, to see the dualic in verbs that mean negative sounds, as in *k8-achiatandichon* 'to groan or moan or complain about something bad' (Potier 1920:162), using the noun root -*chi*- 'mouth' (446); *k8-asenχ8i* 'to utter a cry of sadness, helplessness' (176; see FH1697:44 for the notion of helplessness and FH1697:148–49 for the notion of sadness); *tonta ₗandia8an* 'to vomit' (289); *k8-atsonsti* 'to sneeze' (206); and, admittedly less potent, *k8-astra8an* 'to yawn' (179), which includes the noun root for 'lips' (FH1697:108). The following is an illustrative example:

osontenhaon aθochiatandichon

il n'a fait que se plaindre toute la nuit

[he did nothing but complain all night] (Potier 1920:162)

(1) Sudden and Violent Action

Sudden and violent action typically involves the dualic. This includes the verb *k8-atratati* meaning 'to throw oneself at or to attack someone, the enemy' (Potier 1920:172 and 202), *k8-atoχ8i* 'to jump, dive or fall into the water and disappear' (194), *k8-atsarandi* 'to push, knock or throw someone down' (204 and 328), and *ka'k8an* 'to seize something or someone' (271). This last verb can be found in various forms in the following violence-related words:

a'ki8an ...	aller en guerre [to go to war]
a 'ki8achra	parti de guerre, bande de guerriers [war party, band of warriors]
k8-a'ki8achra'k8an	[with the verb root -'k8a- added] defaire un parti de guerre [to defeat a war party] (Potier 1920:167)

And then there is torture. The verb meaning 'to torture' uses the dualic prefix, the noun root *-onnh-* 'life,' the verb root *-ont-* 'to attach' (418), the distributive (*-anion-*) and the undoer (*-8an*) root suffixes in the following way:

Ti-onnhontanion8an ... tourmenter q., le faire souffrir [to torment someone, to make them suffer] ... retirer, faire sortir la vie des diverses parties du corps en les tourmentant [to take out, to make leave the life from diverse parts of the bodies of those one is tormenting] ... (416).

The same combination with the semi-reflexive voice (*-at-*) emphasizes suffering:

... *k8-atonnhontanion8an* ... quasi dicas la vie se retirer elle-meme des divers endroits du corps ou perdre q.c. de les divers degres, se diminuer (id est) soufrir, endurer divers peines ou tourments [as if to say, life withdraws itself from diverse places of the body or loses something in diverse degrees, or diminishes itself (it is) to suffer, to endure diverse pain or torments]. (416)

Using the dualic prefix with the same verb root (*-ont-*) and the undoer (*-a8an*) with the noun stem *-ondech-* 'country, earth' and the cislocative prefix (*-eti-*), we get another reference to destruction:

t'etiotondechonta8an voila un etrange evenement ... le terre dest renversée [behold a strange occurrence ... the earth is turned over]. (421)

Look what happens when the dualic is added to an action. When the verb *akenhen* 'to raise oneself' has the causative suffix added, it means 'to raise oneself for such a reason' (166). Add the dualic and you get: *'onta8enkenhati* se lever subitement, en sursaut (dcr des esclaves) [to raise oneself suddenly, with a start (said of slaves)]' (166). The suddenness is due to the presence of the dualic—for Huron cultural reasons a sudden action carries a sense of "twoness."

(2) Changes for the Worse
These include being bald (*k8-achar*, Potier 1920:162), hoarse (*k8-asonia₍i*,178), to go or be numb in the legs (*k8-atsisten*, 205), or to have part of the body frozen (*te onθendi*, 423). This category includes the following, in which the undoer root suffix -*a8an*- seems to reverse the sense of the verb root from having something to losing it:

> *k8-atetaroha8an* ... quitter son emploi, sa charge, son office vg. de capitaine, s'en demettre, s'en deposer [to leave one's employ, one's charge, one's office, for example, of captain, to resign from, to leave it]. (Potier 1920:187)

(3) Combative Duality
Combative duality entails the addition of a dualic prefix to create a competition in which someone outdoes someone else, often through negative means. For instance, the verb -*en*- means 'to put' (Potier 1920:219). Adding the distributive -*ton*- to it means 'to put in many places, many times.' Let's look at what you get when we use the noun root -*rih8*- 'matter, affair, news' and the dative suffix:

> ₍*arih8aentondi* ... donner à q. plusieurs bons avis ... le precher ... lui apporter de bonnes raisons [to give someone several pieces of good advice, to preach to someone, to bring to him/her good reasons]. (Potier 1920:220)

Add the dualic (appearing here as the initial -*k*-) and the meaning changes (you will notice that the suffix has also changed—it is now the instrumental, not the dative):

> *karih8aentonk8i.* donner de mauvais avis de part et d'autre, jetter des semences de devil des deux cotés, mettre la discorde, mettre plusieurs choses en avant chez l'un et chez l'autre qui causent des querelles ... trancher des 2 cotes [to give bad advice to one side and the other, to sow the seeds of the devil on both sides, to make discord, to give several things in front of one and the other that causes quarrels ... to contrast two sides] ...
>
> *te harih8aentonk8a* il seme la discorde par ses mauvais rapports ... c'est un boutte feu [he sows discord by his bad reports ... he is a firebrand].

aₗθarih8aentonk8a il a voulu mettre la dissension, il a voulu brouiller [he wished to make discension, he wished to set (people) at odds]. (220)

A similar situation happens with the verb *-ₗenni-* 'to surpass' (245). Adding the noun root *-ndiₗonr-* 'mind, thought' results in the following:

ₗandiₗonkennion sine te dual, surpasser q. in esprit sans tromperie [without the *-te-* dualic, to surpass someone in thought without deception, trickery] (245)

Add the dualic and you get:

kandiₗonkennion ... tromper q., le trahir [to deceive someone, to betray someone] (245)

This kind of combativeness can also be seen with the noun roots *-rih8-* 'matter, affair' and *-eiachi-* 'heart' as well, as in the following:

karikennion ... disputer, debattre de paroles ... vaincre q. à la dispute [to dispute, debate words, to vanquish someone in dispute] ... (245)

k8-eiakennion ... disputer a qui aura le plus de courage, s'entredefier à qui aura le plus de coeur ... vaincre q. en courage [to dispute as to who will have more courage, to challenge one another as to who will have more heart]. (245)

Words that always take a dualic may also feature this combative element:

k8-atandi(g)enti s'entredefier, s'entreprovoquer [to challenge, provoke one another]. (300)

(4) Dangerous Uncertainty

This category is for situations in which one is uncertain about what is going on or going to happen. For instance, consider the following unsuccessful hunt:

k8-atenda8an ... aller a la chasse des betes qu'on tache de rencontrer, et que souvent on est long tems sans pouvoir rencontrer le chasseur allant d'un coté et la bete de l'autre [to go on the hunt for animals that one tries to encounter, and that often one is for a long time without being able to encounter, the hunter going on one side, and the animal on the other]. (Potier 1920:278 and 175)

Also dangerous in its uncertainty is divination. You are dealing with potentially negative spirits after all:

k8-atoχ8i ... jongler, faire le devin avec certaines chansons superstitieuses [to juggle, to divine with certain superstitious songs]. (194)

Confusion also fits into this category:

> *k8-enditsori* ... se peller-meler, se confondre, les unes avec les autres sans order, sans distinction, sans arrangement [to be jumbled, confused, ones with others without order, distinction or arrangement]. (377)

Similar, but perhaps not so extreme, is being astonished:

> *kaskenheati* ... une chose etre etonnante ... faire des choses etonnante agir, se comporter d'une maniere etonnante; faire qu'on s'etonner [a thing is astonishing ... to cause astonishing things to act, to comport oneself in an astonished manner, to make it so that one is astonished]. (323)

And then there is the dangerous uncertainty of being sick, very sad, or very worried. This is expressed in the Wendat language with the noun root *-onnh-* 'life' (455) and the verb root *-ₗarenre-* 'to slant.' Here, the dualic appears as follows:

> *Ti - onharenron* ... rendre q. malade, chagrin, inquiet [to render someone sick, sad or worried], *ondaie ationₗionharenron* [that, it slants our life two ways] cela nous rend malade ... nous jette dans une grande inquietude, nous met fort en peine [that renders us sick ... it casts us into a great anx-iety, it puts us in a [state of] great worry]. (412)

With the semi-reflexive voice we have:

> *k8-atonharenron* ... etre malade; etre entre la vie et la mort ... item etre dans un grande peine et inquietude d'esprit [to be sick, to be between life and death ... also to be in a great worry and anxiety of mind]
>
> *onne ak8aₗatonharenron* me voila malade (en peril de la vie) ... inquiet chagrin [behold, I am sick (in peril of my life) worried, sad] ... (412)

The list presented is representative, not exhaustive. Some verbs do not precisely fit into my categories (e.g., verbs that deal with blocking holes: '*k8atsohanienk8i* ... calfater, boucher les fentes, les ouvertures d'un maison [to caulk, to close up the cracks, the holes of a house]' 206) and '*kachirak8i* ... boucher q. ouverture [to block some hole]' (216). I look forward to someone else tackling the voluminous material in the Wendat language to prove or disprove my hypothesis. Analyses of other Iroquoian languages could be done, although the traditional sense of dualism may be lost on more recent speakers after hundreds of years of change, since the living languages have not been frozen in time as early Wendat language material has.

Chapter Summary

In this chapter we have looked at the structure of the Wendat verb, which entails the greater part of Wendat grammar. We have seen that there are eight structural positions inside the verb, each of which may be filled by a number of alternatives. This system creates in the thousand-some Wendat verbs (a number guessed at by looking at Father Pierre Potier's dictionary, the culmination of all the Jesuits' work with the Wendat language) a great capacity to generate words.

Some of the Wendat verb features discussed here are shared with Canadian Aboriginal languages not in the Iroquoian family. Since Wendat is verb dominated by verbs rather than by nouns, it resembles most other such languages. The complexity of the verb, not surprisingly, is also shared. The first person inclusive and exclusive distinction is found, for example, in Algonquian languages such as Ojibwe (spoken by the historic neighbours of the Huron) and Inuktitut (the language of the Inuit). Other Wendat features are uncommon in Canadian Aboriginal languages. One example is its way of making a grammatical distinction between male and female pronouns. Algonquian, Eskimo-Aleut, and Athabaskan languages do not do this.

I suspect that like a number of other Canadian Aboriginal languages, Wendat can be used as evidence that the Sapir–Whorf hypothesis may have, at least in its weaker form, some validity. (The animate–inanimate distinction in Algonquian languages might be another piece of supportive evidence.) I have explained here how the dualic prepronominal prefix could relate to other "dualisms" in the culture, to make up an active dialogue between language and culture. I suspect another prepronominal prefix, the repetitive, might do likewise.

Note

1 The usual -θ- is replaced by -th- to show the causative form -t-.

2 Huron Nations

A Note on Terminology

Some confusion surrounds the names that relate to the Huron. First, as we have seen, the word "Huron" itself is not the people's name for themselves. It was imposed upon them by the French, much as so many other names were forced upon indigenous peoples by Europeans and other colonizers. Jesuit Father Jérôme Lalemant explained the origin of the word "Huron" in the following way:

> Arriving at the French settlement, some Sailor or Soldier seeing for the first time this species of barbarians, some of whom wore their hair in ridges—a ridge of hair one or two fingers wide appearing upon the middle of their heads, and on either side the same amount being shaved off, then another ridge of hair; others having one side of the head shaved clean, and the other side adorned with hair hanging to their shoulders—this fashion of wearing the hair making their heads look to him like those of boar [hures], led him to call these barbarians "Hurons;" and this is the name that has clung to them ever since. (JR16:229–31)

As Conrad Heidenreich duly notes: "an alternative explanation of the name comes from Old French, meaning a 'ruffian,' 'unkempt person,' 'knave,' or 'lout'" (1971:21).

Secondly, there is the matter of what to call the member groups of the Huron alliance. Some archaeological writers have used the word 'clans' to refer to these groups. As we will see, this is misleading because it ignores the fact that the Huron had an eight-clan structure composed of social units of a different nature than that of these groups. The term 'tribes' is more in keeping with traditional anthropological practice, but instead I will use 'nations.' This reflects the practice of the original French writers, and it reflects the separate existence of the different groups both prior to the forming of, and after the breaking-up of, the alliance of the Huron. Finally, I find it more respectful.

Searching for the Literal Meaning of Wendat

As discussed earlier, we know that the Huron called themselves "Wendat" (typically transcribed as *8endat*). Early twentieth-century scholar J. N. B. Hewitt proposed that this might refer to their being "the islanders" or "dwellers on a peninsula" (Hodge 1971:206). Father A. E. Jones chose the more colourful "The One Island" or "The One Land Apart" (Jones 1908: 419–20; see below for another). They both based their analyses on a noun root *-h8en'd-*, meaning 'island, separated piece of land' (FHO, FH1697, HF59:78, HF62, HF65:93, FH67, and Potier 1920:448).

Later scholars added geographic or cultural justifications for such a translation. Historical geographer Conrad Heidenreich suggested that the island reference could be relating to the fact that "Huron is almost an island, surrounded along 60 per cent of its perimeter by water and most of the remainder by vast swamps." (1971:300). Bruce Trigger added that it might refer to the traditional Aboriginal belief that the world was an island constructed on the back of a turtle (1976:27). Both made reference to two passages from *Jesuit Relations* in support of their views. One 1638 passage speaks of the rumours travelling throughout Huronia of how the Jesuit missionaries were spreading the diseases that were devastating the Huron. The Jesuit Fathers questioned the Huron concerning these stories:

> Their usual answer was that 'this was being constantly said everywhere; and that, besides, all the inhabitants of the Island where these people live had their brains upset[1],—that the death of so many of their relatives had unsettled their minds.' (JR15:21)

In the 1648 *Relation*, in a condolence ceremony following the murder by a Huron or Hurons unknown of a young Frenchman, Jacques Douart, a Huron speaker summed up the perilous position of his people: "This country is an Island; it has now become a floating one, to be overwhelmed by the first outburst of the storm. Make the floating Island firm and stationary" (JR33:237–39).

This evocative image of Huronia as a 'floating island' is reproduced in a name for the Huron that appears in a number of seventeenth-century Jesuit dictionaries, both Huron (the first three entries) and Mohawk (the last two entries):

atih8en'darak	les hurons quod insulat habitabant [the Huron, those who live on an island] (FHO)
hoti8en'darak	les hurons, les insulaires [the Huron, the islanders] (HF62)
atih8endarak	les hurons q[ui]ā insula habitabant [the Huron, who on an island live] (FH1697:97)
hati8endogerha$_l$	les Hurons (quia in insula habitabant)
hah8endagerha$_l$	les Hurons (Bruyas 1970:22 and 55)[2]

The verb into which the noun root *-h8en'd-* is incorporated here is *-a$_l$ra-* 'to float' (FHO, HF59:3, HF62, HF65, and Potier 1920:170). As the following dictionary entry shows, this verb root was used with a variety of noun roots, both to specify a physical state and to speak metaphorically:

A$_l$ra ...	flotter [to float]
ohona$_l$ran'de [with *-hon-* 'canoe']	le canot va sur leau [the canoe goes on the water]
hoata$_l$ [r]an'de [with *-at-* 'body']	il va flottant [he goes floating]
hoti8en'da$_l$rak	les hurons, les insulaires
a$_l$an$_l$ota$_l$ [a]ren [with *-n$_l$ota-* 'cedar'] ...	le morceau de cedre flotte [the piece of cedar floats]
N.[3] *onsahochienda$_l$ren* [with *-chiend-* 'name']	il a fait reparoistre le nom [he has made the name reappear] (HF62)

Does the reference to the Huron as 'they of the floating island' lend credence to the hypothesis that 'Wendat' means 'islanders'? I think that the connection is weak. Let's address the answers to two key questions.

What was the time period for the expression 'they of the floating island'? The words of the 1648 *Relation* might be instructive: the country 'has now become a floating one.' That is, it was not one before, but became one within recent times. This expression may have begun in the late 1640s with the defeat and destruction of village after village in Huronia, or in the late 1630s, with the devastation caused by disease. The term may have lost its accuracy by the late seventeenth century, once the Huron settled at what is now their current home in Loretteville, Quebec. The Potier dictionary, written in the 1740s (but largely a copy of what had been written before), did not have in its entry for *-a$_l$ra-* a reference to the Huron as 'they of the floating island.'

But was the 'floating island' an extension of an older island image? Judging from the very limited use of the noun root *-h8en-* found in the Jesuit

Huron dictionaries, I would say not. Apart from -a₁ra- only one other verb
is shown as incorporating this noun root -o- 'to be (in) water' (Potier
1920:401). This was used with the external locative noun suffix -(ᵢ)e- to
mean 'at the island in water,' referring to Christian Island (see maps 11–15
in Heidenreich 1971). With the populative suffix -ronnon- ('people of' (Potier
1920:66)), it was used to refer to the English (HF62 and FH1697:248). If the
Huron thought of themselves as 'islanders,' a much longer list of verbs would
have incorporated the noun root. Huron speech was, in Brébeuf's terms,
filled with: 'an infinity of Metaphors, of various circumlocutions, and other
rhetorical methods: for example, speaking of the Nation of the Bear they
will say, 'the Bear has said, has done so and so; the Bear is cunning, is bad;
the hands of the Bear are dangerous" (JR10:255).

A translation of an Aboriginal name must pass two tests. The first,
which we have been talking about so far, is cultural: Does the translation
fit with the usage or thinking of the culture? The second is purely linguistic: Does the construction of the name make morphological sense? Applying strict standards, it is not possible to construct the word 'Wendat' using
-h8en'd-. While there is no real problem with the dropping of the -h- (see,
for example, the HF62 entry), because the French-speaking Jesuits often
missed that sound, distinct difficulties arise with the lack of pronominal
prefixes. To be grammatical, nouns and verbs in Huron typically require the
presence of pronominal prefixes, in this case a pronoun that would precede
-8-. It is also difficult to come up with a verb root that would combine suit-
ably with this noun root. Jones suggested -t- 'to be one' (Potier 1920:357)
but using this verb requires the presence of the repetitive prepronominal
prefix typically represented by -s-.[4] Another possibility is -t- 'to stand' (356),
but it was not used to incorporate noun roots, and it required the dualic prefix, typically represented by -te-. The only possible verb that does not bring
with it mandatory prepronominal baggage is -(a)t- 'to be inside' (179 and
357). But even with this, the mystery of the missing pronominal prefixes
remains.

The One Language

Jones (1908:419–20) and respected Iroquoian linguist Floyd Lounsbury
(Tooker 1978c:405) both relate the word 'Wendat' to the noun root -8end-
'word, voice' (Potier 1920:452) and the verb root -t- 'to be one.' From this
we get a combination that could mean 'one language' or 'the same language.' This is a tempting hypothesis in that the Huron term for the Neutral, hati8endaronk, probably meant something like 'their words (or

language) are some distance away' (see Steckley 1990a:21), apparently referring to the differences between the Neutral dialects or languages and those of the Huron. Huron terms for speakers of the different Algonquian languages describe how these people seemed unintelligible:

ak8a₍annen ...	parler un langue mal, avoir l'accent etranger[e] [to speak a language badly, to have a strange accent]
ok8a₍atat	8ta80is [Ottawa] (Potier 1920:168)

The above may contain the noun root -*8*- 'voice' (452). We also have:

asa₍annen ... parler une langue etrangere que ceux a qui l'on parle entendent pas ... [to speak a strange language that the people to whom one speaks do not understand]

* *hondasa₍annen*   les loups (nation[5]) [the wolves (nation)] (174)

This may have the same verb plus the noun root -*chi*- (446), which, combined with the voice prefix -*at*-, could have produced the -*as*- in this word.

The major problem with the "one language" hypothesis is that, again, the prefixes are missing. I believe it is not enough to simply say, as did Lounsbury (cited in Tooker 1978:405) that 'Wendat' was "probably an elliptical shortening of some longer form corresponding to Mohawk *skawénát* 'one language.'" That begs the question of how or why.

Villagers

Marius Barbeau claimed that 'Wendat' meant 'villagers' (Barbeau n.d.; card 436), apparently basing his translation on the noun root -*ndat*- 'village' (Potier 1920:448). Heidenreich supported this claim, based on Sagard's use of the word '*houandate*' to represent Wendat (Sagard 1866).

Two difficulties present themselves, one relating to the prefix, the other to the suffix. First, if the -*8*- or -*w*- that begins the word precedes the pronominal prefix -*e*-, it must also have a vowel before it (see Potier 1920:6 'De 8 euphonico seu adjectitio'). Second, since Sagard used -*te*- to represent a final -*t*-, the word is missing a suffix following the noun root -*ndat*-. This would be ungrammatical; at the very least, there should be the noun suffix -*a*- (see Potier 1920:445–54).

Conclusions

What does that leave us with? As a researcher and as a teacher, I hate to say I don't know. Yet none of these translations is both linguistically and culturally appropriate. The search is still on. We can see, however, that the naming of these people wasn't as static as the traditional ethnohistorical literature supposes. That the Huron renamed themselves as inhabitants of a drifting island could be as significant as the fact that they had previously called themselves 'Wendat.' As we will see later, they also began to apply the name for the Bear nation to themselves when living in Lorette, Quebec. That, too, could have a significance greater than has been supposed.

Member Nations of the Huron Alliance

In our look at the member nations of the Huron Alliance,'[6] we will be investigating the names given to these peoples, as well as what their dialects tell us about their similarities and differences, and what these suggest concerning historical connections between Huron nations (including the non-Huron Wendat: the Petun or *Khionnontateronnon* 'people of the hill').

The Names and Their Meanings

The *Relation* of 1639 gave the following description of the alliance:

> The general name, and that which is common to these four Nations, in the language of the country is Wendat; the individual names are Attignawantan, Attigneenonghnhac, Arendahronons, and Tohontaenrat. The first two are the two most important, having received the others into their country, as it were, and adopted them—the one fifty years ago, and the other thirty. These first two speak with certainty of the settlements of their Ancestors, and of the different sites of their villages, for more than two hundred years back. (JR16:227)

I present now my analysis of these four national names, commonly referred to in the literature as the Bear, the Cord, the Rock, and the Deer. I add a fifth name that was twice recorded in the *Relations:* the Bog.

The Bear

An easily confused point is that the Bear nation was not the same as the Bear clan. In fact, they had different names in Huron. The name for the Bear nation was presented in the following ways, in chronological order:

WORD	SOURCES
attigouautan	Champlain, in Heidenreich 1971:301
atignouaatitan	Champlain, in Heidenreich 1971:301
attigouantan	Champlain, in Heidenreich 1971:301
atingyahointan	Sagard 1939:91
attignawantan	JR16:227

attignaouentan	JR19:125
atignawentan	JR26:217
attinniaoentan	JR34:131
atinnia8enten	FH67:145
hatindia8enten	FH1693:234[7]
hatinnia8enten	HF65:124 and HF59:114
attinnia8enten	Potier 1920:660
hatindia80inten	Potier 1920:154
hatingia80inten	Potier 1920:154
hatindia80inten	Potier 1920:686
hatingia80inten	Potier 1920:686
hatendia8enten	Bruté 1800:55

The word for the people takes three basic dialect forms: *hatinnia8enten* (in Northern Bear and Rock), *hatingia8enten* (in Southern Bear and Wyandot), and *hatindia8enten* (in Lorette). The following sources define the name: '... a part of the Hurons, who are called *Atinniaoenten* (that is to say, the nation of those who wear a Bear on their coat of arms) ...' (JR34:131) '*Hatinnia8enten*. Les ours peuple' [the bear people] (HF65:124; c.f. HF59:114).

The pronominal prefix, imperfectly realized in the earliest entries, is -*hati*-, with a masculine plural form. Without it, we have the following: '*ʇan'nia8enten* pais des Ours' [country of bears] (HF65:124: c.f. HF59:114 and Potier 1920:450). This suggests a meaning of 'they of the bear country' for this nation.

The term appears to be unique to the Huron. No cognate exists in any of the other Northern Iroquoian languages. This is not surprising, given the propensity for names for 'bear' in many cultures to be developed as respectful circumlocutions. Adrian Tanner (1979) discusses this at length concerning the Mistassini Cree. The name of the Bear nation may be derived, possibly as a different dialect or archaic form, from the verb root -*n'nion-ʇen*- 'to be a bear' (Potier 1920:451), which itself may incorporate the noun root -*n(d/n)*- 'finger' (Potier 1920:449). Both names are given in the clan listings, with the latter name first: '*Annionʇen* en ours hommes *hatinnia8enten hatinnionʇ* en femmes *annia8enten*' (FH67:96; c.f. FHO; see Steckley 1982:30). However, there is no clear morphological path to make the linguistic connection between clan name and nation name.

Interestingly, the Bear clan was listed first in the clan lists recorded in the Jesuit dictionaries, and the Bear nation was the largest and most powerful of the Huron nations, which could imply that the two wer actually one and the same. But there is no other compelling reason to think this;

although Northern Bear leaders' names appear prominently as Bear clan names among the Wyandot in the mid-eighteenth century, we know that the Bear nation also had members from outside the Bear clan.

The Lorette Community

In the last six entries of the list presented above, the name of the Bear nation actually refers to the people of the Lorette community. This is curious because the Bear nation was recorded in the *Jesuit Relation* of 1657 as joining the Mohawk. By that time, the Bog had disappeared, the Deer had joined the Seneca, and the Rock had joined the Onondaga. Conventional wisdom has it that this left the Cord to form the basis for the Lorette community. Why then is their community referred to in the eighteenth century as 'Bear'?

I think it worth considering that the Lorette community after 1656 could have been constructed around an amalgam of Bear and Cord. One piece of evidence suggesting this relates to what I call 'Atsena's promise.' Atsena ('plate or spoon'[8]) was a leading figure in the negotiations during the 1650s that led people from the Bear nation to join the Mohawk. In 1657, a Mohawk delegation came up to the Quebec area, and an envoy said to Atsena:[9]

> My brother, it is to you that my words are addressed. Four years ago, you begged me to take you by the arm, to raise you and bring you to my country; you sometimes withdrew it when I wished to comply with your request; that is why I struck you on the head with my hatchet.[10] Withdraw it no more; for I tell you in earnest to get up. It is time for you to come. Here, take this collar to assist you to arise ... Fear not; I no longer look upon you as an enemy, but as my relative; you shall be cherished in my country, which shall also be yours. And, that you may not I doubt it, take this other collar of porcelain beads as a pledge of my word. (JR43:189)

There is no mistaking the finality of the Mohawk envoy's offer. The Mohawk had waited for four years, and now Atsena had to make a move. The Jesuits seemed to have understood the potential threat of the envoy's statement, but still to have placed the responsibility for the fate of the Huron on Atsena's shoulders. They and the French Governor made no promise of French support should Atsena decide to rebuff the Mohawk. In the harsh words of Father Paul Le Jeune:

> The Huron [Atsena] doubtless, would have liked to retract his words; but it was no longer possible to do so—the fault had been his, and he had to

bear the consequences. It was no longer time to delay; he must go, or die by the hand of the Iroquois. (JR43:191)

A discussion ensued that night between Atsena, whom the Jesuits termed 'the Captain of the Nation of the Bear,' and his nation. The next day, he formally addressed the Mohawk representative, stating reluctantly:[11]

> My brother ... it is decided; I am at your service. I cast myself, with my eyes shut, into thy Canoe, without knowing what I am doing. But, whatever may happen, I am resolved to die. Even if you should break my head[12] as soon as we are out of range of the cannon here, it matters not; I am quite resolved. I do not wish my cousins of the two other Nations to embark this time with me, in order that they may first see how you will behave toward me. (JR43:193)

Two other 'Captains' (a French term for a Native leader) were referred to on the same page in that *Relation*. No national affiliation was ascribed, so we cannot assume that they were from the other two nations. One of them simply addressed the Mohawk with a gift, the purpose of which was to ensure the safety of Atsena and those travelling with him. The other "Captain," who was "unwilling to embark, and who did not offer himself to the Iroquois" (JR43:193) spoke of his decision as follows: "I see the whole River, ... bristling with long and great teeth; I would put myself in danger of being bitten, were I to embark at present. It will be for another time" (JR43:193).

Was this another Bear leader, one who would ultimately stay? The associations or connections borne by the name *Atsena* contain the possibility that such is the case.

Iroquoian names are like titles. They belong to particular lineages, ultimately to clans, and have with them particular responsibilities or duties. The name *Atsena* first appeared during the 1630s, as the name of a 'great war Captain' (JR13:59) who was reputably "the foremost War Captain in the whole country" (JR13:131). His house was where "all Councils of war are held" (JR13:59). It was located in the community of Arontaen (JR13:39), in the northern part of the Penetang Peninsula (see Heidenreich 1971: map 17).

This presents two possibilities for divided Bear nation leadership. The Huron were divided politically into "war chiefs" and "peace chiefs" (JR13:59). If Atsena was the name of the traditional war chief of the Bear nation, his promise might only be considered binding on those who chose to follow him. If the other Captain mentioned was the peace chief of the Bear nation, then his decision to stay could represent the choice of others in the nation. Atsena would be keeping his promise without needing to take all the Bear with him.

Secondly, if Arontaen was a Northern Bear community, Atsena might have been representing the Northern Bear, with the other leader representing the Southern Bear. Again, Atsena could be seen by the Mohawk as keeping his promise without taking all the Bear with him.

The Cord

The meaning of the one of the member nations of the Huron, the Atingeennonniahak, has been imperfectly known for years. There is one reference in the Jesuit Relations to the name meaning 'cord' (JR43:191), but no evidence other than that has been forthcoming.[13] This led Bruce Trigger to write in 1976: "It is generally agreed that Cord is a nonsensical gloss ... Until a competent linguist takes the Huron language in hand, further speculation seems unwarranted" (Trigger 1976: 437 fn5). Having taken the language in hand, and with linguistic evidence, I would like to speculate now on the meaning and connotations of the name.

The Name of the Cord in the Ethnohistorical Literature

NAME	SOURCE
Atigagnongueha	Sagard 1866 and 1939:91
Attiguenongha	JR8:71
Atignenonghac	JR10:235
Atignenongach	JR13:125
Attigueenongnahac	JR15:57
Attigneenongnahac	JR16:227
Attinguenongnahac	JR19:125
Attingneenongnahac	JR19:183
Attingueenongnahac	JR21:169
Attingueenonniahak	JR26:259

The most likely realization of this name would be, in Jesuit orthography, *hatingeennonniahak*. A couple of statements are necessary to justify my use of this form. First, I have added an initial *-h-*, because in the name for the Bear nation and the Huron name for the French (*hatinnion ͺenhak*) (HF62:79 and HF65:126)), the *hati-* pronominal prefix is used—a masculine plural, the Huron initial *-h-* being something the French-speaking Jesuit linguists often missed, and so let it seem that the feminine plural (*-ati-*) was being used.

The following entry is from one of the Huron dictionaries. It shows the form I am suggesting here. I think it is too unusual a word to simply appear as an example to illustrate the use of a noun. I find it unlikely that it would be mentioned for any reason other than to translate the Cord's name:

ongeenda   ligne, corde a rets [line, cord for nets]

hatingeennonniahak   ils faisoient des cords [they made cords]
(HF65:115)

The noun root here is *-ngeen(d)-*, which appears in five Huron dictionaries. In most of the dictionary entries, the noun root is presented as meaning 'line or cord used in the making of nets' (HF59:107, HF62:73, and HF63). One dictionary gives it as simply 'line or cord' (FH1697:109), and another as 'Ligne a pecher la barbue [line for fishing for catfish[14]]' (Potier 1920:450). Catfish, being shallow water spawners, were probably fished with nets, so the meaning of the noun root is 'line or cord used in the making of nets.' This distinguishes this noun from the words representing the cords or lines used in bowstrings and in bead necklaces (see discussion in chapter 7). The verb root employed is *-on(n/d)i-* 'to make' (Potier 1920:408), with the habitual aspect plus past suffix (i.e., *-hak-*) giving us the meaning of the whole word as 'they used to make cord for nets.'

The *Jesuit Relations* suggest that the Cord still gathered material used in the making of nets, putting the activity in the ethnographic present as well as in the past. When recounting the story of the death of Thomas *Sawenhati*, a Huron from the main Cord village of *Teanaustaiae*, Jesuit Father Bartholemy Vimont wrote:

> About forty persons [from Tenaustaiae] went to gather some wild plants, of which they make a kind of twine for the nets that they use in fishing. During the night, while they were sound asleep, about twenty Iroquois fell on them, massacred some, and took the others prisoners; a few, more fortunate, escaped by flight ... Our Christian [Sawenhati] was one of the first to fall under the hatchet of the enemy ... During the whole evening and a part of the night, while he was preparing his hemp, he offered his work to our Lord with such fervour that he could not contain his devotion within himself.... (JR26:203–5; see also JR23:55 and 241)

The Rock

The Rock were the easternmost of the Huron nations, and the first to be encountered by the French. Champlain visited them in their home territory during his trip to Huronia in 1615.

The name for this nation takes a number of slightly different forms, as can be seen in the list below. The form began to change in 1642, which is significant because, as we will see later in the study of the dialects of the different nations, the way that the Jesuits recorded the Huron language in the *Jesuit Relations* began to change about that time. This reflects, I believe, the Jesuits' increased exposure to dialects such as Rock which were different from those of the Bear nation. Once the Jesuits were repeatedly exposed to the Rock dialect, they would record the people's name for themselves more accurately. The name was most probably *Arendaenronnon*, with the noun root *-rend-* 'rock' (Potier 1920:452), the verb root *-en-* 'to lie' (221), plus the populative suffix *-ronnon-* (66), to give the meaning of 'people of the lying rock.'

Forms Taken by the Name of the Rock Nation

FORM	SOURCE
Renarhonon	Sagard 1866
Arendarhonons[15]	JR8:7
Arendoronnon	JR10:235
Arendarrhonnons	JR13:37
Arendahronons	JR15:51, 16:227
Ahrendaronons	JR19:125
Arendaronons	JR20:19
1642 CHANGE	
Arendaenhronon	JR23:159
Arendaronnons	JR27:29
Arendaeronons	JR28:149
Arendaenronnons	JR33:81 and 121
Arendae'enr.	JR36: photo of original, facing page 38[16]
Arendageronon	JR43:41

The Deer

The Huron name for the Deer nation was *Atahonta ͺenrat* (JR36:141; also written as *Tohontaenrat* (JR16:227)). This word is composed of the noun root used was *-ahont-* 'ear' (Potier 1920:445), and the verb *-ͺenrat-* 'to be white' (247), and means 'two white ears.' The ears appear to have been a point on which Northern Iroquoian speakers focused. The Cayuga term for deer, which uses the same noun root, means 'long ears' (Froman et al. 2002:81) Interestingly, the name of the one community identified in the 1630s and 1640s as belonging to the Deer nation, *Scanona ͺenrat* (see chapter 5) also incorporated the same verb root as the term for the nation. I do not believe that this is a coincidence.

The Deer spoke a different dialect from those of the Northern and Southern Bear, as was noted by Brébeuf in 1636, when he wrote about a Deer woman:

> I baptized her this Autumn at the village of Scanonaenrat when returning from the house of Louis de Sainte Foy, where we had gone to instruct his parents. The deafness of this sick woman, and the depths of the mysteries I brought to her notice, prevents her from sufficiently understanding me; and besides, the accent of that Nation is a little different from that of the Bears, with whom we live. (JR10:11)

The Bog

Another name, *Ataronchronon*, appeared only twice in the *Jesuit Relations*, in 1637 (JR13:61) and 1640 (JR19:125). It referred to a people who lived in the central part of Huronia. This word appears to have the noun root *-tar-* 'wet earth, swamp, clay' (Potier 1920:453; see discussion of village names in chapter 5) in combination with the verb root *-o-* 'to be in water, wet' (401), which may be nasalized in this word (indicated by the *-n-* following the *-o-*) because of the following nasal vowel. With the addition of the populative suffix *-ronnon-* (66), the translation of the people's name would be 'people of the clay or mud in water.'

As is the case with the Deer nation, there may be a relationship between nation name and village names. There are two village names with *-tar-* in them; *Ataratiri* 'it is supported by clay, wet earth' and *Koutarcano*, used to refer to the Jesuit mission site of Sainte-Marie-Among-the-Hurons, which could possibly be translated as 'where the clay, wet earth is penetrated.' (This describes well what the Wye River does to the Wye Marsh area at that location.) Both villages are in the area where Heidenreich suggests that the Bog nation might have lived (Heidenreich 1971, map 17).

Another putative "translation" was presented by Father A. E. Jones: 'Nation beyond the intervening fen or mud-bottomed lake' (Jones 1908:314). Similar to many of his other ventures into the Huron language, Jones made two major mistakes: first, he used the form of the noun that does not combine with verbs (*-ta-*) in combination with a verb; and second, he used the particle *chi* 'far' (Potier 1920:92) in combination with the verb as well, which is ungrammatical.

Dialects of the Huron Nations

In a series of articles in *Arch Notes* (Steckley 1990d; 1991a, b, c, d, and f; 1992a and d; 1993c; 1995a and b), culminating in a summary piece in

Northeast Anthropology (1997), I investigated the dialects of the Huron language, looking also at the relationships between the various Huron nations and the Petun. I will summarize that research here, and add some further thoughts.

The distinctiveness of the various nations of the Huron has been under-communicated in the scholarly works by archaeologists and historians, and even more in the teaching at elementary and secondary levels of education. The following discussion emphasizes that distinctiveness and demonstrates the dynamic relationship between Huron nations—they were not frozen in one shape as suggested by maps but were ever-changing.

Eleven phonetic or sound features (called phonemes) provide clear evidence of difference between Huron linguistic sources. Based on these features, I have hypothesized five dialects of Huron or Wendat: Northern Bear, Southern Bear, Cord, Rock, and Petun. We have no direct evidence to tell us what the Deer dialect of Huron was like; we just know from Brébeuf's difficulty speaking to a Deer woman that it was different from the Bear dialects (JR10:11). I can only surmise that, like Bog, it was similar to Rock, thereby causing the shift in the 1640s to what I have termed Rock dialect forms in the Jesuits' transcription of the Huron language.

The Dialects of the Bear Nation

The *Hatinnia8enten* or Bear nation of the Huron was the largest of the member nations of the Huron alliance, said to have composed approximately half of the people at the time of early contact (JR10:77), making up some thirteen or fourteen communities. There is written evidence for a split within its ranks. In 1636, the leaders of the five northernmost communities (at the top of the Penetang Peninsula) seem to have had a rift with the leaders of the more populated territory to the south. This led to the drastic step of the northerners holding a separate Feast of the Dead (JR10:281 and 307). According to Brébeuf, "This division has been followed by distrust on both sides" (JR10:281). He reported that the northern leaders complained that "they do not become acquainted as they would like with the affairs of the Country; that they are not called to the most secret and important Councils, and to a share of the presents" (JR10:281).

The dispute was partly caused by a power struggle between two strong figures, *Aenons* in the north and *Anenkhiondic* in the south, and possibly because the Bear nation might have been getting too big for its internal political mechanisms to handle. However, I suspect that the main source of the struggle came from a pre-existing ethnic difference revealed by the linguistic evidence. Clan differences may be a factor here too; the Wyandot data concerning these names suggests that the "Aenons" was a Bear clan name and "Anenkhiondic" was a Turtle clan name.

Brébeuf provides the first main source that can be used to determine features of the Northern Bear dialect. He lived in the community of *Toanche*, a village in the extreme north of the Penetang Peninsula, during his initial stay with the Huron from 1626 to 1628. From that early stay came his "Doctrine Chrestienne" (1830), a translation into Huron of the Ledesma catechism. When he returned to the Huron in 1634 with his Jesuit colleagues, their base of missionary work was the community of *Ihonatiria*, a descendent village of abandoned Toanche (Heidenreich 1971:32), again in the northern part of Bear territory. Although they left Ihonatiria for *Ossossane* in the south in 1637, Brébeuf and the others wrote in the Northern Bear dialect until the early 1640s. As we will see shortly, the oldest surviving Jesuit dictionary, FHO, has Northern Bear dialect features, as does the French–Huron part of the first Huron–French dictionary.

The -y- Phoneme

The -y- phoneme is variously recorded as -ι-, -y-, and -g- (typically before -u-) in the Huron linguistic literature. This phoneme is absent in Northern Bear, not appearing in Brébeuf's catechism, nor in the *Jesuit Relations* until 1646, with the name *houιousta* (JR28:159). It appears with more frequency after that, and is found in all of the Huron dictionaries. All the other dialects have this feature. Along with this, where a -8- or -w follows the -y- in the non-Northern Bear dialects, it is dropped in Northern Bear.

What prompted the dropping of this phoneme? All other dialects of Huron differ from other Northern Iroquoian languages in that they have -y- where the other Northern Iroquoian languages have -g- or -k-. For example, consider the verb root meaning 'to row or paddle':

Cayuga	-*gawe(:)*- (Froman et al. 2002:447)
Onondaga	-*gawe*- (Woodbury 2003:1261)
Huron (not-Northern Bear)	-ιa8e- (FH1697:168)

Perhaps the Northern Bear originally spoke a language that contained the -g- (like that of a non-Wendat-speaking people such as the Neutral or even Laurentian Iroquoian). When they encountered the Southern Bear, they may have dropped the feature that differentiated the two. Such a dropping of differences happened early in the history of the English language, with speakers of various Germanic languages in Britain facilitating communication by levelling the distinctions between them. This hypothesis would be difficult to prove and needs a lot more evidence before it can stated with any authority. To my knowledge, we have no archaeological evidence that suggests that the Northern Bear came from a non-Wendat-speaking people.

From the Huron words written in Champlain's *Works*, we know that the dialect of the Rock (the people that Champlain travelled with and fought alongside) had the *-y-* phoneme, represented by a *-g-*. This can be seen in the following words (with the feature bolded):

Touaguainchain	Bear village (Champlain 1929:48)
Cahiague	Rock village (Champlain 1929:49)
Ochataguain	Rock leader name (Champlain 1929:73)
Asistaguerouon	Mascoutens nation name (Champlain 1929:97)

The sole source for Southern Bear is the writings of Récollet Brother Gabriel Sagard. His phrasebook or dictionary contains two dialects: Southern Bear and Rock. It appears from his writing that Southern Bear drops the *-y-* phoneme when it occurs at the beginning of a word, which could be an example of Southern Bear speakers being influenced by the speech of their Northern Bear neighbours.

-k(h)r- and *-t(h)r-*

Another apparently unique feature of Northern Bear is the *-k(h)r-* that corresponds to a *-t(h)r-* in Southern Bear (and all other dialects). In the following example, note that the Sagard entry contains the Southern Bear feature *-ky-* (see discussion below) expressed as *-qui-*, so the word is clearly Southern Bear and not Rock. Both entries have words composed with the semi-reflexive prefix *-at-* followed by the verb root *-rio-* 'to fight, kill' (Potier 1920:229):

Northern Bear	*nonak**h**riochaens*	aux enemies (Brébeuf 1830:14)
Southern Bear	*Onnen onda**thr**io haquiey N.*	Nous allons combattre contre les N. (Sagard 1866)

Again, the Jesuits seem to have moved away from using the Northern Bear form. The last word in the *Jesuit Relations* bearing a *-k(h)r-* occurs in 1645, in the name *Tokhrahenehiaron* (JR27:52). Beginning in 1646 (JR30:22 and 28:230), *-t(h)r-* forms are found, and these also occur in all Huron dictionaries. In Sagard's dictionary, we find around one hundred entries with *-t(h)r-*, and no sign of a *-k(h)r-*. This can be considered evidence that *-t(h)r-* was both a Rock and Southern Bear form. The fact that the Jesuits shifted away from using the Northern Bear form towards a more common form tells us there is a good chance that the -t(h)r- was shared by the Cord, Deer, and even Bog dialects.

Northern and Southern Bear Sharing Distinctive Features

-ky- and -ty-

Another Northern Bear feature that fades from the *Jesuit Relations* during the 1640s is the use of -ky- (typically written as -kh(i)-) rather than -ty- (typically written as -ti- (Steckley 1991)). We see the shift in two versions of the personal name of a Deer nation man.[17] His name appears as *Okhuk8andoron* (JR22:134 and 138) in 1642, but as *Aotiok8andoron* (JR26:294 and 298) in 1643. While -ky- is a feature shared by Northern Bear, Southern Bear and Petun (Wyandot), all the dictionaries take -ty-. The shift from -ky- to -ty- in the *Jesuit Relations* may have been because the Jesuits found the latter form more prevalent in their expanding missions of the 1640s, suggesting that it must have been a feature of the Rock and the Deer, possibly the Cord and the Bog as well.

-ngy- and -ndy-

A similar case occurs with the move from -ngy- to -ndy- before -a-. Northern Bear, Southern Bear, and Wyandot take -ngy- (Steckley 1993). Rock, as seen in Sagard and the dictionaries, takes -ndy-. The shift seems to have taken place sometime during the 1640s. The earliest recorded instance of -ndy- before -a- in the *Jesuit Relations* occurs in 1648, with the name *Tsoendiai*. The latest occurring example of -ngy- is the place name *Onguiaahra* (i.e., the Neutral name 'Niagara' (JR21:190)) or *Onguiaahra* (JR21:210) in 1641). All of the dictionaries then take -ndy-. This uniformity after 1641 suggests that the -ndy- form was not unique to Rock, but shared by the dialects of Cord, Deer, and Bog as well.

-ndh-, -nth-, and -nnh-

Northern and Southern Bear both take -ndh-, where Wyandot has -nth- and Rock has -nnh-. This can be demonstrated with the verb root -n(d/t/n)hi- 'to be full' (Potier 1920:303).

Northern Bear	*ichiendhi*	'you are full' (Brébeuf 1830)
Southern Bear	*yguendi*	'they (indefinite) are full' (Sagard 1866)\
Rock	*yguenhi*	'they (indefinite) are full' (Sagard 1866)
Wyandot	*ien'tnhi*	'they (indefinite) are full' (Potier 1920:303, with Wyandot superscript)

The 'Northern Bear' dictionaries, FHO and FH62 contain more -*ndh*-forms than any of the other dictionaries (see Steckley 1993:23–4). The *Jesuit Relations* are of mixed use in this regard, as -*ndh*- occurs in early *Relations*—e.g., 'femmes *otiendekhien*' (JR10:70) in 1636, but then between the 1650s and 1670s both -*ndh*- and -*nnh*- are found (for the former, JR36:122, 132, 142, 37:104 and 168 for 1651 and 1652, and JR55:274 for 1672; and for the latter JR41:166 in 1654 and 57:62 in 1673).

-8- and -o-

The contrast between -*8*- (-*u*-) and -*o*- presents a more complicated picture, with slightly different situations occurring depending on whether the phoneme appears at the beginning or in the middle of a word. I have discovered thirty-eight nouns and verbs in which -*8*- or -*o*- can appear in a feminine patient pronominal prefix (she or it). Southern Bear tends to take -*8*- in this situation, demonstrated by the fact that there are twelve nouns and verbs in Sagard in which both -*8*- and -*o*- occur (see Steckley 1992:6). The former reflects the Southern Bear forms; the latter reflects the Rock forms. Brébeuf's catechism, FHO, and FH62 all demonstrate that this is a Northern Bear feature as well (Steckley 1992:6).

In word-central position, Southern Bear is more likely than Northern Bear to take -*8*-. The best demonstrated example of this is in the noun root -*skot*- / -*sk8t*- 'head' (Potier 1920:453). In the Southern Bear words below, the -*8*- is detectable in the -*ou*- spelling:

Southern Bear	La teste [the head]. *Scouta* (Sagard 1866)
	Oscouta [name of a shaman living in the Southern Bear community of Ossossane] (JR14:60 and 62)
Northern Bear	*Oscotarach* Perce-teste [a mythic figure] (JR10:146)
	Condayee oscotaweanaon, 'There is something with which he wipes away the blood from the wound in the head.' (JR10:217)
	Teste. *oskota* (FHO; c.f. FH62)

It should be pointed out, however, that Northern Bear still uses -*8*- word-central in instances when Rock (as found in Sagard) does not. Typically (but not always) when that happens, the Huron dictionaries take the -*8*- form, as in this example with the noun root -*ndoch*-/-*nd8ch*- 'old robe':

Rock	Robe vieille.	*Endocha* (Sagard 1866)
Northern Bear	vieille robe de Castor	₁*And8cha* (FHO:170)
Other Dictionaries	vieille robe	₁*and8cha* (FH1697:186,
HF59:103, FH1693:29 and HF65:111)		

Perhaps, just as Southern Bear may have dropped -y- being influenced by Northern Bear, Northern Bear picked up -8- being influenced by Southern Bear.

Wyandot has the most complete set of -8- forms, as demonstrated by Potier's sporadic -8- superscripts, and by the complete replacement of -o- by -8- in Barbeau's writing.

-ch- and -chr-

In the contrast between -ch- and -chr-, the former is a Northern Bear and Rock feature, while the latter is shared by Southern Bear and Petun (Wyandot). With the noun stem -ondech(r)- 'country,' for example, we get the following:

Southern Bear	*Ondechra, Ondechrate*	la terre, le monde (Sagard 1866)
Wyandot	*ondechra*	terre ... pais (Potier 1920:455)
Northern Bear	*econdechate*	la terre (Brébeuf 1830)

That the -ch- is a Rock form can be seen in the following, in which the Rock form -o- also appears:

Rock	*sanontaha ottecha*	Elle te portera le bled pile (Sagard 1866)
Wyandot (Petun)	*8techra*	farine (Potier 1920:450)

Perhaps, again, there is a Northern Bear influence at play with the Southern Bear. In the following example, with the verb root -ch(r)onni- 'to prepare' (Potier 1920:216), we see the -ch- appearing with the Southern Bear -gya- form:

Asson tesquechongya   Elle n'en scauroit encore faite (Sagard 1866)

Cord Features

So far, I have argued for the existence of four Huron/Wendat dialects: Northern Bear, Southern Bear, Rock, and Petun (Wyandot). In what follows, we will discuss some potential features of the Cord dialect, beginning with those that seem to be shared with Southern Bear.

-m-

The phoneme -m- does not exist in most Northern Iroquoian languages, Wyandot and Laurentian Iroquoian being the exceptions. In Brébeuf's description of the Huron language (based on his experience primarily with the Northern Bear), as recorded in the *Relation* of 1636, he stated that speakers of the language were "not acquainted with [the letters] B. F. L. M. P. X. Z" (JR10:117). None of the Huron dictionaries contains a Huron word with an *-m-*. Words borrowed from other languages, such as the French name Marie[18] and the Ojibwe word 'Mississauga' (Steckley 1990a:24; see JR10:72 for Marie), have the *-m-* changed to a *-w-*.

However, there is evidence for *-m-* existing in Cord and Southern Bear. Of the over three hundred Huron names that appear in the *Jesuit Relations*, the only one to bear the sound *-m-* is the Cord name *Amantacha* (JR5:73, 225, 239–41, 245, 251–53; 6:21–23; 7:215). Sagard's recording of Southern Bear clearly demonstrates the existence of *-m-* as well.[19] It does so by consistently appearing with particular words and by having the *-m-* occur in the same linguistic environments as it does in Laurentian Iroquoian (Barbeau 1961)[20] and Wyandot (e.g., instead of *-w-* and before and/or after a nasal vowel). The best examples come from two different words (possibly cognates) found in Sagard that signify the pointed tool known in English as an 'awl.' Notice how *-m-* corresponds to the *-w-* or *-8-* in the examples:

Two Words for Awl

SAGARD	OTHER HURON SOURCES
-(t)c(h)omat-[21]	*-chion(8)a't-*[22]
-ssiment-	*-chi8ent-*[23]

The *-m-* seen in these examples may have been disappearing from Southern Bear and Cord when Sagard was recording the feature, owing possibly to the relatively recent entrance of the Rock and the Deer nations into the Huron alliance. The lack of an *-m-* in the dialects of these new arrivals may have encouraged it to be lost or replaced in Southern Bear and Cord.

With Wyandot, the feature was innovative, not conservative. That is, it was developed during the latter half of the eighteenth century and was not an ancestral Petun form. Potier makes no reference to hearing it among the Wyandot. The *-m-* does not appear in print until the records of the council of nations that met at Detroit on May 19, 1790. Several of the Wyandot leaders had names with *-m-* in them: 'Ska~hou~mat,' 'Mon~do~ro,' 'Trem~you~maing,' 'She~hou~wa~te~mon,' and 'Meng~da~hai' (Curnoe 1996:220).

-dr- and *-nr-*

Another feature that might be shared by Southern Bear and Cord is the use of *-dr-* after a nasal vowel, where Northern Bear and most of the Huron dictionaries take -nr- (Steckley 1993c). I say "might" here because the five examples of -dr- found in Sagard give no hint as to whether the dialect in question was Southern Bear and/or Rock. The absence of -dr- in most of the dictionaries suggests that it was not a Rock feature. As with -m-, this feature is shared with Wyandot but appears to be a conservative rather than innovative form. It is well recorded by Potier in the mid-eighteenth century.[24]

There are five French–Huron dictionaries or partial dictionaries in my collection. The earliest two, FHO and the partial FH62 date from the mid-seventeenth century and show Northern Bear features. For example, Northern Bear drops -$_\iota$8- after nasal -o- (written as -on-). We can see this occurring in the Huron word translated as 'it is forbidden to us,' written as *onatia8enre* in FH62 and FHO, but as *on$_\iota$8atia8enre* elsewhere (FH67:67, HF59:26, HF65:32, and Potier 1920:188).

The last three French–Huron dictionaries—FH67, FH1693, and FH1697—have features that show up in no other seventeenth-century dictionaries: the -a- suffix for kinship terms (see discussion below) used in verbs meaning 'to have as brother's child' (female speaking), 'to have sister's child' (male speaking), and 'to be cousin,' for example. This suffix appears with the -dr- form appearing in these dictionaries, but not with the -nr-, which occurs in the other dictionaries.

The -dr- appearing in the last three dictionaries is documented as follows:

VERB OR NOUN ROOT	FORM TAKEN	SOURCES
to have as nephew/niece	-dr-	FH1693:257 and FH1697:258
(female reference)	-nr-	FHO, HF62:12, HF59:48, HF65:59
to dance	-dr-	FH67:66, FH1693:88, FH1697:47
	-nr-	FHO, HF62, HF59:121
to get dirty	-dr-	FH67:176
	-nr-	FHO, HG62, HF59, HF65:226, FH1697:190
nest	-dr-	FH1693:239, FH1697:131
	-nr-	FHO:140, HF62:84, HF59:121, HF65:134
stem of an ear of corn	-dr-	FH1693:368
	-nr-	HF62:84, HF59:121, HF65:133
leaf	-dr-	FH1697:76
	-nr-	HF62:85, HF59:121, HF65:134

We see here that only FH67, FH1693, and FH1697 take the -*dr*- forms. Now, the -*dr*- is also presented as a Wyandot superscript in Potier (1920:216, 452, 396, 450, 452 and 452, respectively). I suggest two potential interpretations of this. One, (in line with the above discussion regarding the use of the Bear nation name to refer to the Lorette Huron) is that the Southern Bear form is being used here. In Southern Bear, we find the -*dr*- form, as seen in the following:

Etchondray   Ma niece (maniere de parler aux femmes & filles)
(Sagard 1866)

The other interpretation is that the -*dr*- is a Cord feature (shared with the Southern Bear dialect), with the Cord linguistically dominating the Lorette Huron. Evidence in support of that includes forms that occur in the three dictionaries, FH67, FH1693, and FH1697, that are different from Southern Bear forms found in Sagard's writing. This can be seen in the next two features discussed.

-*nni*-, -*ngi*-, and -*ndi*-

This threefold contrast, in which a phonetic -*ny*-, -*ngy*-, or -*ndy*- occurs before an -*a*-, can be readily seen in the words for 'mouse' and 'Bear nation.' For the former, we have *tsonniatena* occurring in FH62 and HF65, *tsongyatan* in Sagard's Southern Bear (1866), and *tsondiatena* in one of what I will be calling the "Cord dictionaries" (FH1697:199). In the latter, *Atigniouaatitan* (i.e., the -*ny*- form) appears in the Rock dialect recorded by Champlain (Heidenreich 1971:301), as it does in the Northern Bear dialect of the early *Jesuit Relations* (JR16:227 and 19:125). Sagard records *Atingyahointan* (1939:91), a -*ngy*- form, as does Potier with his Wyandot superscript. The -*ndy*- form occurs only in the Cord dictionary of FH1693, and with the non-superscript Lorette forms in Potier. With a few verbs, a mix of -*nya*- and -*ndy*- occurs in some of the other dictionaries, but the -*ndy*- form is still more prevalent in the FH67, FH1693, and FH1697 dictionaries (see Steckley 1995).

Summary of Dialect Evidence

We have seen that Northern and Southern Bear are separate dialects, pointing to a separate ethnic origin of the two groups that made up the Bear nation at the time of first contact with the French (1620s to 1640s). Also to be noted is the influence each dialect may have had on the other— apparently a mutual process. However, more influence appears to have

Summary Chart of Huron Dialect Features

			DIALECT			
FEATURE	Petun (Wyandot)	Cord	Southern Bear	Northern Bear	Rock (Deer/Bog)	Conservative/ Innovative
-y-	-y-	(?)	-y-/-ø-[25]	ø	-y-	-y-/ø
-tr-/-kr-	-tr-	(?)	-tr-	-kr-	-tr-	-tr-/-kr-
-ty-/-ky-	-ky-	(-ty-)	-ky-	-ky-	-ty-	-ty-/-ky-
-ndy-/-ngy-	-ngy-	(-ndy-)	-ngy-	-ngy-	-ndy-	-ndy-/-ngy-
-nr-/-dr-	-dr-	-dr-	-dr-	-dr-	-nr-	-nnr-
-8-/-o-	-8-	(?)	-8-	-8-	-o-	-o-/-8-

been exerted by the numerically larger and politically stronger Southern Bear group.

Southern Bear seems closer linguistically to Petun (Wyandot) than it is to Northern Bear. The two dialects share almost every feature in which Wendat dialects differ. This suggests that the Southern Bear and the Petun (or at least the group of the Petun that formed the basis for the Wyandot) were linked before the former formed an alliance with the Northern Bear, before there was a 'Huron'/'Petun' distinction among the Wendat speakers.

The Cord nation may well have had a closer historic link to the Southern Bear than they did to the Northern Bear, and the forming of the 'Huron alliance' of Bear and Cord some two centuries prior to contact might have been a linking of Southern Bear and Cord.

Finally, the Bog dialect presents even more speculative possibilities. The Rock and the Deer nations were relative newcomers to the Huronia of early contact. The Bog were quite likely newcomers as well. It would make sense that the changes that took place in the dialect recording of Wendat found in the *Jesuit Relations* during the 1640s reflected a move towards representing a majority of Wendat speakers in Huronia. The Jesuits lived in what appears to have been Bog country. When deciding on the majority dialect forms, the Jesuits would necessarily have considered what the Bog nation spoke. This suggests that the Bog shared forms with the Rock and the Deer, and perhaps had been linked with them prior to their coming to the shores of Georgian Bay.

Notes

1 This is a reference to *onnonh8aroria;* see discussion in chapter 7.
2 The *-o-* in *hati8endogerha*, and the *-ha-* rather than *-hati-* in *hah8endagerha* would appear to be mistakes. I suspect that these words were borrowed into Mohawk, or at least in Jesuit Mohawk from Huron, as the Mohawk cognate for 'island' does not have a *-d-* (see Michelson 1973:118).
3 The 'N.' here is a short form for 'nomme' or name.
4 Sometimes it takes the coincidental prefix *-chia-* instead of the repetitive, but this is likewise nowhere in sight.
5 This could be a reference to the Mohican, whose name means 'wolf.'
6 Arnold and Gibbs, in their elementary-school textbook, mistakenly refer to the Huron Alliance as being composed of the Huron, Petun, Neutral, and Erie (1999:53). I suspect that this is a common error in such books.
7 Also in this dictionary is the only use I have discovered of using the pronominal prefix *-e-*, which signifies 'they (indefinite)': 'Les hurons 8endat item *Endia8enten*' (FH1693:182).
8 Potier 1920:454 '*ₗatsen, ₗatsena* ... plat, cuilliers [dish, spoon].'
9 I have updated the translation by changing "thou"and "thee" to "you," "thy" to "your," "thine" to "yours," "mayst," to "may," "didst beg," to "begged," "didst ... withdraw" to "withdrew," and "shalst" to "shall."
10 This is a symbolic expression indicating that the Mohawk attacked the Huron. See the short section on axe metaphors in the material culture chapter. The promise or request referred to was made by Atsena in the fall of 1653 (JR41:19).
11 I have again updated the language, changing "betide" to "happen," "shouldst" to "should," and "wilt" to "will."
12 This is a metaphorical reference to killing.
13 The lack of good evidence in this regard led Heidenreich to speculate that the name might mean 'They of the barking dogs' (Heidenreich 1971:302).
14 This could also be a reference to burbot (see discussion in chapter 5).
15 The *-s-* here is added by the original French writer.
16 In the published French and English versions, the *-n-* following the second *-e-* is missed (JR36:141 and 142).
17 This name, which written in full would be *aₗotiok8andoron* 'it is a difficult or valuable group,' referring to Deer, later became a prominent name among the Wyandot.
18 For the similar fate of 'mess' ('mass') and 'Rome,' see Steckley 1978:111.
19 We can tell that it is Southern Bear and not Rock that has this feature, as the Southern Bear feature *-ky-* appears five times in the same word or sentence with the *-m-*. An example is the following: 'L'alesne est rompue. *Tachomatakiaye*' (Sagard 1866).
20 An example is 'Water, fresh water ... *ame*' (Barbeau 1961:158). Compare this with 'Eau ... *a8en*' (FH1697:58).
21 The same form is found in Wyandot (Barbeau 1960:200 #10), mistakenly printed as 'owl' rather than 'awl.'
22 In FH67:7, it appears as *ₗachiona'ta*; in Potier 1920:446, as *ochion8ata*.
23 FH1697:11, HF62, HF59:49, HF65:59.
24 Examples are the superscript *-d-* found in the words for 'leaf,' 'mushroom/fungus,' 'to look at,' and 'to dirty oneself' (Potier 1920:452 for the first two examples; 234 and 396 for the last two).
25 This symbol indicates that the feature is absent.

3 Clans and Phratries of the Huron

Clans are central to understanding the traditional culture of the Huron. They provided names, songs, teachings, medicine, identity, and social support to the individual. And yet, unfortunately, little has been written about them. Even the number of Huron clans was for a long time a mystery. Prior to my writing an article entitled "The Clans and Phratries of the Huron" (Steckley 1982), it had long been suspected, but not known, that the Huron had eight clans at the time of first contact with the French. The main early source for this belief was the *Jesuit Relation* of 1648, in which Father Paul Ragueneau gave an account of the condolence ceremony for a murdered young Frenchman called Jacques Douart. Father Ragueneau mentioned that there were eight "nations" of the Huron, but did not name them (JR33:243, 247; also see Bressani in JR38:283 and 287). It is important to keep in mind here that Ragueneau had no term for "clan" and that the nation-state as we think of it now did not then exist as a well-formed concept (see Anderson 1983). Drawing upon the *Jesuit Relations*, and on material published in the nineteenth and early twentieth centuries on the Wyandot (Barbeau 1915 and 1917; Clarke 1870; Connelly 1900; Finley 1840; and Powell 1881), Elisabeth Tooker suggested that the eight clans were the Deer, Turtle, Wolf, Bear, Beaver, Snake, Porcupine, and Hawk (Tooker 1970).

Linguistic evidence further supports the idea of the eight-clan structure but changes the composition by excluding the Snake and the Porcupine of the Wyandot and including instead the Loon/Sturgeon and the Fox clans.

In the same *Relation* of 1648, Ragueneau also refers to "three principal Captains of the Huron," similar to the three representatives that were
found among the Wyandot in the late seventeenth and eighteenth centuries.[1] Like Trigger (1976:749), I believe that these were the heads of three
phratries (i.e., collections of three or more clans within a tribe or nation).
I will provide evidence to support this belief by comparing two Huron clan
lists with another list from the mid-eighteenth-century Wyandot. I will also
discuss entries in Huron dictionaries that mention something known in
Huron as the *Aiheonde* burial relationship.

The Huron Dictionary Evidence for an Eight-Clan Structure

The earliest surviving clan list comes from FHO. For a few reasons, we
can say that this dictionary was written in the mid-1650s. It contains some
Northern Bear forms (see chapter 2). More importantly, the Onondaga
entries in the right columns of the pages are few, showing that linguistic work
was only then beginning. Fathers Pierre Chaumonot (who wrote later Huron
dictionaries) and Claude Dablon made the Jesuits' first visit to Onondaga
country in the mid-1650s. Under the dictionary's entry for "Aumoirie"
(meaning 'an armorial sign'; the word appears as "armoirie" elsewhere
and in modern French) we find evidence of the names, number, and some
affiliations of the clans. A similar list is found in a later dictionary (FH67:96).
Father du Peron shows us why the armorial sign is such an important source
of information:

> Each family ['famille'] ... has its distinctive armourial bearing ['armoiries'],
> one having a deer, another a serpent, another a crow, another the thunder,
> which they consider a bird; and like objects. (JR15:181; additions from
> French on page 180)

Each dictionary list mentions eight of these signs, said by the author to
represent the "nations" or "familles" of the Huron. The term "famille"
was often used by the Jesuits to refer to clans, as can be seen in the following example, in which reference is made to two Huron clans:

> Famille ... de quelle famille est tu?
> [Family ... of which family are you?]
> *ndia8eron esendio'k8ten?* [Which clan are you?]
> *andia8ich* de la tortue [of the turtle][2]
> *annion,en* de l'ours [of the bear] (FH1697:74; c.f. FH1697:15, FHO:58 and
> FH1693:141)

The Huron noun stem[3] used to refer to clans here is *-ɩentiok8-*, with the verb root *-8ten-* 'to be of such a nature' (Potier 1920:441) added. This was derived by adding the instrumental suffix *-k8-* to the verb root *-ɩentio-* (Potier 1920:391, HF62, HF59, and HF65), which referred to relatives on the mother's side.[4] With the external locative noun suffix *-ɩe-*, you get dictionary entries such as the following:

> *gentioɩe*   1. etre parens de c[oté] maternal
> [to be relatives on the mother's side]
> *onɩ8entioɩe*
> [we are mother's side relatives]
> ils sont mes par[ens] du c[oté] maternal
> [they are my relatives on my mother's side]
>
> 2. av[oir] les par. matern. en tel lieu
> [to have maternal relatives in such a place]
> *θo aɩitioɩe*
> [there, on my mother's side]
> J'ay la des parens du c[oté] de ma mere
> [I have there relatives on my mother's side] (HF59; c.f. HF62, and Potier 1920:391)

The following is a presentation of the FHO dictionary list, which is the most complete of the two lists. The headings are mine, but the words that follow come from the list:

SIGN	FRENCH GLOSS	"NATION" OR CLAN	WORD STEM
An'nionɩen	ours	*Atinnia8enten* *hatin'nionɩen*	*Annia8enten*
oskennonton	cerf	*sontennonk*	*skiatennon*
Andia8ich	tortue	*tionnenria honnentre[a]* *hotienrotori*[5]	*ontrea* *oenrotori*
Ets8tai	castor	*Satichiohare*	*tsochiohare*
Annaarisk8a	loup	*hatinnaarisk8a*	*Ahonrek*
h8enh8en	huart	*hoti'raɩon*	*o'raɩon*
Andesonk	epervier	*hatindesonk* *hatiraenre*	*Araenre*
Andatsatea	renard	*Andatse'ronnon*	*Skandaɩona*

Translation and Analysis

Bear Clan

An'nion₁en (the name of the first sign) and *hatin'nion₁en* (one of the clan names attached to it) are both derived from a verb root meaning roughly 'to be a bear' (Potier 1920:451 and the FHO entry for 'animaux'), a term unique to Huron among the Northern Iroquoian languages. The first term translates as 'it is a bear,' the second as 'they [masculine] are bears.' The other terms—*Atinnia8enten* and its stem *Annia8enten*—are derived directly from the name of the Bear nation (discussed in chapter 2).

Deer Clan

Oskennonton (along with various cognate terms) is used to refer to deer in several Iroquoian languages (Barbeau 1961:168, Michelson and Doxtator 2002:959 for Oneida, Woodbury 2003:1074 for Onondaga, and Michelson 1973:102 for Mohawk). It has the literal meaning of 'one goes to or is in the land of the dead' (Potier 1920:352). The terms *sontennonk* and *skiatennon* seem to be derived from a verb root *-ennon-* meaning 'to take care of, keep' (Potier 1920:308). This could be a reference to taking care of or keeping some political office.

Turtle Clan (and the Wenro)

Andia8ich was the Huron word for 'turtle' (Potier 1920:449; FHO 'animaux'). The last word of the phrase in the "Nation" or "Clan" column makes reference to the Wenro. They were one of the nations that were termed "Neutre" or Neutral by the French in Ontario during the early seventeenth century. The French referred to them as Neutral because they appeared to be uninvolved in the battles that existed between the Huron and the Iroquois. This appearance would prove false. The Neutral were a grouping of loosely allied nations living from around the west end of Lake Ontario, in southwestern Ontario, and in the Niagara Frontier of western New York. The Wenro, who lived about thirty miles east of the Niagara River, were the Neutral nation closest to the westernmost member of the Iroquois Confederacy, the Seneca. This put them in a precarious position.

Sometime during the 1630s, life became much more dangerous for the Wenro, as described by Father Jerome Lalemant:

> As long as this Nation of Wenrohronons was on good terms with the people of the Neutral Nation, it was sufficiently strong to withstand its Enemies, to continue its existence and maintain itself against their raids and invasions; but the people of the Neutral Nation having, through I know not what dis-

satisfaction, withdrawn and severed their relations with them, these have remained a prey to their enemies. (JR17:25–7)

The Wenro decided to ally themselves with the Huron, so in 1638 some six hundred refugees, most of them women and children, moved into the major Huron community of Ossossane (the main village of the Southern Bear) and some of the surrounding smaller villages.

The name "Wenro" was written in a variety of ways, presented here in chronological order:

NAME	SOURCE
Ouaroronon	Sagard 1866
Ahouenrochrhonon	JR8:115–16
Weanohronon[6]	JR16:252–53
Wenronronon	JR17:24–25
Oneronon	JR18:234–35
Awenrehronon	JR21:230–31
Oenronronnon	JR39:138–39

Wenro[7] is composed of the noun root *-8enr-* 'moss' (Potier 1920:454) and the verb root *-o-* 'to be water, wet' (Potier 1920:401–2). Adding the populative suffix *-ronnon-* 'people of' (Potier 1920:66), we get 'people of the wet moss.' To delve further into what this term signifies, we need to analyze the reference to the Wenro in the Turtle clan dictionary entry: *hotienrotori*. It appears to be made up of, not one word, but two separate words jumbled together by the writer: *hotienro* and *otori*. The first word contains the pronominal prefix *-hoti-* 'they (masculine),' giving the meaning 'they (male) are moss on something wet.' The second word is based on the verb root *-ori-* 'to cover, be covered' (Potier 1920:431), and should be translated as 'it is covered.' The combined translation would be 'they are covered with moss.'

A combination of *-8enr-* and *-ori-* was used in the Wyandot dialect of Huron, as the term for the 'moss-backed turtle' (Barbeau 1915:72 fn2 and 86 fn1). Significantly, it was the usual term for the Big or Large Turtle clan, the leading clan of the Turtle phratry.

My hypothesis is that, like the Bear and Deer nations of the Huron, and the Deer and Wolf divisions of the Petun, and the Erie ('it has a long tail') or Cougar nation, the Wenro were named after an animal: the turtle. Let's return now to the rest of the phrase in the "Turtle" entry in the list of armorial signs. The word *tionnenria* appears to combine the cislocative prefix (*-ti-*), the noun root *-nnenr-* 'forces, group' (Potier 1920:450) incorporated into the verb root *-a-* 'to be such a number, magnitude' (Potier

1920:161), and the diminutive, giving the meaning 'when a group was small.' The next word, *honnontre[a]* is based on the verb root *-atrea-* 'to have as maternal grandchild' (Potier 1920:203), with the pronominal prefixes that give us the meaning 'they have them as maternal grandchildren.' The combined translation is: 'when they were small in number, they had as maternal grandchildren those who are covered with moss (i.e., the Wenro).' This suggests that the Wenro were adopted by the Huron Turtle clan because the Wenro were also socially defined as turtle.

There is some evidence to suggest that the Turtle clan was the leading clan at Ossossane at the time of the Wenro's arrival. The principal headman for the community was Hannenkhiondik ('he is a protruding fir tree'). His nephews (most probably his sister's sons) were the brothers Joseph Chi-hoatenh8a and Tehaondechoren. Joseph had gone back to Wenro country to help bring the people back to Ossossane.

In order to obtain the clan identity of the Hannenkhiondik and his two nephews, we need to look to the Wyandot of the mid-eighteenth century. The Jesuit missionary, Father Pierre Potier, recorded a house-by-house census of the Wyandot in 1747 (see Toupin 1996:170–265). Sometimes it is possible to discern the clan identity of certain individuals; both of the brothers' names appear in the census, and they can be identified as belonging to the Large Turtle clan. Although the name of their uncle appears once (Toupin 1996:868), his clan membership cannot be determined directly. We can only surmise from the clan identity of his nephews that Hannenkhiondik belonged to the Large Turtle clan too. Therefore, we can say that the Turtle clan provided the leadership of Ossossane when the Wenro were adopted.

Beaver Clan

Ets8ai is the usual Huron word for 'beaver.' It literally means, 'it is very shiny or brightly coloured' (Potier 1920:180 and FHO), and is cognate with the word for 'black squirrel' (see discussion below). The Laurentian Iroquoians used a cognate word (Barbeau 1961:168). *Satichiohare* and *Tsochiohare* are derived from the noun root *-chi-* 'mouth' (Potier 1920:446) and the verb root *-ohare-* 'to wash' (Potier 1920:405). With the repetitive prefix *-(t)s-* we get something like 'they (probably masculine) are characterized as washing their face' and 'it is characterized as washing its face.'

Wolf Clan

Annaarisk8a and *hatinnaarisk8a* refer to 'wolf' and 'they (masculine) wolves' respectively (FH1697:231). Among Northern Iroquoian languages, this way of constructing a word for 'wolves' is unique to the Huron language. In his dictionary, Potier (1920:450) claimed that this word was derived from the noun root -nna- 'bone' (FH1697:135; also -nne- Potier 1920:450) and the verb root -ri$_l$- 'to bite, chew' (Potier 1920:346), thus giving the two words the meanings 'it chews bones' and 'they (masculine) chew bones' respectively.

Both clan lists show the word *ahonrek* in the word stem section (FHO and FH67:96). This term is clearly cognate with *Atiaonrek*, a Neutral group whose name appears in the following list of nations defeated by the Iroquois, recorded in the *Jesuit Relation* of 1656 as part of the vision speech of an Iroquois spirit: 'I made you conquer the Hurons, the Tobacco Nation, the Ahondironons, Atiraguenrek, **Atiaonrek**, Tekoulguehronnons and Gentuetehronnons' (JR42:197; my emphasis).

The difference between the two terms exists only in the pronominal prefix, with *Ahonrek* apparently containing the feminine singular -($_l$)a-, while *Atiaonrek* probably has the masculine plural -hati-, the same two forms that appear with the root for wolf. I suspect that the people referred to lived in the Niagara region, as the terms *Niagara* and *Ahonrek* never appear in the same nation lists. Although no linguistic clues suggest this, it is possible that these people were identified with wolves just as the Wenro were with turtles.

Loon/Sturgeon Clan

The word *h8enh8en* means 'loon' in Huron (FH1697:232). It is curious that the name is connected with the words *hoti'ra$_l$on* and *o'ra$_l$on*, which mean 'they (masculine) sturgeon' and 'sturgeon,' respectively (FH1697:232). I do not know the spiritual or symbolic connection between the two creatures. While sturgeon and loon clans exist among Algonquian peoples of the Great Lakes area (e.g., Ojibwa and Menominee), they have no special connection that I am aware of. Even more interestingly, in the Wyandot nation, the Sturgeon clan has two names;[8] its other name, *ti$_l$ata$_l$entsi*, refers to the first woman on earth in traditional Huron belief (e.g., *$_l$aata$_l$entsik* 'her body is old').

Hawk Clan

The names *Andesonk* and *hatindesonk* refer to 'hawk' and 'they (masculine) hawks,' respectively (FH1697:232). They both appear as personal names (see chapter 10). In both clan lists, we find the terms *hatiraenre* (which has the masculine plural pronominal prefix) and *Araenre*. The *Atiraguenrek* in the nation list above is cognate with the *$_l$era$_l$enk* recorded in the early 1670s in *De Religione* (Potier 1920:662 and Steckley 2004:132–3, line 16). Both refer to a Neutral group. The term is close enough to the Oneida word for hawk, *kalhakúha* (Michelson and Doxtator 2002:1035), to bear consideration that it too refers to hawks.

Fox Clan

The word *Andatsatea* means 'fox' (FH1697:231), and *Andatsate'ronnon* adds the populative suffix *-ronnon-* (Potier 1920:66) to give the meaning 'fox people.' In both clan lists, the term *Skanda₍ona* is included, which does not relate to any readily discernible nation name. Neither does it relate to any term for 'fox' in the Iroquoian language literature.

Relating Huron Clan Structure to That of Other Northern Iroquoian Peoples

The Huron clan structure differs only slightly from that of the traditional Seneca, Cayuga, and Onondaga (Tooker 1970:94), as can be seen from the following chart:

Clan Structures in Four Northern Iroquoian Nations

HURON	SENECA	CAYUGA	ONONDAGA
Bear	Bear	Bear	Bear
Deer	Deer	Deer	Deer
Turtle	Turtle	Turtle	Turtle
Beaver	Beaver	Beaver	Beaver
Wolf	Wolf	Wolf	Wolf
Hawk	Hawk	Hawk	Ball
Fox	Snipe	Snipe	Snipe
Loon/Sturgeon	Heron	Eel	Eel

Phratries

A number of kinds of evidence support the idea that the Huron had three phratries (i.e., three groupings of clans). First is the known fact that the Mohawk and Oneida have a three-clan structure: Bear, Turtle, and Wolf. This is the grouping pattern I am suggesting for the phratries of the Huron. A second kind of evidence is in the records of the Wyandot clan structure, specifically Potier's list of Wyandot clans and phratries in the mid-eighteenth century. This is presented below along with the list of Huron clans. All names are presented in the order in which they appear in the dictionaries. The Huron clans are spaced according to the phratries I believe they belonged to:

WYANDOT CLAN	WYANDOT PHRATRY	HURON CLAN
Deer	Deer	Bear
Snake	Deer	Deer
Bear	Deer	
Large Turtle	Turtle	Turtle
Porcupine	Turtle	Beaver
Striped Turtle	Turtle	
Prairie Turtle	Turtle	
Wolf	Wolf	Wolf
Hawk	Wolf	Loon/Sturgeon
Sturgeon/Yaatayentsik	Wolf	Hawk
		Fox

Several points are worth noting here. The Snake clan originated with the Deer clan (Barbeau 1915 and 1960), so there is an even closer link than first appears between the first two Huron clans and the first three Wyandot clans. Secondly, the beaver being a water animal like the turtle, an easy logic could connect the two in a phratry. Thirdly, we see that the Sturgeon clan exists as a double-named clan in proximity to the Wolf in both instances. Further, it seems not surprising that a Fox clan would be linked conceptually to a Wolf clan, both named after animals from the dog family.

Reciprocal Burial: The Aiheonde *Relationship*

Another form of evidence for the possible grouping of clans into phratries comes from what I have termed the *Aiheonde* relationship. Jesuit Father Jean de Brébeuf's *Relation* of 1636 makes two references to people whose function it was to take care of the dead. In the first such reference, Brébeuf was speaking of single burial: "Each family has someone who takes care of the dead, these latter come as soon as possible to take care of everything, and determine the day of the funeral" (JR10:269).

In a later passage in the same *Relation*, he speaks of what occurs at the mass burial that took place at the Feast of the Dead: "In each village they choose a fair day, and proceed to the cemetery, where those called *Aiheonde*, who take care of the graves, draw the bodies from the tombs in the presence of the relatives ..." (JR10:281–83).

The term *Aiheonde* is derived from a Huron verb root -ɩenhe(on)- 'to die' (FHO, FH1697:126, and Potier 1920:387). The entries for this verb recorded in the Huron dictionaries give evidence that suggests three significant points when combined with other linguistic documentation (i.e., clan names) and with information from more conventional ethnohistorical

sources. First, the *Aiheonde* relationship was reciprocal. Second, the relationship was not purely hereditary but had some element of negotiation or
contract involved. Third, the relationship might have been inter-clan and
might also have formed the basis of such clan-linking socio-political groups
as moieties or phratries among the Huron.

Linguistic Evidence for the Reciprocal Nature
of the Aiheonde Relationship

Although most Huron dictionaries have entries that relate to the *Aiheonde*
relationship, my main linguistic evidence comes from two sources. The
earliest is the French-Huron-Onondaga (FHO) dictionary of the 1650s.
The other is Potier's much more elaborated dictionary of the 1740s. Below,
I present four entries, all of which appear in both dictionaries. They provide evidence for the reciprocal nature of the *Aiheonde* relationship. In
each instance, the earlier FHO entry appears above the one in Potier's
work.

Heading both sections on the *Aiheonde* relationship is an entry for
ɪenheonde:

> *[ɪ]Enheonde* avoir soin des morts des uns des autres
> [to take care of each other's dead] (FHO 'Mourir,' c.f. HF65:215, HF62, and
> HF59)
>
> *ɪenheonde* care. sing … avoir soin d'ensevelir, d'enterrer les morts, des uns
> des autres, preparer tout ce qui est necessaire pour l'enterrement, faire la
> fosse, accomoder les corps dans les sepulchre
> [not in the singular … to be responsible for burying each other's dead, for
> preparing all that is necessary for the interment, for preparing the grave,
> for placing and arranging the body in the tomb] (Potier 1920:387)

This basic form takes the verb root with two features added. The first is the
dislocative root suffix, which adds a sense of motion. The second is the
purposive aspect suffix, which gives the sense of 'going to (do something).'
This produces a word with the meaning of 'going to (handle) each other's
dying.'

Examples of sentences using this form of the verb are almost identical in the two dictionaries, with the difference being that there were longer,
more developed French translations in the later Potier dictionary. The
following is a representative sample. The pronominal prefixes are key to
the notion of mutuality. Here, for instance, we see the pronominal prefix
-sti-, a second person dual (as opposed to plural) form, i.e., 'you two':

Tsinnen stiheonde. [Who, you two are going to (handle) each other's dying?] qui a charge des morts? [who is in charge of the dead] (FHO)

tsinnen stiheonde [Who, you two are going to (handle) each other's dying?] qui est-ce qui et vous auez soin des morts l'un de l'autre [who is it who with you takes care of each other's dead?] (Potier 1920:387)

In the second example (only the Potier version has a translation) we have the pronominal prefix *-andi-*, a first person exclusive form, referring to 'we two (excluding the listener)':

ondaie andiheonde [he/she, we two are going to (handle each other's dying] Lui et moy avons soin des morts l'un de l'autre [(s)he and I take care of each other's dead] (Potier 1920:387)

Finally, we have the examples using *-ai-*, an indefinite pronominal prefix that can be translated as 'people, one' or a gender-neutral 'they.' This is the form used in Brébeuf's description of the Feast of the Dead quoted earlier, and in the following:

on'd[aie] d'aiheonde. [they, those who are going to (handle) dying] ceux qui ont charge des morts des uns des au[t]res [those who are in charge of each other's dead] (FHO)

Ondaie d'aiheonde.
Ceux qui ont soin de s'entresevelir et enterrer leurs morts [those who prepare and bury each other's dead] (Potier 1920:387)

The key element here is in the reciprocal nature of the relationship. This is indicated not only in the French translations "l'une de l'autre" and "des uns des autres," but also in the Huron pronominal prefixes used (i.e., the dual and the plural), or perhaps more to the point, those not used. No singular pronoun forms appear no forms that can be translated as 'I, you, she or he.' Further, while Huron pronominal prefixes allow for both a subject and an object to be expressed in a verb (e.g., *ha₁atatiak* 'he talks to me'), no such prefix can be found in any of the examples found in the dictionaries. Clearly, then, the relationship was one of equal players—a reciprocal one.

Contracting an Aiheonde Relationship

Those dictionaries both go on to suggest that the *Aiheonde* relationship involved a contract or choice. The evidence for this is the causative-instrumental root suffix *-st-*, which adds the idea of causation or creating. In Potier, we have the following:

ᵢenheondesti
contract ensemble une alliance mutuelle pour avoir soin d'ensevelir et d'en-
terre les morts les uns des autres [to contract or form together a mutual relationship for taking care of the burial of each other's dead] (Potier 1920:387)

Compare that to the following, developed from the verb roots *-nnonhonk-*
'to be related' (Potier 1920:310) and *-atio-* 'to be brothers-in-law' (Potier
1920:190) respectively:

ᵢannonhonsti ...
adopter q[uelqu']un, le faire son parent [to adopt someone, make him a rel-
ative] (Potier 1920:310)

Atiosti ...
devenir beau frere par un mariage ... contracter alliance reciproque [to
become brothers-in-law by marriage, to contract such a reciprocal alliance]
(Potier 1920:190)

Inter-Clan Relationships

What level or levels of socio-political groups were involved in the *Aiheonde*
relationship? Was it established between lineages of the same clan, or with
lineages of other clans? In the quotation from Brébeuf with which I introduced this subject, the word 'family' was employed, a translation of the
French word 'famille.' 'Famille' also occurs in a Potier dictionary entry that
appears to refer to the *Aiheonde* without mentioning the word. This time
Potier is explaining a verb created from the noun root *-rih8-* 'matter, news,
affair' (Potier 1920:453) and the verb root *-ont-* 'to attach, be attached'
(Potier 1920: 418).

[ᵢ]arihont ... [to have a matter attached]
y avoir q[uelque] liaison, q[uelque] affinite entre 2 familles qui son recipro-
quement de leurs morts.[there is a relationship, an alliance between two families regarding taking care of each other's dead] (Potier 1920:419)

As we have seen above, the term 'famille' was often used by the Jesuits
to refer to clans. So do we have here a funeral version of clan exogamy
(i.e., marrying outside your clan)? The Iroquois literature seems to suggest
this. Lafitau, speaking of the Mohawk in 1724, wrote:

Each household has another (opposite) one in which are found its under-
takers and those who wash the corpse and prepare it for burial ... that is
to say, those who take care of the dead. These are usually, I believe the
households which have alliance with that of the deceased. (Fenton 1974:217)

William Fenton, pioneering Iroquoianist and editor of the Lafitau text, specified the cross-clan nature of this alliance through references to more modern Iroquois practices:

> When anyone in Iroquois society dies ..., persons of households and clans to which the family is linked by marriage, his wife's or her husband's families and clans perform the necessary duties. In Seneca-Cayuga-Onondaga society today, the clans of the opposite moiety perform these functions. (Fenton 1974:217 fn1)

What were these 'moieties' to which Fenton referred? The word "moiety" is based on the French word for one half. A society that has moieties is divided into two groups for certain ritual purposes. The groups are typically made up of more than one clan. Elisabeth Tooker, in her important work "Clans and Moieties in North America," asserted that the obligation of the opposite moiety to take care of the deceased is "an old Iroquois custom" (Tooker 1971:361). Further, she pointed out that moiety reciprocity (i.e., two families, one from each moiety, taking care of each other's dead) in ritual following death "is the most basic" function of the moiety among Aboriginal groups.

Did the Huron have moieties? We know they engaged in competitive endeavours, such as athletic competitions and gambling, which are often handled by having moieties as opposite sides. However, the *Jesuit Relations* state that when the Huron played lacrosse or gambled at the plum stone or bowl game (shaking the bowl so that three plum pits coloured differently on two sides will all show the same colour), they competed "village against village" (JR10:185–7 and JR17:201). While one's moiety identity could depend on where one lived, this would typically divide groups with a village, not between villages. It is interesting to note, though, that the Huron did have double villages (i.e., ones with two living areas) the best-known being *Cahiagué*, (Heidenreich 1971:125). Also, six of the Huron village names began with the dualic prepronominal prefix (see chapter 5). It is conceivable that the villages divided into moieties, but if they did, these do not seem to have acted as competitive groups.

Moieties can be seen as being much like phratries, except that they exist in twos. A common symbolic expression of moiety distinction among the Iroquois was that of "sitting across the fire" (Fenton 1951:49 and Tooker 1978:426). The Mohawk and Oneida collapsed their three clans of Turtle, Bear, and Wolf into two moieties for some ritual purposes. The Wyandot used the expression to refer to their different phratries: Deer, Turtle, and Wolf. In 1911, Barbeau talked to Smith Nicolas, an 83-year-old Wyandot, who described in the story of the "Origin of the Phratries" how members of the Deer and Turtle clans would sit on opposite sides of the fire, with the Wolf clan (the sole clan of the Wolf phratry at that time) sitting at the end of the longhouse. Nicolas said the three groups were "across the fire" from each other (Barbeau 1915:85—87 and 1960:99–100).

The practice of one Huron group sitting across the fire from another was only recorded once in the *Jesuit Relations*. At a council meeting, the Bear nation sat on one side, while two other, smaller Huron nations sat on the other side (JR13:39). This weakens the case for the Huron moieties, as these units are not typically aligned tribally. Linguistic evidence is similarly negative. To the best of my knowledge, the expression "across the fire" does not ever appear in any Huron dictionary. The absence of such a significant symbolic statement in the Jesuits' linguistic works certainly suggests that it was not important in Huron culture. The Jesuits were highly aware of Huron metaphor and were generally reliable recorders of meaningful political expressions in the Huron language. We can conclude, then, that if moieties were present at all in Huron ceremonial-political culture, their influence was limited. I think it is likely, however, that the Huron did have incipient or simple phratries (Bear, Turtle, Wolf) or moieties (Bear/Deer/Turtle/Beaver and Wolf/Sturgeon/Hawk/Fox) that expressed themselves in the *Aiheonde*.

The Father's Clan's Possible Significance: Speculation Regarding Huron Infant Burial

Over the years there has been significant discussion of infant burial in and around the longhouses of Ontario Iroquoians (see, for example, Melbye 1983). In what follows, I will attempt to add a linguistic voice to this discussion. I will begin with concrete linguistic evidence concerning Huron recognition of the father's role in the conception of a child, and move toward more speculative suggestions concerning the clan affiliation of infants buried in longhouses and along pathways.

Strong linguistic evidence demonstrates overt Huron recognition of the father's role in conception. For example, the verb root *-ak8eton-* presented by Potier as meaning 'enfanter, engendrer, produire ou avoir des enfans [to give birth to, beget, produce, or have children]' (Potier 1920:170), was often used to refer to men. The following are typical examples:

> *Stante hak8etonk* [he doesn't produce children]
> *il n'a point d'enfans, il est sterile [he doesn't have children; he is sterile]

ndak ihok8eton [four, he has produced children]
il a 4 enfans [he has four children] (Potier 1920:170)

Other evidence suggests that the Huron may even have regarded the male genetic role as primary. The term for human semen in Huron was *onnenha* (Potier 1920:450, FHO:173, and FH1697:192 and 239), a noun usually used to refer to corn (FH1697:23 and Potier 1920:450). The analogy would seem to be to seed, which was probably the base meaning of the word prior to the coming of corn to the Huron. The cognate in Oneida, the noun root *-nʌh-*, means 'seed, pit (of a fruit), grain, oats' (Michelson and Doxtator 2002:1168).

Another interesting word here begins with the verb root *-ondi-* 'to make' (Potier 1920:408). With the semireflexive prefix *-at-*, which typically adds a sense similar to the passive in English, the literal translation is 'to be made.' However, it was used with the following meanings or connotations: 'to be born,' '(for a seed) to germinate and rise above the ground,'and 'to be on the paternal side of a person's family' (Potier 1920:409). Not only does this linguistically continue the identification of human birth with plant germination, but it also expresses the notion that it is the father who 'makes' the child. The following is an example showing the use of the third meaning in a sentence:

8endake hotondi [at (the country of) the Wendat, he has made him]
il a ses parens du cost de pere aux hurons [he has his relatives on his father's side among the Huron] (HF62)

When the nominalizer (noun-maker) suffix *-ch-* is added to this combination, you get a noun, *atondicha*, which means 'the father's side of the family' (HF59:185 and Potier 1920:409). With the verb root *-en-* 'to have' (Potier 1920:221), we get "etre ne de tels ou tels, les avoir pour parens du coté de son pere [to be born of such and such, to have them as relatives on the father's side" (Potier 1920:408; c.f., HF59:185). Examples are the following:

aₜatondichen [I have as my makers]
mes parens du coté paternal [my relatives on the paternal side]

te sk8aₜatondichen [I no longer have my makers]
je n'ai plus de parens du coté de mon pere [I no longer have relatives on my father's side] (Potier 1920:408)

62

Clan Affiliation

Names belong to matrilineal clans in Iroquoian culture. There is, to my knowledge, no direct evidence of the age at which Huron children were given their first names (i.e., ones to be replaced later on by adult names). Generally, in traditional North American Aboriginal culture, naming did not take place immediately after birth (Driver 1970:368). Nicholas Perrot (as recorded in Kinietz 1965:276) wrote that around the beginning of the eighteenth century, Algonquians from the Great Lakes area held their naming ceremonies for children aged five to six months. Thus, it would seem reasonable to assume that the infant burial practice described by Father Jean de Brébeuf in the *Relation* of 1636 would have occurred with children not yet given a name:

> There are even special ceremonies for little children who die less than a month or two old; they do not put them like the others into bark tombs set up on posts, but inter them on the road—in order that, they say, if some woman passes that way, they may secretly enter her womb, and that she may give them life again and bring them forth ... This fine ceremony took place this winter in the person of one of our little Christians, who had been named Joseph at baptism. I learned it on this occasion from the lips of the child's father himself. (JR10:273)

This suggests that children who were not yet named, not yet made the incarnation of ancestral members of the mother's clan, were not yet members of that clan. As the father's seed, they still belonged to their "makers." Admittedly, the evidence for this is indirect. Part of it comes from the term for the father's family discussed above. Another part comes from how the Jesuits viewed baptism. Baptism would, as in the case above, typically involve naming. It is instructive, then, that in the Huron text, *De Religione*, written by Jesuit Father Philippe Pierson during the early 1670s but incorporating ideas that had been developed earlier in the Huron mission, the writer speaks of the Jesuits creating a lineage (using *-h8atsir-* 'matrilineage') (Potier 1920:447), as can be seen in the following:

> Admire, my brothers, that the Charcoal [the Jesuits] will be a lineage in the sky. They will have made them their children in the sky. They will form a lineage of those they will have baptized.
> Would it be unimportant that I would rejoice that one hundred I would baptize all would arrive in the sky when they die, as those I made my children would have formed a lineage? I, by myself, would make a lineage. I, by myself, would have a large lineage....
> They would be very pleasing to me, the several hundreds I would have baptize, as I find those in the sky that I made my children by baptism.

There my lineage would form a group, surrounding me. (Steckley 2004:177 and 179)

I suspect that Pierson, and the Jesuits generally, learned this idea from Huron naming. If a child that dies before naming is considered his or her father's seed, then it would seem appropriate that incest taboos would affect the place of such an infant's burial. Entering the womb of a woman from the child's father's clan would be considered incest, because the woman would be seen as the child's (and the father's) sister. The Huron, like every other people, had well-established rules against incest (JR10:213).

Some suggestion that incest considerations were important in the birth or rebirth of children who had been in the ground can be seen in the story of a short, hunch-backed Huron shaman. He claimed:

I am a spirit. I formerly lived under the ground in the house of the spirits, when the fancy seized me to become a man; and this is how it happened. Having heard one day, from this subterranean abode, the voices and cries of some children who were guarding the crops and chasing the animals and birds away. I resolved to go out. I was no sooner upon the earth than I encountered a woman. I craftily entered her womb and there assumed a little body. I had with me a she-spirit, who did the same thing. As soon as we were about the size of an ear of corn, this woman wished to be delivered of her fruit, knowing that she had not conceived by human means and fearing that this *ocki* [spirit] might bring her some misfortune. So she found means of hastening her time. Now it seems to me that in the meantime, being ashamed to see myself followed by a girl and fearing that she might afterward be taken for my wife, I beat her so hard that I left her for dead; in fact, she came dead into the world. This woman, being delivered, took us both, wrapped us in a beaver skin, carried us into the wood, placed us in the hollow of a tree, and abandoned us. (JR13:105–7)

The shaman's fear that his sister would be taken for his wife shows how incest rules were considered for those reborn from inside the ground.

Conclusion: Infant Burial

I am suggesting here that, in terms of incest, the socially safest place for an unnamed infant (his or her father's seed) to be buried would be where a member of its mother's clan would be the future mother in the rebirth. In this way the child would not be reborn in the womb of a fellow clan member. The burial would be either in or around a longhouse of the mother's clan, or on the paths leading to or in the fields worked by females of that clan.

I think that there is a broader significance to the linguistic documentation of what, in a matrilineal society, the Huron felt the role of the father
(and his family) was in the creation of a child. More clues as to the nature
of this relationship will come later in this text when we look at Huron kinship more generally.

Huron Bridewealth

The Huron verb stem -8arinnhech- relates to marriage gifts. That much is
straightforward. There is, however, a somewhat fragmented collection of
dictionary entries pertaining to this verb that can at first be very frustrat-
ing for the student of Huron culture. In what follows, the fragments will be
pieced together to give insight into Huron marriage customs.

The entries in Huron dictionaries are as follows:

ga8arindhechon	nou[velle] mariee aller porter aux parens les pre-sens de mariage [a newly married woman to go to carry marriage presents to her relatives] (HF59)
₁a8arinnhechon	nouvelle mariee porter dans la cabane de son mary ce qu 'on luy a donne [a newly married woman to carry in her husband's house that which people have given her] (HF62:87)
₁A8arindhechon	Dot Douaire [dowry] (HF62)
₁a8arinnhechon	nouvelle mariee porter çe qu'on luy a donne en la cabane de son mary [a newly married woman to carry that which people have given her in the house of her husband] (HF65:136)
₁a8arinnhechon	... le present que le mari donne à la mariee [the present that the husband gives to his wife]
o8arinnhechon	elle a le present des noces [she has her marriage present] (Potier 1920:318)

There is also an entry in a seventeenth-century Mohawk dictionary that
contains a cognate:

Gak8arinna	... dote d'une femme qui se marie [dowry of a woman who marries]
Gak8arinnionton	... la porter dans la cabane ou l'on se marie [to carry it in the house where one marries] (Bruyas 1970:56)

What can be determined by these entries? We know that the gifts are presented to a new bride. And I believe we can determine where this presentation takes place. My reading of the French translation of two of these entries (HF62:87 and HF65:136) has her receiving the gifts in the home of her husband's family. Perhaps, consistent with the Mohawk entry, that is where the couple got married.

But she does not remain there. She is carrying the gifts to somewhere. The -ch- in this verb stem is a dislocative suffix, typically used to express the notion that someone is going somewhere when he or she is performing or experiencing the semantic content of the verb.

Where is the bride going? One of the entries (HF59) has her going to take the presents to her relatives. If we assume that the Huron were predominantly matrilocal, with married couples going to live with or near the wife's relatives, then the bride would probably be taking the gifts to those whom the couple will be living with in the longhouse.

The fact that we have gifts brought by a woman to her marital home could be the reason why in two cases (one Huron and one Mohawk) the Jesuits translated this verb with words meaning 'dowry.' I believe this to be a mistaken translation, as a dowry is provided by the bride's family. This is not the case here—her family receives rather than gives the gifts. Potier claims that the husband provides the gifts, but it is more likely that ultimately the husband's family does this. A dowry is a relatively rare social phenomenon, existing in roughly four per cent of Murdock's World Ethnographic Sample (Ember and Ember 1990:333), and confined fundamentally to Europe and South Asia, usually in patrilineal, patrilocal societies involved in intensive agriculture and experiencing significant inequalities in wealth (Nanda 1987:216). It appears that what we have here is a form of bridewealth, goods given by the groom's family to the bride's family. This is much more common than the dowry, occurring in forty-seven per cent of societies (Ember and Ember 1990:332).

Bridewealth is typical of a patrilineal society (Kottak 1987:184), as its usual role is to formalize the incorporation of the children (along with the mother) into the descent group of the husband/father. For that reason, bridewealth is sometimes referred to as 'progeny wealth' (184). But the Huron were matrilineal. I suspect that the main reason for bridewealth among the Huron would be to smooth the entry of the groom into the bride's family and into their home. In the next chapter we will discuss further the strong possibility that the Huron had matrilocal-preferred post-marriage residence, that is that their preferred marital home was with the wife's family. The son-in-law would be an outsider, not of their clan. He would actually be more responsible for his sisters'children—who belonged to his clan—than for his own, who did not. This created a reasonably high potential for conflict.

In sum, I believe that the verb stem -8arinnhech- refers to a ceremonial or symbolic gift-carrying journey made by a newly married woman. This journey took her from her husband's family home to the place in which the couple were going to live, the home of the bride's family. The gift-giving was to assuage potential problems with a non-clan newcomer entering a clan home. To use a Huron expression, it would make the minds of his in-laws 'like a field (prepared for planting).'

Summary

One can go a long way toward understanding the nature of seventeenth-century Huron society by having a feel for their clan system. This has been neglected or misrepresented over the years. We find archaeologists, even recently (Williamson and Steiss 2003:112), referring to the member nations of the Huron as "clans." We also find people writing elementary school textbooks containing mistaken clan lists of the Huron (Arnold and Gibbs 1999:61).

This chapter has identified the names of the Huron clans as: Bear, Deer, Turtle, Beaver, Wolf, Sturgeon/Loon, Hawk and Fox. We also looked at the clan logic of totem identification (i.e., in the case of the Turtle clan and the Wenro) linking a Huron clan with an Iroquoian people of the same totem animal, a logic that may have been used more generally in inter-tribal relations among Iroquoians in the area. I argued that the clans of the Huron were probably organized at least ceremonially and in terms of burial relationships as phratries, perhaps as a sign of their growing socio-political complexity. Further, I tentatively linked both infant burial practices and the system of bridewealth among the Huron with the clan structure. Doubtless, the logic and influence of clans will be found to play a part in other aspects of Huron culture not yet researched.

Notes

1 In a conference on August 15, 1682, the Wyandot were represented by three people: "*Soüaïti*, called the Rat, *Ondahiaste chen*, Burnt tongue ..., and *Oskoüendeti*, the Runner" (NYCD9:181). In 1701, three leaders again represented the Wyandot: Kandiaronk, Houatsaranti, and Quarante Sols (Havard 2001:120).

2 This might indicate that this entry was first composed when Brébeuf was working with the Huron Christian, Joseph Chihoatenhwa, who was of the Turtle clan.

3 A noun stem is distinct from a noun root in that it includes a verb root plus a suffix, usually a nominalizer, but sometimes (as in this case) the instrumental suffix.

4 While other Northern Iroquoian languages have the form with the instrumental suffix,
   which they don't use to refer to clans, but to any group (a meaning also found in Huron,
   e.g., 'troup, assemblee [troup, assembly]' (HF59)), they do not seem to still have the
   verb root from which it came.

5 In the other dictionary, only part of the idea is captured by the words that follow the
   word for turtle: '*andia8ich* tortue *Hennontrea ontrea*' (FH67:96). Whoever copied this version of the dictionary must not have known the story the verb attached to the Turtle entry
   (see below).

6 The -*8*- of the original has been transposed to -*w*- here.

7 J. N. B. Hewitt translated Wenroronnon as 'the people of the place of the floating scum'
   (Hewitt 1910:932). While the morphemes chosen are correct, I question his interpretation.

8 After Potier listed the two names, he wrote: "ne fait qu'une bande [it makes only one
   band]" (Toupin 1996:260).

4 Huron Kinship

In 1993, I published a paper entitled "Huron Kinship Terminology." One feature the paper lacked was a good set of comparative material coming from modern Northern Iroquoian languages. Since that time, several comprehensive dictionaries have been published, allowing me to refer here to the Cayuga dictionary of Frances Froman, Alfred Keye, Lotte Key, and Carrie Dyck (2002); the Onondaga dictionary by Hanni Woodbury (2003); and the Oneida dictionary compiled by Karin Michelson and Mercy Doxtator (2002). This updated version of that paper benefits greatly from the stellar work of these people.

The study of Huron kinship terminology presents a unique opportunity to anthropologists. No other Aboriginal group is so extensively documented for the early contact period of the seventeenth century, and no other such group offers us such a long period of written evidence through which to observe changes, with material coming from the 1620s up to 1911.

The goals of this kinship terminology study are varied. Simple description is important, as the source materials, particularly the Huron dictionaries, are not generally known or readily available to the researcher. Secondly, observing change gives us an opportunity to discuss the effect on Aboriginal kinship terminology of long-term contact with European-based societies. The description of the kinship terminology of the Huron of the early contact period, and the documentation of how it changed are particularly important to the study of kinship terminology among speakers of other Northern Iroquoian languages such as Mohawk, Oneida, Onondaga, Cayuga, Seneca, and Tuscarora. Seventeenth-century material about kinship terms in these languages is either non-existent or is considerably less extensive.

A third goal of this study is to describe how the Huron and the French (primarily Jesuit missionaries) interacted with each other using kin terms. These usages demonstrate key aspects of the nature of the relationship between the two peoples, and how that relationship changed after the initial contact period.

Fourthly, this study investigates two aspects of Huron social structure. First, we can learn something about the politics of social distance, power, and solidarity by looking at the use of pronominal and reflexive prefixes and of the -a- possessive suffix. We saw earlier that pronominal prefixes either immediately precede the verb root or are separated by the reflexive (-atate-) or semi-reflexive (-ate-) prefix. The forms of these prefixes depend on which of the five conjugations the verb root belongs to. Pronominal prefixes can contain an agent, a patient or both. A transitive verb (i.e., one that takes an object) has both agent and patient, acting as subject and object respectively. A sociological significance exists in who appears as the agent and who the patient in transitive kinship verbs. It comes down to which person or group is older.

Finally, we consider more evidence regarding post-marital residence (i.e., where a couple would live after their marriage) and some of the social dynamics relating to that residence pattern (e.g., mother-in-law avoidance).

Sources

The most extensive documentation is from the seventeenth century, although there is a rich vein of material from the early twentieth century from one Wyandot source (Marius Barbeau). The early sources are the four French–Huron and four Huron–French dictionaries dating from mid 1650s to the 1740s, as well as Sagard's phrasebook. The rest of the early Huron material comes from the *Jesuit Relations*, which provides examples that were originally in Huron, but most often are presented just in translation.

Three sources of Wyandot kinship data are used in this study. The earliest comes from Potier, who in copying Huron material for his grammar and dictionary sometimes added or substituted Wyandot features or terms to the original Huron ones. A later source is the material published in Lewis Henry Morgan's famous *Systems of Consanguinity and Affinity of the Human Family* (1966), originally collected in 1859 with the assistance of two Wyandot men, Matthew and William Walker. Finally, most of the Wyandot data comes from Marius Barbeau's fieldwork of 1911–12, either published (Barbeau 1915 and 1960) or in his unpublished field notes.

While I will be presenting some examples of seventeenth-century Mohawk (Bruyas 1970 and Shea 1970), and modern Mohawk (Michelson 1973 and Bonvillain 1973), Oneida (Michelson and Doxtator 2002), Onondaga (Woodbury 2003), Cayuga (Froman et al. 2002), Seneca (Chafe 1963) and Tuscarora (Rudes 1987), the main time period represented in the Iroquois comparative material is from the nineteenth century. My main body of Iroquois data was obtained by Morgan from 1859 to 1861. Since that time, some changes have taken place, making the terms more like the English model (for Mohawk examples, see Bonvillain 1973:160–62).

The Kinship Terms

Mother

We will look now at the Huron words for a person's kin, beginning with the mother. Two verb roots in Huron can be translated as 'to be mother to,' and they seem to have stood in a complementary relationship to each other. The term with the broadest variety of pronominal prefixes was typically recorded as *-nd8en-* (Sagard 1866, 1939:71; Brébeuf 1830:3, 7 and 9; FHO; FH1693; FH1697:253—54; HF59; HF62:71; HF65:113; and Potier 1920:68 and 297). It appears in one source as *-ndoen-* (FH67:130).

Barbeau recorded a Wyandot cognate (Barbeau 1960:64–66, 68, 71 passim, and field notes, cards 553, 690, 702–4, 721 and 723). (Morgan was just dealing with the term for 'my mother,' and so used the other verb root, discussed below.) Such cognates appear in all other Northern Iroquoian languages except Mohawk, which instead uses a term cognate with the Huron 'to be father' (see Chafe 1963:23, Lounsbury 1971:193 and Morgan 1966:295 for Seneca; Morgan 1966:295 and Froman et al. 2002 for Cayuga; Morgan 1966:295 and Woodbury 2003:1237 for Onondaga; Morgan 1966:295 and Rudes 1987:67 for Tuscarora; Michelson and Doxtator 2002:608 for Oneida; and Barbeau 1961:149 for Laurentian Iroquoians).

The second verb root signifying mother, *-nnen-*, appears to have been confined, except in one source, to forming the term of address 'my mother.' It is represented in several slightly different ways in the Huron literature, all with the same meaning: *Anan* (Sagard 1866:104), *Annen* (FHO), *Annen-en* (FH67:130, FH1693, FH1697:254, HF62, and Potier 1920:297), and *Annenhen* (Potier 1920:108). The only Huron exception to this form of representing the term is representation is *Sanan* in Sagard, alongside

sendouen as a way of saying 'your mother' (Sagard 1866). This may be a feature of Southern Bear, one of the two Huron dialects that appear in Sagard's
writing.

A cognate for this verb root appears in Wyandot in both Morgan (Morgan 1966:295) and Barbeau (Barbeau 1960:78 and 234, and field notes,
cards 566, 703–4 and 765). While Wyandot words for 'my mother' come
from both roots (something that does not occur in Huron), those coming
from the *-nd8en-* cognate are terms of reference rather than of address
(contrast Barbeau, field notes, cards 658 with 704). According to Barbeau,
the *-nnen-* cognate "seems to be more sacred and refer to the heart" (card
703). (An equally limited cognate occurs in Tuscarora, again with the term
for 'my mother' (Rudes 1987:108).)

The pronominal prefixes used with the verb root *-nd8en-* have the
mother as the agent and the child or children as the patient, as in the following examples:

sand8en	ta mere	('she' is the agent and 'you (sing.)' is the patient)
	[your mother]	[she is mother to you]
hond8en	c'est sa mere, de luy	('she' is the agent and 'he' is the patient)
	[it is his mother]	[she is mother to him]
ond8en	c'est sa mere d'elle	('she' is the agent and 'her' is the patient)
	[it is her mother]	[she is mother to her] (HF65:113)

The reflexive prefix *-atat-* occurs with this verb root, although judging
from its rarity in the dictionaries, its use was not extensive:

ontatend8ten	Estre mere et enfant	('they' (indefinite) is the patient)
	[to be mother and child]	(HR62; c.f. HF65:113)

In both Huron and Wyandot, *-nd8en-* refers not only to a person's biological mother, but also to one's mother's sisters (FHO for Huron; Barbeau
field notes, cards 553, 702–4; and Morgan 1966:339, Morgan contains a
Wyandot *-nnen-* cognate). This is to be expected in an 'Iroquois' system of
kinship terminology, as that system is defined within the six basic termino-
logical system types (Nanda 1987:245). Such a system merges terms for
mother and mother's sisters (i.e., both were called 'mother'), father and
father's brothers (i.e., both were called 'father'), as well as merging the
terms for father's brothers' and for mother's sisters' children, having them
both called 'brothers' and 'sisters,' rather than 'cousins.' The children of

everyone you call father and everyone you call mother, you call brother or sister. As we will see, the Huron had such a system in every detail.

In modern Onondaga, the cognate is applied not only to the mother and mother's sisters, but to the father's sister as well (Woodbury 2003:715). According to Woodbury, there is a linguistic device used to distinguish between the different kinds of 'mothers': "For the aunt types, the term is often modified to mark that extension: *gnohá'dekhenųhę* 'my aunt,' literally: my mother, I greet her with it" (Woodbury 2003:715). In contemporary Cayuga, the cognate is applied just to the mother and mother's sisters (Froman et al. 2002:523). With Oneida, it has been extended to both mother's siblings, male and female (Michelson and Doxtator 2002:608).

Father

The Huron term for 'father' was the verb root usually represented as -ɩisten- by seventeenth- and eighteenth-century writers (FHO, FH67:148), FH1693:256–7, FH1697:253–4, HF59:82, HF62:45, HF65:99, and Potier 1920:108 and 270), or sometimes as -istan- in the early literature (Sagard 1866 and 1939:71; Brébeuf 1830:2, 4, 6 and 9; and JR10:69 and 267). A Wyandot cognate was recorded in both Morgan (1966:295, 313, 348, and 362) and Barbeau (1960:73, 135, 137, 144, and 212). The only cognate for this term in other Northern Iroquoian languages is the Mohawk term for 'mother' (Morgan 1966:295, 339, 358, and 368; Bruyas 1970:79; and Michelson 1973:62). All the other languages, with the exception of Tuscarora, share a term that may have a cognate in the Huron term for the paternal grandparent/grandchild relationship.

This verb root follows the pattern of 'to be mother to' in that the father occupies the agent position, the child or children the patient position:

ton pere	*hiaɩisten*	('he' is the agent and 'you' is the patient)
[your father]		[he is father to you]
son pere	*hoɩisten*	('he' is the agent and 'him' or 'her' is the patient)
[his/her father]		[he is father to him or her]
notre pere	*sonɩ8aɩisten*	('he' is the agent and 'us' is the patient)
[our father]		[he is father to us] (FH1697:253)

The Huron used -ɩisten- to refer to a father's brother as well as to the biological father (FHO, FH1693:256–7 and Potier 1920:270). Other Northern

Iroquoian languages in Morgan's time also have terms with such a double meaning (Morgan 1966:295), but contemporary counterparts do not. The unrelated Oneida term refers to father only (Michelson and Doxtator 2002:854); the same is true for Cayuga (Froman et al. 2002:115) and Onondaga (Woodbury 2003:9620).

Morgan and Barbeau offer contradictory evidence concerning extension of the father term. Morgan has the mother's brother term applying to the husbands of both mothers' and fathers' sisters (Morgan 1966:322 and 339). However, while one of Barbeau's Wyandot informants, Allen Goligas, agreed that this reflected current usage, he claimed that both of those relationships earlier had -ₗisten- applied to them (Barbeau, fieldnotes, card 656). He appears to be describing a change from a system in which all those who were not mothers' brothers by narrow definition were called father (as did Morgan's Mohawk and Oneida), to one more like the English speaker's system of using an alternative term (i.e., 'uncle') to refer to all related males of the ascending generation who were not biological fathers. The "new" Wyandot system would be just one person away (i.e., father's brother) from having such a pattern.

The Jesuits introduced two extensions of the meaning of the term 'father' to the Huron language: these referred to God and to the Jesuits themselves. Neither was immediately successful. Brébeuf first used -ₗisten- for God as father in the catechism he composed after his 1626–28 stay with the Huron. In this early work he used *Aistan* 'my father' for God as 'le Pere' (Brébeuf 1830:2 and 4) and the grammatically incorrect (as it would literally mean 'she or it is father to me') *Onaistan* for 'Nostre Pere' (Brébeuf 1830:6). The appropriate Northern Bear prefix would have been -sona- ('he' being the agent and 'us' being the patient), not -ona- ('she' as agent and 'us' as patient). Brébeuf was falsely generalizing the often occurring -ona- as a pronoun meaning 'our.'

In a prayer included in the *Jesuit Relation* of 1636, Brébeuf used *d'Oistan* (probably actually '*d'hoistan*,' the masculine form) for God as father (JR10:9). This could imply that Brébeuf had learned of sorcery implications of referring to God specifically as his father, implications that he would want to avoid. Or he may just have been applying his improved learning of Huron pronominal prefixes. Still, this usage did not last either. Later works would replace the use of this verb with -en- 'to have as child' (see below), with the masculine singular as the agent and the third person indefinite ('they, one, someone') as the patient: 'he has them as children.'

The Huron seemed to have accepted at least the notion of God as father, as there are a number of examples in the *Jesuit Relations*, in which

Huron Christians used the term. Unfortunately, we do not have records of whether they used -*ꞑisten*- or -*en*-. The first such instance involved the young Huron seminarist Robert Satouta in 1637 (JR12:55; see also JR19:147, 26:241–75, 28:73 and 29:167).

That the non-Christian Huron may have accepted the notion of a Creator as father can be seen in the report in the *Relation* of 1646 of a vision of a powerful Native-generated spirit figure to compete with the Christian God-as-father figure. To have competing spiritualities, they must have similar traits. After claiming to have created humans and provided them with the necessities of life, the spirit stated that, 'he recognized [the Huron] as children although they did not recognize him as their father—just like an infant in the cradle, who has not firm enough judgement to recognize those to whom he owes all that he is, and all the support of his life' (JR30:25).

I have come across one reference to Jesus as father, in a translation into Huron of Luke 5:5: "And Simon answering said unto him, Master, we have toiled all the night, and have taken nothing: nevertheless at thy word I will let down the net." In the Huron text, 'Master' is translated as *aꞑisten*, 'my father' (Potier 1920:471).

It was difficult to get the matrilineal Huron to refer to the Jesuits as their fathers. The mother's brother/sister's son relationship was more appropriate to their culture. While the patrilineal Algonquians made such reference frequently in passages recorded in the *Jesuit Relations*,[1] the Huron, even the converted ones, rarely did so (JR20:289, 24:107, and 39:181 and 191). That the Jesuits encouraged the Huron to think of them as their fathers can be seen in a passage from Father Philippe Pierson's *De Religione*, written during the early 1670s. After an invidious comparison of what non-Christian Aboriginal parents and Jesuits do for children, he has a hypothetical child say: "He who is a Jesuit continually worked at preparing something for me by praying for me. He did good things for me while my parents did not. The Jesuit made me his child. He is my father [*aꞑisten*]" (Potier 1920:678; translation mine).

When Potier was working with the Wyandot in the 1740s, using 'my father' to address a Jesuit priest was probably the general practice. In a letter of 1746, the Huron of Lorette used *aꞑisten* to address Father Daniel Richer (Potier 1920:687). The term may have developed into a term of respect for leading French figures in general, as suggested by the fact that Longueuil, the French leader in charge of Detroit, was, along with Father Armand Richardie, referred to as *aꞑisten* in another letter of 1746 (Potier 1920:685). The Lieutenant Governor of Quebec in 1873 was addressed with the same term (Le Moine 1882:446).

Child

The Huron verb root for 'to have as child' was -*en*-.[2] Cognates exist in Wyandot (Morgan 1966:296 and Barbeau 1960:64, 72, 77, and 89 passim), Tuscarora (Rudes 1987:332), Mohawk (Morgan 1966:296, Bruyas 1970:60, and Michelson 1973:125), and Oneida (Morgan 1966:296 and Michelson and Doxtator 2002:823). Seneca (Chafe 1963:22 and Morgan 1966:296), Cayuga (Morgan 1966:296 and Froman et al. 2002:503), and Onondaga (Morgan 1966:296 and Woodbury 2003:492) do not have a cognate term.

With the pronominal prefixes we have the parent(s) in the agent position and the child(ren) in the patient position:

je t'ai pour pere.	*endi skiena* ('you' is agent and 'me' is patient)
[I have you for father]	[I, you have me as child] (FH1693:256)

The reciprocal prefix -*atat*- also occurs with this verb root, with dual or plural pronominal prefixes:

ta mere ...	*tsatatiena*
[your mother]	[you two are reciprocally parent and child]
(FH1697:254)	

The -*a*- suffix occurs in most instances. One exception occurs when a person is addressing his or her child:

k8e a₁ien	(bonjour mon fils)
	[hello, my child] (HF65:62)

Another form that frequently does not take the -*a*- suffix is *hoen* ('he' or 'she' as agent and 'him' as patient; see JR10:69 and 71; but also see FHO, FH1697:255, Potier 1920:108 and FH67:98 for exceptions). The main source of evidence I have that the -*a*- suffix is often dropped in this form is a passage of New Testament translation written in Huron. In the passage I studied (Potier 1920:461–69), the verb -*en*- appears forty-one times. The -*a*- suffix is missing in thirteen instances, ten of which are with *hoen*. The *hoen(a)* form appears sixteen times, ten of which lack the -*a*- suffix.

With the causative-instrumental suffix -*st*- you get the meaning of 'adopting a child' (FHO, FH67:5, FH1693:256, FH1697:7, HF59:51, HF62, HF65:63, and Potier 1920:219). A reciprocal prefix can be added to this to speak of the relationship between the adopter and the one adopted (HF59:51 and FH1697:7).

In the Huron material, -*en*- refers only to one's children, either biological or adopted (even adopted prisoners; JR18:31). I feel that it is a safe assumption that the Huron extended this term to include reference to the children of a father's brother and of a mother's sisters, consistent with those children calling such people 'father' and 'mother.' Further, both Morgan and Barbeau provide examples of the Wyandot extending the term to a male referring to his brothers' children (Morgan 1966:302–3 and Barbeau field notes, cards 632 and 662). This kind of extension is shared by all other Northern Iroquoian languages during Morgan's time (Morgan 1966:302–3), but the major modern sources do not document it for the twentieth century.

A contradiction in Barbeau's material may show a change taking place in the direction of an English model. In some fieldwork cards he claimed that -*ɪenh8aten*- 'to have as nephew, niece (male speaking)' was used to refer to a man's brothers' children (Barbeau fieldnotes, cards 596–97 and 532).

A similar situation exists with the term used for a woman's sisters' children. Barbeau claimed that the term -*chionnrak*- 'to have as nephew, niece (female-speaking)' applied to these children. Again, this would seem to make sense as a way of conforming to the North American majority in having nephew and niece terms apply to a greater diversity of people than child terms.

The Jesuits eventually came to use the verb root -*en*- to refer to the 'Father' and the 'Son' of the Trinity, through a grammatically innovative use of the indefinite third person 'they, one, people, someone' as patient in the first case and agent in the second case. In Pierson's *De Religione*, for example, we find *saɪoen* ('he' as agent and 'they (indef.)' as patient) 'he has them as children' and *honaen* ('they (indef.)' as agent and 'him' as patient) 'they have him as child' (Potier 1920:629).

Concerning interaction between Jesuits and the Huron, we find no examples in the *Jesuit Relations* of the former addressing the latter as 'my child(ren).' The earliest such examples I have found are in two letters written in Huron in 1746, one by Father Richardie, the other by Father Richer. In both cases, we have Huron speakers addressed as *ɪ8aena* 'I have you (plural) as children' (Potier 1920:684 and 687).

Finally, the Jesuits add the causative-instrumental to this verb to speak of baptism as a kind of adoption ceremony. This can be seen in the following quotation from *De Religione*:

> It is not insignificant that it is pleasing that parents and children exist together in the sky. They will be good to look at, a beautiful family that I engender. They are pleasing to me, the several hundred I baptized, as I will find in the sky those people made into my children. There they would be a lineage. My family would surround me. I would not leave any out.

They would not break their word to honour my name. I would live with my beautiful family. They would be pleasing to me. We would praise each other as parents and children forever. We would not abandon nor separate from each other.

Now, my brothers, you know why we baptize. We will make a lineage in the sky. We keep people from suffering inside the earth. We prepared them for happiness in the sky. We believe that the Great Voice adopts people when we baptize them. (Potier 1920:679; my translation)

Mother's Brother

The Huron term for 'mother's brother' was -atennon'ron- (Sagard 1866, 1939:71, FHO, FH1693:257, FH1697:253 and 258, HF59:24, HF62, HF65:29, and Potier 1920:108 and 186). A cognate exists in Wyandot (Morgan 1966:330 and Barbeau 1915:130 fn2 and 250 fn3, 1960:142, 144, 198 passim). There are no cognates, however, in any other Northern Iroquoian language, although all had terms for the relationship in Morgan's time. In modern times, the Oneida use the verb root of the term for 'mother' (Michelson and Doxtator 2002:608); the Onondaga (Woodbury 2003:1415), Cayuga (Froman et al. 2002:613), Seneca (Chafe 1963:23), and Tuscarora (Rudes 1987:145) use a distinct term. The Mohawk use a general 'uncle' term (Michelson 1973:81). This suggests that the Huron/Wyandot term could have been a Huron creation. Perhaps this came about because an earlier word, cognate with those names in the other Northern Iroquoian languages, somehow became taboo.

One possibility is that the Huron word was developed from the verb root -ndoron- 'to be difficult, valuable' (Potier 1920:295), which was used in another form to express the relationship between fellow parents-in-law. This would involve the semi-reflexive prefix -ate- and a nasalization of the -o- in assimilation to the following nasalized -o- (nasalization being indicated by the Jesuits with an -n- following a vowel). This would entail the dropping of the -d- according to the phonetic rules of Huron. The mother's brother is in the agent position, as seen in the following:

hiatennonron ton oncle [your uncle]
[he is mother's brother to you]

son₁8atennonron notre oncle [our uncle]
[he is mother's brother to us]

honendatennonron leurs oncles [their uncles]
[they (masculine) are mother's brothers to them (masc. or fem.)] (Potier 1920:186)

There is also a term of address using the same verb root:

a8atennonron mon oncle ou mes oncles in vocativo [my uncle or my uncles]
(Potier 1920:186)

The typical translation of *-atennonron-* in the Huron dictionaries was 'oncle maternal' (HF1697:253, HF59:24, and Potier 1920:108) or just 'oncle' (Sagard 1866, FH67:140, HF62, and HF65:29). In only one Huron dictionary source (FHO) is the meaning spelled out completely, with the entry headed by the Latin '*Matris frat.*' According to Morgan, the Wyandot cognate signifies mother's brother (Morgan 1966:330). Both Barbeau and Morgan record it including father's sister's husband (Barbeau, card 656 and Morgan 1966:322) and mother's sister's husband (Barbeau, card 656; Morgan 1966:339). This made it unique at that time. No other Northern Iroquoian language recorded by Morgan used the same term for these two other relationships. This may have been caused by a move to make the mother's brother term more like the English word 'uncle.'

The move to include these extra meaning was made easier by was the fact that both the Huron and Wyandot already had another, more abstract, extended application of the mother's brother term. In the *Jesuit Relations* we find evidence for 'mother's brother' being a term of respect used by younger males when addressing older men (JR10:215, 13:67–69, 17:247, 23:77, and 40:175). This happened even when the younger man was addressing an older man he was torturing (JR13:67–69).

The Wyandot shared this respect term usage, in the following quotation from Barbeau:

This term … , is not used by the Wyandots in the same sense as in English. It implies no blood kinship, but only the fictitious tie of relationship that exists between an old protector or educator apparently selected in the maternal line and his protegé. (Barbeau 1915:130 fn2)

Wyandot stories suggest that this uncle/nephew relationship contained ambivalent feelings. On the negative side is the story "The Old Bear and his Nephew," in which the nephew needs the power of an *oki* spirit to outwit and outdo a bear uncle who wanted to kill him because they were competing for the same woman (Barbeau 1960:32–35). As in other cultures, a potentially tense relationship can contain humour. In "Tawidi'a and his Uncle" (Barbeau 1915:224–33 and 1960:40–44), an older man and his nephew live together, with the main line of the story being how the nephew constantly misunderstands his uncle's instructions, usually through lack of comprehension of metaphor or homophony (words that sound alike).

The stories can also reflect the positive nature of the relationship. In "The Bear and the Hunter's Son," the mother's brother brings a child mistreated by his stepmother back into Wyandot society (Barbeau 1915:128–31 and 1960:20–22). In the story of "The Witch's Daughters and the Suitors" (Barbeau 1915:154–60), the nephew hero is protected by spiritual advice from his uncle.

Concerning the relationship between the Huron and the Jesuits, it is instructive to note that at no time in the *Jesuit Relations* do we find the Huron addressing the French Jesuit missionaries as 'my uncle(s),' nor did the Jesuits respond to being called 'my nephew(s)' (see below) by dutifully addressing the Huron as 'my uncle(s).'

Father's Sister

The Huron term for 'father's sister' was *-ar(a)hak-* (Sagard 1866, FHO, FH1693:257, FH1697:253 and 258, HF59:11, HF62:14, HF65:18, and Potier 1920:108 and 170). The Wyandot cognate appears only in Morgan (1966:322), not being recorded in Barbeau's writing at all. Cognates exist with the Seneca (Morgan 1966:322, Lounsbury 1971:260 and Chafe 1963:23), Tuscarora (Morgan 1966:322 and Rudes 1987:93) and seventeenth-century Mohawk (Shea 1970:97). Morgan records that Cayuga, Onondaga, Oneida and Mohawk used a variant of their different terms for 'mother' (Morgan 1966:322). A modern Oneida dictionary, however, includes a unique term for father's sister (Michelson and Doxtator 2002:607), one that does not appear cognate with the Huron/Wyandot term. The modern Cayuga dictionary has what the writers term an 'old word' for 'aunt' which appears to be a cognate (Froman et al. 2002:616).

The father's sister is in the agent position:

sarahak	ta [tante paternelle]	['she' is agent and 'you' is patient]
	[your paternal aunt]	[she is paternal aunt to you]
orahak	sa [tante paternelle]	['she' is agent and 'she' is patient]
	[her paternal aunt]	[she is paternal aunt to her]
onₜ8arak	n[otr]e tante	['she' is agent and 'us' is patient]
	[our aunt]	[she is paternal aunt to us]
(FH1697:258)		

No *-a-* suffix appears, even in the following phrase of address:

k8e arahak   bon iour ma tante (HF62:14, c.f. HF65:18 and HF59:11)

The Jesuit Huron dictionaries have *-ar(a)hak-* translated as 'tante' (Sagard 1866, FH1693:257, HF59:11, HF62:14, and HF65:18), 'Patris soror'

(FHO), 'Tante paternelle' (FH1697:258 and Potier 1920:108), or they spell it out more clearly as a term used by 'enf[ants] du Fr[ere] d'une f[emm]e' ('children of the brother of a woman') (FH1697:253). According to Morgan, this term extended in Wyandot beyond 'father's sister' to include father's brother's wife (Morgan 1966:313) and a mother's brother's wife (Morgan 1966:313). In other words, he was stating that the Wyandot used *-ar(a)hak-* to refer to all the women of the ascending generation that were not specified as mother (i.e., the biological mother and mother's sister(s)).

In Morgan's compilation, neither the Seneca nor the Tuscarora cognates, nor the different terms used by the Mohawk, Oneida, Onondaga, and Cayuga extended from father's sister to include these other two relationships (Morgan 1966:322).

It appears as though the Wyandot were expanding the use of the verb root so that it was more like the English term 'aunt.' The term seems to have been somewhat equivalent to the mother's brother term being used to show respect across generations. For example, Father Isaac Jogues (JR25:45) addressed an older Mohawk woman taking care of him as 'my aunt,' much as he would have called an older man 'my mother's brother.' I believe the Huron would have had similar usage.

I argue below that the linguistic forms taken or not taken by the verb root also constitute evidence for 'father's sister' being a general respect term for women.

Nephews/Nieces (male reference)

The Huron verb root used by a man when speaking to or of his sister's children was *-ɩenh8aten-* (Sagard 1866, 1939:71, FHO, FH67:140, FH1693:257, FH1697:253 and 258, HF59, Potier 1920:108 and 387, JR13:69, and JR14:95). Barbeau's Wyandot contains a cognate form (Barbeau 1960:144, 197, 205, 209, 236, and 251). Cognates exist in all other Northern Iroquoian languages, including Laurentian Iroquoian (Barbeau 1961:149). The pronominal prefixes used with this verb have the uncle in the agent position, as can be seen in the following examples. It should be noted that the term can be used in address as well as in reference:

hi8aten	mon nev[eu] in voc. et nom[3] (in reference and in address) [I have him as sister's child]	
ɩih8aten	ma niece [I have her as sister's child]	
hechih8aten	ton nev[eu] [you have him as sister's child]	
chih8aten	ta niece [you have her as sister's child] (FH1697:258)	

The Huron evidence contains one instance of the -*a*- suffix (FH1693:257); it occurs in all the Wyandot examples (Potier 1920:387–88;[4] and Barbeau 1960:144, 197, 205, 209, 236, and 251), so the former may be a dialect feature. Generally speaking, Wyandot had the -*a*- suffix more than any other Huron dialect. I do not know whether this is due to change over time after contact, or whether a difference existed at the time of contact.

The primary Huron use of -*ɩenh8aten*- was 'un hom[me] avoir pour neveux et pour nieces les enfans de sa soeur [a man having for nephews and nieces the children of his sister]' (Potier 1920:387; compare FHO, FH1697:253 and FH1693:257). Barbeau states that it referred to both a man's sister and his brother's children (Barbeau fieldnotes, cards 596–97 and 632), fitting more closely into the English 'uncle' model.

Morgan incorrectly saw this verb as the Wyandot female reference term for nephew/nieces (Morgan 1966:308, 318–19, 327, 335–36, 344–45, 349–50 and 356–57). He thought a man's brothers' children called for the verb -*en*- 'to have as child' (Morgan 1966:302 and 303). All the other Northern Iroquoian languages Morgan refers to have their cognates signifying the male reference term (Morgan 1966:305–6, 319–20, 328, 336–37, 345–6, 352, 359–60, and 364). This is supported by other sources for Mohawk (Bruyas 1970:108, Shea 1970:73, and Michelson 1973:164), Cayuga (Froman et al. 2002:548), Seneca (Chafe 1963:23), and Tuscarora (Rudes 1987:31). In modern Onondaga, although the traditional meaning is known, the cognate has broadened so that 'contemporary speakers use it for both a man's and a woman's brothers' and sisters' children' (Woodbury 2003:400). Oneida seems also to use it as a generalized term (Michelson and Doxtator 2002:748).

The verb -*ɩenh8aten*- had an extended use as a form of address occurring when older men spoke to younger males. This is amply demonstrated for both the Huron and the Iroquois in the *Jesuit Relations* (JR13:69 and 205; 26:257 and 275; 33:43; 40:175; 43:279; 25:259; 57:63; and 62:101). This even included the relationship between captor/torturer and captive/torture victim (Sagard 1939:178 and 180; JR13:41, 53–55; 24:301; and 40:175).

When the Huron first encountered the French, they addressed these newcomers to their country as 'my nephew(s).' This is found in the *Jesuit Relations* from 1635 to 1639 (JR8:93; 10:45; 13:171 and 181; 14:23; 15:25, 27–9, 33, 57 and 113; and 17:209). The Iroquois used the term similarly during the 1640s (JR24:301 and 27:255–57). Use of this term even included Jesus: "An old man, looking at our Crucifix, asked who that was fastened to it. Having told him, he began to speak to our Lord in these words, *Etsagon ihouaten [hi8aten] etsagon taouacaratat*, 'Courage, my nephew, courage, take care of us!'" (JR14:95–97).

Perhaps in doing this the Huron and Iroquois were thinking of the French as dependent upon them, as boys or young men were to their more knowledgeable elders. According to Connelley, the Wyandot spoke of the Delaware in that way (Barbeau 1915:324).

Not surprisingly, no instance is recorded in the *Jesuit Relations* of the Jesuits reciprocating to this nephew address by politely calling the Huron or the Iroquois 'my uncle(s).' There is even a record of a French Governor's attempt to reverse the 'nephew' usage. The *Jesuit Journal* of February 1654 describes a meeting between the Jesuits and Huron concerning the Onondaga's bid to have the Huron join with them. During this meeting, the French Governor reportedly "found nothing to gainsay in the essentials of this project, since he did not intend to keep his nephews, the hurons, in captivity" (JR41:23).

Nephews/Nieces (female reference)

The Huron verb for nephews/nieces (female reference) varies slightly with dialect: *-chionnrak-* (JF59:48, HF62:12, HF65:59, and FHO) for the Rock and Northern Bear dialects and *-chiondraka-* (Sagard 1866, FH1693:257, FH1697:253) for the Southern Bear and Cord dialects. The Wyandot cognate resembles the latter (Potier 1920:108 and 216; Morgan 1966:304–6 and Barbeau, fieldnotes, cards 594 and 767).

No other Northern Iroquoian language has a cognate. Onondaga and Cayuga appear to have an archaic term that fulfills basically the same function (Woodbury 2003:893 and Froman et al. 2002:612).[5]

The pronominal prefixes have the aunt in the agent position, as is predictable: This can be seen in the following dictionary entry:

hechiondra'ka mon neveu	*ˌechiondra'ka* ma niece
[I have him as brother's child]	[I have her as brother's child]
hechiondra'ka ton nev	*chiechiondra'ka* ta niece
[you have him as brother's child]	[you have her as brother's child]
hochiondra'ka son n.	*ochiondraka* sa n[iece].
[she has him as brother's child]	[she has her as brother's child]
(FH1697:258)	

The *-a-* suffix would appear to be a dialect feature, co-existing with the *-d-*.

Unlike the male reference term, the female equivalent does not appear as a term of address in the recorded evidence (see for example Potier

1920:216). Perhaps this is because it was simply not considered as important, or heard as often by the male-centric Jesuits. That there was a term
of address can be seen in the following quotation from the *Jesuit Relations*,
in which an older Huron woman addresses a French boy:

> *ho, ho, ho. Echiongnix* [i.e., *hechionnrak* (?)[6]] *et sagon achitec,*
> Ah, my nephew, I thank thee;[7] be of good heart for the morrow (JR13:255).

The verb refers to 'vne femme avoir p[ou]r neveux ou nieces les enf[ants]
de son Frere [a woman having as nephews or nieces the children of her
brother]' (HF59:48; compare FH1693:257, HF62:12, HF65:59, Potier
1920:216, and FH1697:253 and 258). As we have seen above, Morgan (or
his informants) confused the meaning of this term with the male-reference
term. Other Wyandot sources (Potier 1920:108 and 216; Barbeau fieldnotes, card 594) have the correct term.

One of Barbeau's cards has *-chionnrak-* extended to include 'mother's
brother's (or sister's) children' (fieldnotes, card 767). I believe this means
that, for at least one of his informants, the term applied not just to a
woman's brothers' children, but to her sisters' children as well. This seems
to be taking a step towards generalizing the term in the manner of the English 'aunt.'

Maternal Grandparents

The Huron verb root for maternal grandparents was sometimes written in
the dialect form *-chiot-* (Sagard 1866, FHO, HF59:48, HF62, and HG65:59),
sometimes as *-chi8t-* (in one instance in HF65:59, HF62, and HF59, and in
all instances in FH1693, FH1697:253–54 and Potier 1920:108 and 216).
The Wyandot had a cognate that mirrored the latter form (Morgan
1966:293–94 and Barbeau 1915:48 and 283, 1960:102, 307, and 311). Cognates exist in all other Northern Iroquoian languages (Morgan 1966:293–95;
plus Bruyas 1970:57 and 59 for Mohawk; Michelson and Doxtator 2002:406
for Oneida; Woodbury 2003:558–59 for Onondaga; Froman et al. 2002:480
for Cayuga; Chafe 1963:24 for Seneca; and Rudes 1987:572 for Tuscarora).

As is expected, the grandparents are in the agent position with this verb
root:

> *hia'chiotaa*   c'est grand pere
> [he is maternal grandparent to you]
>
> *sachiotaa*   elle est ta grand mere
> [she is maternal grandparent to you] (HF62)

The -*a*- suffix was used as a device that differentiated situations in which a grandchild was addressing a grandparent from the grandparent's response. *Achiotaa* or *achi8taa* would be used when a grandchild was addressing a grandparent (FHO, FH1693, FH1697:254, HF59:48, HF62, HF65:59, and Potier 1920:216). The grandparent would respond with -*achiot*- or -*achi8t*-. The -*a*- suffix seems generally to have been added in all other forms (FH1693, FH1697:254, HF59:48, HF62, HF65:59, and Potier 1920:216, but not FHO).

The causative-instrumental suffix was present in two of my dictionaries in identical entries, interestingly with the -*aa*- that included the -*a*- suffix kept:

₁*Achio'taa'sti*	prendre pour petit fils [to take as grandchild]
ahonachiotaasθa	on a la pris pour [petit fils] [they take her as grand-child] (HF62; c.f. HF65:59)

The verb root -*chiot*- could be used to address or refer specifically to the parents of one's mother (FH1693, FH1697:253–54, HF59:48, HF62, HF65:59, and Potier 1920:216). As we will see in the discussion of the term for the paternal grandparent/grandchild relationship, -*chiot*- could be generalized to refer to grandparents on both sides (FH1697:254).

The Wyandot lacked the paternal grandparent term, so -*chiot*- always referred to grandparents on both sides (Potier 1920:108 and Morgan 1966:294–95). Morgan and Barbeau have its Wyandot use extended to include mother's sister (Morgan 1966:358 and Barbeau fieldnotes, card 720). Morgan, but not Barbeau (perhaps an oversight), also includes the father's siblings (Morgan 1966:348 and 351). According to Morgan, these extensions existed in his time in the other Northern Iroquoian languages as well. I could find no evidence for its extension in more modern Iroquois.

For both the Huron and the Wyandot, the figure of the maternal grandmother was a significant one. In their origin myth, the first woman on earth was the maternal grandmother of the culture-hero twins *Ioskeha* and *Tawiskaron* (Sagard 1866, as cited in Barbeau 1915:289, JR8:117,[8] 10:129 for Huron; Barbeau 1915:44, 298, 306, 318–20 for the Wyandot).

Additionally, in the Wyandot version of the origin myth, the toad successfully dives deep into the water to bring up the soil necessary to build a world for the first woman on the back of the Great Turtle. For that reason, the Wyandot referred to the toad as 'our grandmother' (Barbeau 1915:48 fn1; see also Barbeau 1915:304 and card 701). Also called 'our grandmother,' according to the nineteenth-century Wyandot scholar Connelley, was the Little Turtle who, among other achievements, created the sun and the moon (Barbeau 1915:305–6).

The figure of the grandfather seems to have been less significant myth-ically, although for the Wyandot 'Hinnon' the thunderer(s), received the term 'grandfather' (Connelley, in Barbeau 1915:318–19 and Hale in Bar-beau 1915:322), with Connelley suggesting that perhaps this character mar-ried the first woman.

The Jesuits used -chi8t-, as did the Huron, to denote one who began a lineage. When the Jesuits wanted to speak of Joseph being of the lineage of David (Luke 2:4), they wrote:

> *handarek joseph hochi8taa* [he lived, Joseph, he was his maternal grand-parent] (Potier 1920:464 line 2; see also 461 lines 51 and 52).

Interestingly, also in parallel with Huron usage, the Jesuits referred to Adam as follows:

> [n]ot[re] g[ran]d pere adam   *son₁8achi8taa ₁ehen adam haatsinnen* [he
> was maternal grandparent to us; Adam he
> was called] (FH1693)

Maternal Grandchildren

The Huron verb root referring to maternal grandchildren was -*atre*- (Sagard 1866, FHO, FH1693:256, FH1697:253–55, HF59:36, HF62, HF65, and Potier 1920:108 and 203). Cognates exist in Wyandot (Morgan 1966:296–98; Barbeau 1915:117 fn1, 1960:101–2 and cards 620–21, 662, 665, 680, 691, 712–13 and 768), and in all other Northern Iroquoian languages (Morgan 1966:296–98 for all; Bruyas 1970:41 and 88, Michelson 1973:31 for Mohawk; Michelson and Doxtator 2002:230 for Oneida; Woodbury 2003:124 for Onondaga; Froman et al. 2002:611 for Cayuga; Chafe 1963:24 for Seneca; and Rudes 1987:70 for Tuscarora).

The pronominal prefixes have the grandparent as agent:

ton p. fils … matern.	*hechiatrea*	[you have him as maternal grandchild]
ta p. fille … matern.	*chiatrea*	[you have her as maternal grandchild]
son p. fils … matern.	*hotrea*	[she or he has him as maternal grandchild]
sa p. fils … matern.	*hatrea*	[he has her as maternal grandchild]
(FH1697:255)		

The -*a*- suffix is almost universally used with this verb, the sole excep-tion being the response given by grandparents when greeted by their grand-children with this as a term of address (FHO). The only example I know of in which the causative-instrumental suffix appears with this verb occurs with a Wyandot addition to a Huron entry in Potier's dictionary for the paternal grandparent/grandchild, suggesting a loss of this term from Wyandot by that time:

> *andichiasti* non (dic *atreasti*) adopter pour grand pere our grand mere [to adopt as grandfather or grandmother] (Potier 1920:290)

The verb root *-atre-* was used to refer to maternal grandchildren specifically, and, more generally, to all grandchildren when the maternal/paternal distinction was not important (FH1697:254). In Wyandot, which did not distinguish terminologically between maternal and paternal grandchildren, *-atre-* referred to all grandchildren (Morgan 1966:296–97). In both Morgan and Barbeau, the term was extended to refer to the grandchildren of a woman's sister or brother (Morgan 1966:309 and Barbeau card 665). Morgan also included a man's brother's grandchildren (Morgan 1966:304).

From a single example developed more fully in the section on the Wenro, we can see that *-atre-* could be used when a group was adopted by a clan. In a dictionary entry referring to the clans of the Huron, we get this statement following the name of the Turtle clan:

> *tionnenria honnontre hotienrotori* [when it was small, the Wenro were their grandchildren] (FHO)

Paternal Grandparents/Grandchildren

The Huron verb for the paternal grandparent/grandchild relationship was *-ndichi-* (FHO, FH1693, FH1697:253–55, HF59, HF62:64, and Potier 1920:109 and 290). Its use was more restricted than that of *-atre-*, which could be used to speak of grandparents generally. This restriction is spelled out in one of the dictionaries:

> Qu'on n'employe le mot *andichia*, que quand il faut (absolut) distinger de quel cote et le gr. p. our le gr. m[er]e dont on parle
> [one only uses the word *andichia* when it is absolutely necessary to distinguish on which side is the grandfather or grandmother one is speaking of] (FH1697:254)

It may have been one of the first kinship casualties of contact. The term did not exist in Wyandot. When the verb appeared in Potier's copy of the Huron–French dictionary, the writer crossed out the term and substituted the maternal terms he had heard among the Wyandot speakers he lived with (Potier 1920:108). According to Morgan, no other such term, cognate or otherwise, existed in the other Northern Iroquoian languages.

No contemporary Northern Iroquoian dictionary has a term specifically for the paternal grandparent/grandchild relationship. I feel that they lost their equivalent terms after contact, much as the Wyandot had.

Predictably, the pronominal prefixes have the grandparent in the agent position:

> ton gr. p [your grandfather] ... ta gr. m. [your grandmother]
> *hiandichia* [he has you as paternal grandchild]
> *sandichia* [she has you as paternal grandchild] (FH1697:254)

The use of the -*a*- suffix appears somewhat confused in the different sources. Two dictionaries say that when a grandparent greeted a grandchild, the older relative would say "*K8e* [hello] *andich*," not only missing the -*a*- suffix, but dropping the final -*ia*- as well (FHO and FH1697). The grandchild would reply with "*K8e andichiaa*." This is in line with what maternal grandparents would do when using -*atre*- or -*chiot*- (see above). Another source claims the opposite, that *andich* would be used when the grandchild was addressing the grandparent, and that the grandparent would use *andichiaa* (HF62:64). Potier, writing the last of the dictionaries, and just copying what he had not heard himself, states that it could be used either way (Potier 1920:290). In only one source (FH1693) is the use of the -*a*- suffix extended to include more terms than just one of the terms of address. Perhaps this lack of consistency in the written sources reflects both the infrequency with which the Jesuits heard this verb, plus its lack of significance. Rules are more important where the relationship itself is more important.

Interestingly, when the causative-instrumental suffix -*st*- is used with this verb, the French translation refers to adoption:

> *gandichiasti*   adopter p[ou]r p. fils ou fille, com[men]cer a etre gr. pere our
>   gr. mere [to adopt as grandson or granddaughter, to begin
>   to be grandfather or grandmother] (HF59; c.f. Potier 290)

This is curious. Would someone really adopt someone else just as a paternal grandchild rather than as the more meaningful maternal grandchild? It might occur when the father's parents are not alive. Perhaps one would do this if the child needed grandparents, but belonged to a different clan, a situation that could occur with the depopulation from disease and warfare that affected the Huron before these dictionaries were written.

Just as intriguing is the possibility of grandchildren adopting paternal grandparents. In Potier's dictionary we have the following entry:

andichiasti   non (dic *atreasti*) adopter pour grandpere our pour grand-
mere [to adopt as grandfather or grandmother]
(Potier 1920:290)

With the Huron stress on the independence of the individual, does this mean that children could adopt a grandparent if they felt they needed someone in this role? Or was this just a way of expressing the grandchild part of reciprocal adoption?

Same-Sex Siblings

The primary Huron verb for siblings was *-ɩen-*.[9] Cognates exist in Wyandot (Morgan 1966:298–300; Barbeau 1915:275 fn1, 1960:62, 65 passim) as well as in all other Northern Iroquoian languages (Morgan 1966:298–99; Bruyas 1970:47, Shea 1970:30 and Michelson 1973:128 for Mohawk; Michelson and Doxtator 2002:848 for Oneida; Woodbury 2003:944 for Onondaga; Froman et al .2002:449 for Cayuga; and Chafe 1962:21 for Seneca).

The age principle could be added with the suffix *-(i)a(ha)-*, with the eldest sibling in the agent position:

si l'on veut dire, ainé ou cadet on se sert du diminutif
[if one wishes to speak of older or younger (siblings) one uses the diminutive]

ɩaɩeniaha   c'est mon fr. cadet
[It is my younger brother]
[h]eɩeniaha
[I have him as diminutive sibling]

c'est ta cadete
[you have her as diminutive sibling]
chieɩeniaha
[it is your younger sister]

c'est mon fr. ainé
[It is my older brother]
haɩeniaha
[he has me as diminutive sibling]
idem il m'a pr cadet ou cadete
[also, he has me for younger brother or sister]

c'est mon s. ainée
[It is my older sister]
ɩaɩeniaha
[she has me as diminutive sibling]
idem ell. m'a sr cadete
[also she has me as younger sister] (FH1697:256)

This is a different from other Northern Iroquoian languages, which use
the -ₗen- cognate without the diminutive as the term for 'to be younger sibling' (Bruyas 1970:46, Shea 1970:30 and 94 and Michelson 1973:128 for
Mohawk; Michelson and Doxtator 2002:848, and 1176–7 for Oneida; Woodbury 2003: 944 and1341 for Onondaga; Froman et al. 2002:610 for Cayuga;
Chafe 1963:21–2 for Seneca and Rudes 1987:333 for Tuscarora).

For the elder sibling, these languages use a verb stem that has no cognate in Huron or Wyandot that I can see. In Onondaga, the verb root is
-(h)tci?áh- (Woodbury 2003:1341; see Bruyas 1970:57 and Michelson
1973:110 for the cognate in Mohawk; Michelson and Doxtator 2002:1176
in Oneida; Froman et al. 2002:612 in Cayuga; Chafe 1963:22 in Seneca;
and Rudes 1987:127 and 144 in Tuscarora).

The verb root -ₗen- expresses equality rather than the inequality of the
older/younger distinction by having the reflexive prefix -atat- added. In
such cases, the brothers or sisters are placed in the same position, the agent
position, with nothing in the patient position. This can be seen in the following entry:

Aₗiataχen	... luy et moy n[ou]s sommes freres v[el] n[ou]s som[m]es fr[ere]et s[oeu]r
[we two are siblings]	[he and I, we are brothers or we are sisters or we are brother and sister] (FH1697:256)

There are two forms of first person in Huron: inclusive (including the
listener(s)) and exclusive (excluding the listener(s)). Some Huron kinship terms allow for the term of address (as opposed to a term of reference) by using the first person inclusive. For example the verb root -ₗen-
with the reflexive can appear as tiataχen 'we two brothers or sisters' in the
dual and k8ataPen 'we plural brothers or sisters' in the plural (Potier
1920:243).

There appears to be a dialect difference in how the -a- suffix is used with
the reflexive prefix. While Wyandot universally uses the suffix, Huron
seems to make a distinction by including the final -a- only when the reference is cross-gender. In 1697, for example, we get the following:

Les Freres, les Soeurs.	ₗaₗena ...
[brothers, sisters]	
fr. et soeurs simul	Atateₗena
[brothers and sisters together]	
les Freres seuls.	Ataxen.
[brothers only] (FH1697:253)	

This verb root takes the causative-instrumental suffix with the reflexive prefix, giving us the notion of people adopting each other as brother or sister:

Atakensti adopter pr Fr ou Sr [adopt for brother or sister] (HF59:65; compare Potier 1920:243)

In Huron the verb -*ɩen*- referred to biological siblings, usually those of the same gender and to those adopted as siblings (HF59:65; Potier 1920:180 and 243). Potier's dictionary indicates that the word may have stretched more broadly to include parallel cousins (i.e., mother's sister's children and father's brother's children). He translates the verb root -*ɩen*- as "avoir pour frere, soeur, cousin & ..." (Potier 1920:243).

The information concerning this extension in Wyandot is more forthcoming. Both Morgan and Barbeau are in agreement that -*ɩen*- was used with respect to one's mother's sister's children (Morgan 1966:340 and 342–43, and Barbeau fieldnotes, cards 580 and 736), as was the case in all Northern Iroquoian languages in Morgan's time (Morgan 1966:340 and 342–43). The situation seems to have changed later on. In Woodbury's Onondaga dictionary, she states concerning the cognate term: "The term was traditionally used for brother, sister, mother's sister's child, and father's brother's child; now it is used for one's own brother and sister" (Woodbury 2003:945). No modern Northern Iroquoian dictionary makes reference to a contemporary use of the extension to parallel cousins.

For the Wyandot, -*ɩen*- could be extended to include people of the same phratries. In Potier's 1740s listing of clans in the three phratries of Deer, Turtle, and Wolf, he wrote *hontaχen* 'they (masculine) are siblings' after each phratry name (Potier 1920:152). Barbeau spoke of this more than a century and a half later, when he wrote:

Now then, (the four clans of one side of the five formed "one house," while the four opposite clans made up another ... The four clans in each house were 'brothers' to each other). (Barbeau 1915:86–87; see p87 fn 2; see also Barbeau 1960:11)

It was explained to Barbeau through his Wyandot informant for this story, Smith Nicholas (and an interpreter), that a cousin relationship existed for those clans who were "across the fire" of the council house from each other, but that:

The Deer, the Bear, the Porcupine, and Beaver peoples, being on the same side, don't call each other "cousins," but "brothers" or "relatives." The three Turtles [i.e., Turtle clans] and the Hawk, on the other hand, call each other "brother." It does not mean that they were blood brothers, but simply that they acknowledged being brothers. Two persons belonging to the same side of the fire, it was further explicitly stated, could not call each other "cousins." (Barbeau 1915:87 fn3)

Smith Nicholas explained (through interpreter Eldridge Brown) that "the only reason why they arranged themselves in this manner was (their desire) of making marriage regulations" (Barbeau 1915:87 fn6). This appears to mean that people could only marry those belonging to clans on the opposite side of the fire. Preliminary research done on the Wyandot community in the 1740s suggests that they practised clan exogamy only, not phratry exogamy as Nicholas claims. Perhaps in this regard there was a distinction between "ideal" and "real" cultures. Barbeau acknowledges this when he adds to the quotation above "(which is, of course, partly true only)" (Barbeau 1915:87 fn3).

The *Jesuit Relation* of 1639 recorded that the Bear and the Cord, the two Huron nations longest in Huronia, "term each other 'brother' and 'sister' in the councils and assemblies" (HR16:229). The member nations of the Iroquois confederacy also traditionally used sibling terms to address each other (Tooker 1967:10 fn4).

Nations establishing peace between each other also made use of this term. One example of this in the Huron literature came in the 1640s. After an exchange of gifts between the Iroquois, Huron, Algonquin, and French, the Huron leader Jean Baptiste Atironta optimistically stated: "It is done … we are brothers. The conclusion has been reached; now we are all relatives—Hiroquois, Hurons, Algonquins, and French; we are now but one and the same people …" (JR31:289; see Mohawk example JR41:45).

The Wyandot had such a practice as well. Barbeau recorded a story in which the Wyandot and the Seneca made peace. In conclusion, the narrator of the story stated: "That is how it came that a pact was agreed upon. The Seneca now said, 'We are brothers! Never again shall we fight, for here I do surrender now!'" (Barbeau 1915:275).

The sibling term became a statement of relationship between Huron Christians, and between Huron Christians and Christians of other Native nations. The Christian Charles Sondatsaa said the term was used because "we have henceforth but one Father, who is God, and but one common Mother, which is the Church; behold, then, thy brothers who declare to thee, that thy friends are their friends, and thy enemies are their enemies" (JR20:221).

Conversely, sometimes Huron who wanted to become Christian were forced to deny former kinship with those family members who remained traditional and did not convert. We can clearly see this in the following speech made by Joseph Chihoatenhwa, a prominent early Huron Christian, to his brother: "[A]s long as thou shalt be the devil's slave, I will not regard thee as my brother, but as a stranger, from whom I am separated forever, for the little time that we have to live together is not considerable" (JR19:159).

'My brother(s)' became the customary address between Christian Huron and Jesuits, rather than the uncle/nephew address of the more traditionally minded or the more European father/son terminology, throughout the Jesuit Relations.[10]

Cross-Sex Siblings

While, as we have seen, -ₗen- could sometimes be used to refer to a sibling of a different sex, another Huron was confined solely to such usage: -ₗenron- (Sagard 1866, FHO, FH67:103, FH1693:257, FH1697:253 and 256, HF59, HF62, HF65:216, and Potier 1920:108 and 388). The term apparently existed in Wyandot during the 1740s at least. Potier's dictionary contains the expression 'dic *nienronha*' (Potier 1920:388). The Latin short form 'dic' indicates that this is was what Potier heard the Wyandot say. By the nineteenth century -ₗenron- had disappeared from the Wyandot language. It also does not appear in Morgan's list of terms, as cognate or concept, in any Northern Iroquoian language (Morgan 1966:299).

In terms of pronominal prefixes, this verb appears to be unique in that the person being referred to was put in the agent position, as in the following entry. This could mean a kind of respect similar to that grammatically shown for age (see the discussion below).

ond[aie] horon	elle est sa soeur
[she is cross-sex sibling to him]	[she is his sister]
sonₗ8en'ronha	il nous a pour soeurs
[he is cross-sex sibling to us]	[he has us for sisters]
hien'ronha	Il t'a pour soeur
[he is cross-sex sibling to you]	[he has you for sister] (HF62)

The reflexive prefix -*atat*- was used in forms such as the following, when speaking purely of the relationship and not of a particular individual. With the -ₗen- /-I- conjugation, the reflexive prefix takes the form -*and*-:

tsandirhonha	vous etes frere et soeur
[you two are brother and sister]	[you are brother and sister]
(FH67:103)	

a₁iatandironha   Lui et moi sommes freres et soeurs
[frere et soeur]
                                        [he and me are brother and sister]
(Potier 1920:388)

This reflexive-plus-verb-root also takes the first person inclusive, *tiatandironha* (dual) and *k8atandironha* (plural) (Potier 1920:388). As that includes the listener, that means that this verb can function as a term of address as well as of reference.

As can be seen in this entry, the verb root typically takes the suffix *-ha-*, although in two instances in my sources there appears *horon* 'his sister' (HF62 and FH67:103). This appears to be similar to what occurs with *-en-* 'to have as child,' in the word *hoen* 'she or he has him as child' (discussed earlier). In one instance the suffix *-ha-* was dropped: with *senrhon* 'your sister' (FH67:103).

Cousin

The Huron verb root for cousin was *-arase-*.[11] Cognates exist in Wyandot (Morgan 1966:322–25, 331–34, 352, 355, 364, and 366 and Barbeau 1915:250 fn4, 1960:77–84, 86, 99–100 and fieldnotes. They can be found as well in all other Northern Iroquoian languages in Morgan's time (Morgan 1966:322–25, 331–4, 352, 355, 364, and 366), and more recently (Bruyas 1970:25 and Michelson 1973:29 for Mohawk; Michelson and Doxtator 2002:98 for Oneida; Woodbury 2003:77 for Onondaga Froman et al. 2002:610 for Cayuga; Chafe 1963:22 for Seneca; and Rudes 1987:37 for Tuscarora).

The agent is taken only by dual and plural forms. The equality of and lack of social distance between cousins is implied by the absence of the patient form.

a₁iarase   mon cous[in]. id[em] ns som. cousins
[we two are cousins]   [my cousin, also, we are cousins] (FH1697:247)

As with the verb root for same-sex sibling, this root can form part of a term of address with the first person inclusive dual, *tiarase*, and plural *k8arase* (Potier 1920:171).

While in most cases the suffix *-a-* is not used, it does appear in three instances (FH1697:253, FH67:60, and Potier 1920:462 line 6).

In the Huron dictionaries, the most specific translations we get for *-arase-* are "estre issue du frere our de la soeur, cousin" (FHO) or "fils du frere, de la soeur, ou cousin" (Potier 1920:108). In other words, these sources show no distinction between parallel cousins (mother's sister's children and father's brother's children) as siblings and cross cousins (mother's brother's children and father's sister's children) as cousins. Yet such a distinction existed in Morgan's reference to Wyandot and in all other Northern Iroquoian languages. For instance, we find -arase- applying to cross cousins such as father's sister's son (Morgan 1966:332–3), father's sister's daughter (Morgan 1966:322–5), mother's brother's son (Morgan 1966:331–4) and mother's brother's daughter (Morgan 1966:333–4). Barbeau's Wyandot writings did not include such a distinction, although he does point to mother's sister's children being called 'siblings' (Barbeau fieldnotes, cards 580 and 736). Likewise, the distinction is not made in today's Northern Iroquoian languages.

The basic sociological notion surrounding -arase- in Wyandot culture would appear to be that of the "other." In Barbeau's recording of the story of how the Wyandot clans and phratries were founded, the Wyandot used -arase- to apply to members of clans not part of one's phratry (Barbeau 1915:86 fn7, 87 fn4 and 6, and 88 fn1, 1960:11–12, 99–100). Also, -araseexpressed the relationship between trickster and victim in a good number of Wyandot stories, which also fits with the idea of the "other" (Barbeau 1915:190, 192, 193, 197, 200, and 209–10).

Brothers-in-Law

The Huron verb root for the brother-in-law relationship was -atio- (FHO, FH1697:253 and 257, HF59:28, HF62:31, HF65:34, and Potier 1920:109 and 190). Southern Bear (Sagard 1866) and Wyandot have -k- replace the -t- (more accurately, having a -ky- rather than a -ty-; Potier 1920:190, Morgan 1966:317, and Barbeau 1960:248–49). Cognates exist in seventeenth- and twentieth-century Mohawk (Bruyas 1970:37, Shea 1970:27, and Michelson 1973:38), modern Oneida (Michelson and Doxtator 2002:309), Cayuga, as a general sibling-in-law term (Froman et al. 2002:617), and Seneca (Chafe 1963:25), but not Onondaga or Tuscarora.

As this is a relationship of equality, we just get dual and plural forms taking the agent position, with nothing in the patient position:

aɪiatio	mon b. fr. idem ns sommes beau freres
[we two (excl.) are brothers-in-law]	[my brother-in-law, also we are brothers-in-law]
tsatio	ton b. fr.
[you two are brothers-in-law]	[your brother-in-law]

hiatio	son b. fr.
[they two are brothers-in-law]	[his brother-in-law]
a₁8atio	mes b. fr.
[we (pl. excl.) are brothers-in-law]	[my brothers-in-law]
sk8atio	tes b. fr.
[you (pl.) are brothers-in-law]	[your brothers-in-law]
hontio	les b. fr.
[they (pl.) are brothers-in-law]	[brothers-in-law] (FH1697:257)

There are no first person inclusive forms—ones that include the listener(s), which suggests that there might not have been a form of address used by brothers-in-law. This might have made for a kind of brother-in-law avoidance.[12]

Of interest is the fact that the causative-instrumental suffix -*st*- can occur with -*atio*-, especially as the combination is translated not only as "devenir beaux freres [become brothers-in-law]" (HF59:28; see also Potier 1920:190), but additionally as "contracter alliance reciproque" (Potier 1920:190). This suggests that prospective brothers-in-law could play active roles in the arranging of marriages.

Morgan is the only Huron/Wyandot source that includes cross-sex references with females speaking: sister's husband (Morgan 1966:317), father's sister's husband (Morgan 1966:335) and mother's sister's daughter's husband (Morgan 1966:343). I believe that, as with the terms for nephews/nieces, Morgan or one of his informants confused two terms. He also mistakenly records the cross-sex sibling-in-law term -*nda8et*- as applying to relationships between siblings-in-law of the same gender (male reference), including wife's brother (Morgan 1966:379) and sister's husband (Morgan 1966:378; also see 317, 326, 334, and 343).

Sister-in-Law

The Huron term used between sisters-in-law was -*a(₁)iek*- (FHO, FH1697:256, HF59:4, HF62, HF65:8, and Potier 1920:109 and 164). While Barbeau records a Wyandot cognate (Barbeau fieldnotes, cards 576, 616, and 695), Morgan does not. Instead, he translates the Wyandot cognate of -*atio*- as 'sister-in-law' (Morgan 1966:380), and presents -*nda8et*-, the cross-sex sibling-in-law term, as meaning 'brother's wife' (female reference), along with other relationships that could be interpreted as meaning 'sister-in-law (Morgan 1966:324, 333, and 381). As with -*atio*-, I suspect that Morgan got it wrong. Cognates exist in all other Northern Iroquoian languages as recorded by Morgan, albeit with a broader range of meanings (Morgan

1966:380–81). Cognates exist in other sources in Mohawk (Shea 1970:27 and Michelson 1973:29), Oneida (Michelson and Doxtator 2002:100), as a general sibling-in-law term in Onondaga (Woodbury 2003:881), Cayuga (Froman et al. 2002:610), Seneca (Chafe 1963:25), and Tuscarora (Rudes 1987:48).

As with the brother-in-law term, there are only dual and plural agent forms, with nothing in the patient position. Likewise, there are no first person inclusive forms. This suggests that there was no term of address for one's sister-in-law, which could imply that such in-laws practised avoidance. In the following dictionary entries, the abbreviation 'B. Srs.' Stands for 'Belles Soeurs':

aₗiaₗiek [we two (exclusive) are sisters-in-law]	ma b. sr. ide ns som. B. Srs. [my sister-in-law, also we are sisters-in-law]
tsaₗiek [you two are sisters-in-law]	ta B. Sr. [your sister-in-law]
ₗiaₗiek [they two are sisters-in-law]	sa B. Sr. [her sister-in-law]
aₗ8aₗiek [we (pl. excl.) are sisters-in-law	mes B. Srs. [my sisters-in-law]
sk8aₗiek [you (pl.) are sisters-in-law]	tes B. Srs. [your sisters-in-law]
ₗonₗiek [they are sisters-in-law]	ses B. Srs. [their sisters-in-law] (FH1697:257)

In both Huron and Wyandot, the evidence clearly demonstrates that the meaning was confined just to sisters-in-law:

> *aiek* 2 ou plusieurs femmes etre belles soeurs (Potier 1920:164; c.f. FH1697:253 and Barbeau fieldnotes, cards 576 and 616)

As we have seen, other Northern Iroquoian languages extend this meaning. The absence of a cognate for *-nda8et-* in most of these languages would seem to have had an effect in broadening the meaning of this verb.

Cross-Sex Siblings-in-Law

The Huron verb root for cross-sex siblings-in-law was *-nda8et-* (Sagard 1866, FHO, FH1697:253 and 257, HF59:88, HF62, HF65:107, and Potier 1920:108 and 278). This is matched by the form appearing in the Wyandot sources (Morgan 1966:315 and 317; Barbeau 1915:67, 1960:84). A cognate appears to exist in Mohawk (Michelson 1973:14), and possibly in Tuscarora (Rudes 1987:54 and Morgan 1966:380), both carrying the same range of meanings.

The verb root *-nda8et-* is similar to the previous two sibling-in-law terms in that all the grammatical players are lumped into the same position. This time, however, the pronominal prefixes are in the patient position. I cannot honestly say why. The forms do not distinguish between inclusive and exclusive in the first person, so the expression is not confined to the first person exclusive, but I believe that there is no term of address using this verb root. This continues the theme of in-law avoidance referred to earlier.

Beau fr. et Bel. Sr.

on̜inda8et
[we 2 are cross-sex siblings-in-law]

mon b. fr ma b. Sr.
[my brother-in-law, my sister-in-law]

tsinda8et

[you 2 are cross-sex siblings-in-law]

ton b.f ta b. sr. ide vs etes tous deux B. fr. ou B. Sr.
[your brother-in-law, your sister-in-law, also we two are brother-in-law and sister-in-law]

hotinda8et

[they (m) are cross-sex siblings -in-law]

son b. fr. sa b. sr. ide luy et elle sont b. fr. et b.sr.
[her brother-in-law, his sister-in-law, also he and she are brother in law and sister in law]

otinda8et

[they (f) are cross-sex siblings-in-law]

s. b. sr. ide elles sont belles soeur ambae
[her(?) sister-in-law, also they are sisters-in-law]

on̜8anda8et
[we (pl) are cross-sex siblings-in-law]

mes b. fr. mes b. srs
[my brothers-in-law, my sisters in-law]

hotinda8et
[they (m) are cross-sex siblings-in-law]

ses b. fr a elle
[they are brothers-in-law to her]

otinda8et
[they (f) are cross-sex siblings-in-law]

ses b. srs.
[her sisters-in-law] (FH1697:257)

With exceptions to be noted shortly, the verb *-nda8et-* referred exclusively to cross-gender siblings-in-law. In Wyandot, this view is reinforced (Barbeau fieldnotes, cards 616 and 690), with some suggestion that, at a time before Barbeau collected his material, the term could be extended to the relationship between a man and his friend's wife (Barbeau 1915:67 fn4).

In the quotation given above, we see that *otinda8et* was used to express the relationship between sisters-in-law. This term uses the feminine plural patient pronominal prefix, a form confined to usage among a group of two or more females. It contrasts with *hotinda8et*, the masculine plural form, which can refer either to a mixed group or one that is exclusively male. (Its translation here suggests that it related to a mixed group.) Only one other dictionary (Potier 1920:108) providing this list included the feminine plural forms. Three other dictionaries (FHO, HF62, and HF65:107) also provide this list, but do not include the feminine plural. As the dictionaries that exclude this form were written earlier than those that include it, this greater extension may be the result of change taking place during the seventeenth century.

Father-in-Law/Son-in-Law

The father-in-law/son-in-law relationship was signified by a verb which appears in at least one dialect appears as *-nnhes-* (Sagard 1866, HF59:112, HF62:77, and HF65:112), and in Northern Bear as *-ndhes-* (FHO and HF62:62). There is no Wyandot cognate. However, cognates exist for the son-in-law term in the other Northern Iroquoian languages in Morgan's time (Morgan 1966:370 and 372–73). Its use is more generalized in more modern Oneida, where it is cognate with the term for 'in-law, different generation' (Michelson and Doxtator 2002:1054), and in Onondaga, in which it means 'have a parent-in-law; have a son-in-law' (Woodbury 2003:1177), matching the form in Cayuga (Froman et al. 2002:611) and Tuscarora (Rudes 1987:132).

The verb *-nnhes-* would appear to be an incomplete one. Its main use is in complementary distribution to the verb *-nnenh8ak-* (see below). The most often reported form of this verb was as a term of address, reciprocally used between father-in-law and son-in-law:

> *A͟ɩennhes* dit le gendre a son beau pere, et le beau pere a son gender [says the son-in-law to his father-in-law and the father-in-law to his son-in-law] [HF65:122; c.f. HF59:112, and HF62:62]

The only other way in which this verb is presented in the dictionaries is with the reflexive prefix *-atat-* and the indefinite agent pronominal prefix, to speak generally of the relationship (HF59:112, HF62:77, and HF65:122).

Parents-in-Law/Son-in-Law

The verb root used to express the relationship between parents-in-law and their son-in-law in Huron was *-nnenh8ak-* (FHO, FH1697:253 and 256, HF59:110, HF62, HF65:119, and Potier 1920:108 and 302). A Wyandot cognate exists in the writings of both Morgan and Barbeau (Morgan 1966:370 and 372–73; Barbeau 1960:86, 203, 231, and 233). The other Northern Iroquoian languages appear not to have a cognate, with one exception (see below).

The pronominal prefixes for this verb have the parent-in-law expressed in the agent position, the son-in-law in the patient position. It should also be noted that this verb has no term of address from parents-in-law or son-in-law. As this term, unlike the previous one, could include mother-in-law as well as father-in-law, this could be indicative of mother-in-law avoidance:

Mon beau pere	*ha₁ennenh8ak*	il m'a pr gendre
	[he has me as son-in-law]	[he has me as son-in-law]
ma belle mere	*a₁ennenh8ak*	elle m'a pr gendre
	[she has me as son-in-law]	[she has me as son-in-law]
mon gendre	*hennenh8ak*	
[my son-in-law]	[I have him as son-in-law] (FH1697:253)	

Equality in the relationship is expressed using the reflexive prefix *-atat-* with dual or plural forms in the agent position (Potier 1920:302, FHO, and HF59:110).

The causative-instrumental suffix *-st-* is used with this verb to produce the sense of "prendre q. pour son gendre pour mari de sa fille [to take someone for one's son-in-law, for the husband of one's daughter]" (Potier 1920:302). Prospective parents-in-law, apparently, had a significant, active role in at least approving or disapproving a suggested match for their daughter.[13] This role is also suggested in another entry, in which a man apparently requests permission to become someone's son-in-law:

| *ta₁enn'enh8asθa* | prends moi pr. ton gendre |
| [make me your son-in-law] | [take me for your son-in-law] |

In the Huron dictionaries *-nnenh8ak-* is typically translated as expressing the relationship between a son-in-law and his parents-in-law, including his stepfather-in-law:

Auoir pr. gendre, ou pr. beau pere ou belle mere ou mary [to have as son-in-law, or as father-in-law or mother-in-law or [her] husband] *₁An'nen'h8ak* (FHO)

In Wyandot, the use extended beyond that. Both Barbeau and Morgan state that -*nnenh8ak*- could refer to the relationship between parents-in-law and a daughter-in-law (Morgan 1966:373; Barbeau, cards 690 and 708). I see two potential explanations for this: One is that, as Morgan's Wyandot had no separate term for daughter-in-law, -*nnenh8ak*- must have replaced -*sk8ak*- for his informants. He did not record the latter term, and Barbeau only recorded it twice. Another explanation speaks to the matter of where a couple would go to live once they were married. Barbeau wrote the following:

> ha‾tènḘ‾mạ' cḘ (*he-self-lives with parents-in-law* or *he becomes a son-in-law*) is applied to a married man who stays with his wife's relatives or parents-in-law. In the old time, the informant added, a man generally went to live at the home of his wife's parents. (Barbeau 1915:69 fn4)

Perhaps, then, the verb -*nnenh8ak*- expressed the relationship between parents-in-law and children-in-law who lived together, with suitable, respectful avoidance being communicated by not using this verb in a term of address. If the preferred pattern was matrilocality (i.e., to live with the wife's family), the term would then typically apply to the relationship between parents-in-law and a son-in-law. Modern Onondaga appears to have a cognate verb -*nęhwashę*-, which Woodbury translates as "be an in-law, be living with one's spouse's family" (Woodbury 2003:287).

That the connotation of in-laws living together across generations applied not just to the Wyandot, but to the Huron as well, can be seen in an early Huron dictionary entry in which -*nnenh8ak*- was used with a locative suffix -*ıe*- meaning 'at, on, or in.' In three dictionaries this form appears as follows:

> hannenh8aıe ihentron   il demeure ches son beau pere
> [at his parents'-in-law's he dwells]   [he lives with his father-in-law]
> (HF65:119; c.f. HF62 and Potier 1920:302)

However, in the oldest surviving Jesuit Huron dictionary (FHO), we find the same combination used not only in the way presented above, but also with the feminine prefix in the agent position:

> Hann'en'h8aıe ihentron   il demeure ches femme
> [at his parents-in-law's he dwells]   [he lives at the home of his wife]
> ıann'enh8aıe ihentron[14]   elle demeure ches son mary
> [at her parents-in-law's (she) dwells]   [she lives with her husband] (FHO)

Not only does the verb imply living with in-laws, but, with the weight of evidence of three dictionaries against one, it also suggests that the

Huron may have had matrilocality as a preferred pattern, with occasional patrilocal exceptions. The fact that no such locative form occurs with the daughter-in-law term is also instructive. Morgan's Wyandot informants also extend the use of this term to the relationship between a person and his or her siblings' children's spouses (Morgan 1966:303, 305–6, 309, and 311). Barbeau also presents the term as applying in Wyandot to the grandparents of a man's wife (Barbeau, card 708).

Daughter-in-Law

The Huron verb root for the parent-in-law/daughter-in-law relationship was -sk8ak- (FHO, FH1697:257, HF59, HF62:123, HF65:78–79) or -sχ8ak- (Potier 1920:109 and 353). A Wyandot cognate appears only twice in Barbeau (Barbeau 1960:203 and card 624), but not at all in Morgan. Cognates existed in all other Northern Iroquoian languages in Morgan's time (Morgan 1966:370–71 and 373), and can be found in more modern Onondaga (Woodbury 2003:1177), Cayuga (Froman et al. 2002:610), Seneca (Chafe 1963:26), and Tuscarora (Rudes 1987:261), but not in modern Mohawk and Oneida.

With respect to pronominal prefixes, the parent-in-law is always in the agent position:

chiesk8ak	tu l'as pr. Bru, c'est ta Bru
[you have her as daughter-in-law]	[you have her as daughter-in-law, it is your daughter-in-law]
haₑesk8ak	il m'a pr. Bru.
[he has me as daughter-in-law]	[he has me as daughter-in-law]
(FH1697:257; c.f. Potier 1920:108 and HF59)	

The reflexive prefix -atat-[15] has first person inclusive forms—*tiatatesχ8ak* for dual and *k8atatatesχ8ak* for plural—so there is a term of address.

The causative-instrumental suffix -st- is used in cases similar to those used with the parents-in-law/son-in-law term -nnenh8ak-. The active role of the prospective parents-in-law can be seen in examples such as the following:

ₑask8asti	R. prendre pour Bru
[to take as daughter-in-law]	[R. to take as daughter-in-law]
haₑesk8asti	il m'a prise pr bru
[he makes me his daughter-in-law]	[he takes me as daughter-in-law]
(HF65:179; c.f. HF59, HF62:123, and Potier 1920:353)	

Based purely on evidence from Huron and Wyandot sources, -sk8ak- would seem to be confined to the relationship between a woman and her parents-in-law. In Morgan's time, however, the cognates in other Northern Iroquoian languages could refer also to a sibling's son's wife (Morgan 1966:303, 305, 308, and 311), an extension he gives as occurring with -nnenh8ak- in Wyandot. Conceivably, then, -sk8ak- in Huron could have had a similar extension of meaning, without the Jesuits being aware of it.

Parents-in-Law

The Huron had a term that referred to the relationship between the two sets of parents of a married couple. The verb involved is -ndoron- (FH1697:12, Potier 1920:296, HF59:104, HF62:70, and HF65:112). No cognates appear in Wyandot. Potier wrote "non utere" (not used') in his entry for the verb. Cognates exist in nineteenth-century Mohawk (Cuoq 1966:147) and in modern Seneca (Chafe 1963:25), but not in modern Mohawk, Oneida, Onondaga, or Cayuga. This term is probably derived from the verb root -ndoron- 'to be difficult, valuable,' which has the following set of meanings when referring to a human being:

> ... etre difficile a contenter, etre un personner de merite, de distinction, considerable, qu'on estime qui a du credit et de l'autorite en q.c. & [to be difficult to satisfy, to be a person of merit, of distinction, of substance, who people esteem as one of credit and of authority in something] (Potier 1920:295)

Not only do the two verbs appear to be homophonous, but their meaning connects concretely in one instance when the verb referring to the co-parent-in-law relationship takes the causative-instrumental suffix -st-. It is translated as "rendre q[uelqu'un] considerable [to render someone important]" (Potier 1920:296). I believe that the main implication of -ndoron- here is has to do with merit, distinction, and substance, although I suspect the 'difficult to satisfy' connotation was not lost on the Huron.

The pronominal prefixes are those of equality, with both parties in the agent position. Again the first person is confined to the exclusive form, thereby not forming a term of address. An example is the following:

$a_l$indoronch

[we two (excl.) are co-parents-in-law, 'valuable']

nous que sommes leurs B.P. et M., le P de ma Bru. la mere de mon gendre [we that are their father-in-law and mother-in-law, the father of my daughter-in-law, the mother of my son-in-law] (FH1697:258)

In one source, the pronominal prefixes are confined to the dual (Potier 1920:296).

Two of the Huron–French dictionaries show a form of this verb that refers to a different person and uses a different pronominal prefix:

Endoronch   ma belle mere
[one is valuable (or difficult) to me]   [my mother-in-law] (HF62:70 -71 c.f.
HF65:112)

This word may work to describe the relationship, rather than simply specify the connection. A description of being valuable and/or difficult would seem to suggest another example of in-law avoidance.

Step-parents/Stepchildren

The Huron term for the relationship between step-parents and stepchildren was -*ndo*- (Sagard 1866, FHO:148, FH1697:258, HF62, and Potier 1920:109 and 449). A cognate exists in all Wyandot sources (Potier 1920:109; Morgan 1966:374–75, and Barbeau 1960:133 and 135–37 and cards 608–15). Cognates are also found in every other Northern Iroquoian language in Morgan's time (Morgan 1966:374–75), except for Tuscarora. In more modern versions of the languages, a cognate can be found in Mohawk (Michelson 1973:81), Onondaga (Woodbury 2003:718), Cayuga (Froman et al. 2002:613) and Seneca (Chafe 1963:26). In modern Oneida, the verb form used appears to be homophonous with their cognate of -*ndoron*-, both taking -*nolu*- as the root (Michelson and Doxtator 2002:598).

The verb appears to be incomplete, with unusual construction surrounding their terms of address. A stepson addressed his stepmother as *a₁on* (HF62 and HF65, and in "Responds" in Sagard 1866), his stepfather as *₁ando* (FH1697:258, HF62, and HF65). The term of address for 'my stepson' may have been *ando* (Sagard 1866 and FHO:148).

The -*a*- suffix appears in Wyandot (Potier 1920:109 and Barbeau 1960:133, 135–37, 210 and 213, cards 608–15, 690, and 760), as does the causative-instrumental suffix -*st*- (Barbeau 1960:133 and card 760), but in only one Huron source, perhaps as a Northern Bear feature (FHO:148). Curiously, in both Huron and Wyandot, reference using this verb is confined in almost every instance to the relationship between a stepson and his step-parents. The only exception occurs in Morgan (Morgan 1966:374). Interestingly, the Wyandot stories that involved step-parents spoke of the bad treatment that stepsons, not stepdaughters, received from their step-parents (see Barbeau 1960:20–22 and 35–40).

A late seventeenth-century Huron dictionary claimed that Huron Christians were then beginning to substitute the term meaning 'father' for the term 'step-father,'and 'mother' for 'step-mother': "parmi les sauvages Xtiens, ils donnent le nom de pere det de mere au B.P. et a la B.M" (FH1697:258). It is hard to know how truthful that was, as Barbeau spoke of a similar occurrence among the Wyandot (Barbeau, cards 608–9), and the step-parent terms were still being used.

Conclusions

Comparing Huron with Wyandot and the
Other Northern Iroquoian Languages

Huron and Wyandot share cognates with the terms for mother (both terms), father, child, mother's brother, father's sister, sister's children (male reference), brother's children (female reference), maternal grandparents and grandchildren, sibling (same-sex and cross-sex), cousin, brother-in-law, son-in-law, daughter-in-law, and step-parents/stepchildren.

Sometimes changes take place from earlier to later in Wyandot. Morgan records a term for father's sister, but Barbeau does not. The term for a cross-sex sibling occurs in Potier's eighteenth-century dictionary, but not in Morgan or Barbeau. Sometimes, too, there is an extension of meaning to become more like the English-speaking version: niece/nephew (female reference) and possibly the extension of the mother's brother term to include father's sister's husband.

Absent from all three Wyandot sources are the terms for the paternal grandparent/grandchild relationship, and the limited father-in-law/son-in-law term of address. Like the losses that occurred within recorded Wyandot kinship terminology history (e.g., cross-sex sibling and father's sister), these can be seen as victims of extensive contact. The terms have no equivalent in French or English, and are easily covered by the extension of reference of terms more in line with French and English equivalents (e.g., by the maternal grandparent/grandchild becoming simply a grandparent/grandchild, and by having a single term for the son-in-law relationship, and also by eliminating the reference in verb root forms to a person being of the opposite gender.

We find similar differences between Huron and the other Northern Iroquoian languages as we do between Huron and Wyandot, suggesting that, likewise, these difference are due to change since the speakers of the other languages came into contact with Europeans. Both the terms and concepts of paternal grandparent/grandchild and cross-sex sibling are missing from these languages. Further, one of the two parent-in-law/son-in-law terms was dropped too—the one that Wyandot kept. I suggest that these languages once contained such terms and concepts, but again, like with Wyandot, they lost them through contact with French and English speakers.

The same may be true for the term and concept of nephew/niece (female reference), and may explain having two rather than three terms for siblings-in-law, both areas in which some Northern Iroquoian languages differ from Huron. Since Morgan's time, changes towards a European model have taken place in the kinship terminology of the Iroquois. According to Nancy Bonvillain (1973:161–62), among the Akwesasne Mohawk of the early 1970s the terms for father, child, and cousin refer to the same people as do their English equivalents; older and younger sibling terms only apply to those who are biologically brother and sisters; their nephew/niece term (male reference) applies to all the children of one's siblings; and the mother's brother term is used when speaking of or to one's father's brother.

Less easy to deal with are the differences concerning the terms for 'father' and 'mother's brother.' These leave a number of questions unanswered. Did the general Northern Iroquoian term for mother's brother become subject to taboo in Huron so that a circumlocution took its place? As for 'father,' was this an innovative term, possibly with a meaning lost through time? How could that be when a cognate term in Mohawk means 'mother'? Is it a shared conservative term that the other languages have lost? And, finally, why does it mean 'father' in one language (Huron) and 'mother' in the other (Mohawk)? Does this relate to some pre-contact shift from patrilineality to matrilineality? No answer can be presented with certainty at this time.

Pronominal Prefixes: Social Distance and Solidarity

A well-developed sociolinguistic literature describes the social dimensions of the use of second person pronouns in European languages as with 'tu' and 'vous' in French (Hudson 1980:122–28 and Trudgill 1974:103–4). Two key social elements have been identified: power and solidarity (Brown and Gilman 1960). The expression of power or rank difference involved the non-reciprocal use of the familiar second person singular "T-form" (from the French word 'tu') and polite or formal second person plural "V-form" (from the French word 'vous'). The more highly ranked individual would address the more lowly ranked one with the T-form; the lowly one replied with the V-form. This is comparable in English to a situation in which an employer or boss uses an employee's first name in addressing that person, but the lower-ranked employee responds with the appropriate title of Mr., Miss, Mrs., or Ms. followed by the employer's last name.

A more recent development in European second person pronominal usage involves the almost universal reciprocal use of either the T- or V-form depending on the degree of intimacy or familiarity shared between those addressing each other. Soldiers of unequal rank would use the more formal V-form. Brothers would use T-forms. Brown and Gilman (1960) labelled this element "solidarity."

Applying this type of analysis to the pronominal prefixes that occur in Huron kinship terms yields insights, although to adapt it from more hierarchical European society to a more egalitarian Aboriginal society requires some change in terminology and in attendant concepts. Solidarity can stand as it is. However, rather than expressing "power" as such, something absent in a tribal society such as that of the Huron, Huron pronominal prefixes convey a social distance, if you include in that term's purview differences in respect owing primarily to age, and avoidance owing primarily to gender.

The pronominal indicators to be examined in looking for markers of solidarity and social distance are the agent and the patient. As expressed above, when the verb is transitive, the agent acts as the subject, the patient as the object.

Mandatory Respect

The Huron had several ways of using kinship terms to express a respectful social distance due to a difference in age. The main method, used primarily with terms of reference, was to put the senior relative in the agent and the junior relative in the patient. The following are examples:

WENDAT TERM	LITERAL TRANSLATION	ENGLISH EQUIVALENT
sand8en	**she** is mother to **you**	your mother
saena	**she** has **you** as child	your mother
son₁8a₁isten	**he** is father to **us**	our father
hiatennonron	**he** is mother's brother to **you**	your mother's brother
on₁8arahak	**she** is father's sister to **us**	our father's sister
₁echiondraka	**I** (female) have **her** as brother's child	my niece
he₁eniaha	**I** have **him** as younger same-sex sibling	my younger brother

ha₁eniaha	**he** has **me** as younger same-sex sibling	my older brother

This pattern differed somewhat for terms of address, with social distance expressed by having the speaker in the patient position. I would argue that this permitted an expression of solidarity, mitigating the social distance, by having the same term reciprocated, rather like the European soldiers of unequal rank addressing each other with V-forms, which were formal yet more egalitarian than using two different forms. In both the Huron and the European cases, the same formal term was used by both parties.

Solidarity

Solidarity was expressed by grouping both parties in the relationship together as agents (or in one case as patients). This could be done directly with the verb root, or with the addition of the reflexive prefix coming between the pronouns and the verb root. With some verbs, relationships could be expressed in two ways. Separating the parties into agent and patient articulated a social distance. The reflexive prefix, in contrast, could be used with all parties as agents, expressing more familiarity or solidarity:

HURON WORD	TRANSLATION	ENGLISH EQUIVALENT
a₁iataxen	we two are same-sex siblings	my brother, sister
a₁iarase	we are cousins	my cousin
on₁8anda8et	we are siblings-in-law of the opposite sex	my brothers-in-law or my sisters-in-law
hiatio	they (two males) are brothers-in-law	his brother-in-law

In-Law Avoidance Relationships

There are seven different verb roots denoting in-law relationships. Of these, five do not allow for terms of address. This is demonstrated by the absence of first person inclusive forms, dual or plural. The verb roots and the relationships they depict are as follows:

a) *-atio-*   'to be brothers-in-law'
b) *-a(₁)iek-*   'to be sisters-in-law'
c) *-nda8et-*   'to be cross-sex siblings-in-law'
d) *-nnenh8ak-*   'to be parents-in-law and son-in-law'
e) *-ndoron-*   'to be (fellow) parents-in-law'

In contrast, two verb roots allow for terms of reference by having first person inclusive forms:

f) -sχ8ak-   'to be parents-in-law and daughter-in-law'
g) -nnhes-   'to be father-in-law and son-in-law'

This would seem to suggest that a son-in-law could address his father-in-law—someone potentially of his clan—with -nnhes-, but not his mother-in-law. On the other hand, a daughter-in-law could address both parents-in-law with -sx8ak-. (Again, the father-in-law was at least potentially of the same clan.) We might conclude from this that a son-in-law was expected to practise respectful mother-in-law avoidance.

In the discussion of the verb root -nnenh8ak-, I described how the evidence suggests that couples generally lived with the wife's family after marriage. Further, the discussion of bridewealth in the previous chapter also points to the fact that this matrilocality was the preferred residential pattern for Huron couples. Fred Eggan made a connection between matrilocality and mother-in-law avoidance for the Plains people that he studied:

> By the general rule of matrilocal residence he must reside in his parents-in-law's camp and must help support them economically, though to begin with he may feel an intruder. The mother-daughter relationship is a respect relationship; this respect is intensified in the case of the son-in-law by the difference in sex. There is a further factor in the rivalry of the mother-daughter and husband-wife relationships; in order that the affairs of the camp may run smoothly, the son-in-law and the mother-in-law avoid each other completely, though manifesting the highest respect for each other. (Eggan 1971:142)

The other in-law avoidance relationship appears to be that of equals: siblings-in-law of all three sorts and parents-in-law. Clans may be relevant here. These in-laws are almost always from different clans. Due to the practice of clan exogamy, sisters-in-law and brothers-in-law and cross-sex siblings-in-law could not be of the same clan. As for fellow parents-in-law, the mothers-in-law would not be of the same clan as each other, and neither would the two fathers-in-law.

Use of the -a- Suffix

The use of the -a- suffix is difficult to discuss. Some dialects are more likely to use it (e.g., Cord and Wyandot) than are others. Also, in one case we find it used by the younger party; in another by the older party. When, for example, grandparents and grandchildren addressed each other, they used the same pronominal prefixes, but the grandchild used the -a- suffix, while the grandparent did not.

Between two generations, some terms of address could be used by the ascending (older) generation (using the verb roots *-en-* 'to have as child,' *-ˌenh8aten-* '(male speaking) to have as sister's child,' *-chionnrak-* '(female-speaking) to have as brother's child.' Different verbs were used by the descending (younger) generation (*-nnen-* 'to have as mother,' *-ˌisten-* 'to have as father,' *-atendoron-* 'to have as mother's brother,' and *-arahak-* 'to have as father's sister.' In some dialects, the ascending generation verbs take the *-a-* suffix, but the descending generation verbs do not. This occurs with terms of reference as well as terms of address. We can see this by re-ordering the terms from the chart above:

WENDAT TERM	LITERAL TRANSLATION	ENGLISH EQUIVALENT
Ascending Generation Terms		
saena	**she** has **you** as child	your mother
ˌechiondraka	**I** (female) have **her** as brother's child	my niece
heˌeniaha	**I** have **him** as younger same-sex sibling	my younger brother
haˌeniaha	**he** has **me** as younger same-sex sibling	my older brother
Descending Generation Terms		
sand8en	**she** is mother to **you**	your mother
sonˌ8aˌisten	**he** is father to **us**	our father
hiatennonron	**he** is mother's brother to **you**	your mother's brother
onˌ8arahak	**she** is father's sister to **us**	our father's sister

I suggest here that the *-a-* suffix is a form of diminutive (most clearly seen in the younger same-sex sibling terms above), a suffix of endearment, one that lessens potential social distance.

Summary

The study of Wendat kinship terms is important because the evidence begins at such an early date, and continues for such a long time. Both of these elements are unique. We can see change among the Huron as well as suggest changes that took place for other Northern Iroquoian peoples. Not surprisingly, the changes that took place reflect the loss of forms that do not have counterparts in English or French.

We get some clues as to social relations as well. We see hints of Huron mother-in-law avoidance. We discover that the Huron referred to the French as nephews (i.e., sister's son, male speaking); they must have thought of them as children in the Huron world, needing to be taught some of the basics of how to live. Also, we see that when a significant age difference exists between kin, the senior figure is shown respect by being put in the agent position. The patient part of the pronominal prefix is used to refer to the younger one. Finally, the diminutive is used when there is a significant age or status difference, and this, I speculate, might be a way of adding an aspect of closeness to a respect relationship.

Notes

1   JR22:69–71 and 223; 24:213; 25:185; 26:143; 27:147, 191, 217, and 237; 29:75–77, passim; 30:271; 31:145 and 281; 32:207, 233, 271, and 285; 33:53; 36:37 and 77; 37:179, 205, and 207; and 38:273.

2   Sagard 1866, 1939:71; Brébeuf 1830:2, 3, and 4; JR10:267; FHO, FH67:98; FH1693:256–57; FH1697:253–55; HF59:51, HF62:14–15; HF65:63; and Potier 1920:108–9 and 219).

3   Potier 1920:387 distinguishes between *hih8atena* 'my nephew' (in reference) and *ih8atena* 'my nephew or my niece' (in address).

4   Not all the entries have the *-a-;* for those that do, it was clearly added some time after the initial writing.

5   This term appears to me to use the noun root *-at-* 'body' plus the verb root *-8an-* 'to own,' but I cannot be sure.

6   This is the word given as the term of reference in Potier (1920:216). Perhaps, in paralleling the male-speaking term, this might be more like *ehechionnrak* or *hechionnrak.*

7   No word here directly translates as 'thank you.' Perhaps that word was left out.

8   A bad translation of 'petit fils' as 'little son' rather than 'grandson' in the JR8 passage may have been what led Elizabeth Tooker into thinking that for the Huron this figure was the mother rather than the grandmother of the culture-hero twins (Tooker 1967:153).

9   Sagard 1866, 1939:71, JR10:119, 19:147, FHO, FH67:103, FH1693, FH1697:253 and 256, HF59:19 and 65, HF62, and Potier 1920:108, 180, and 243.

10   JR13:135, 175; 15:83 and 93; 19:141, 147, 153, 159, 169; 20:57; 26:207, 289; 27:33; 33:235–7, 39:70; 40:53 passim for Huron to French: JR15:47; 17:41, 31:35; 34:91; 35:111; 39:79 passim for French to Huron.

11   Sagard 1866, 1929:71, FHO, FH67:60, FH1697:253 and 257, HF59:11, HF62, HF65:18, and Potier 1920:108 and 171.

12   As the term is generally used in anthropology, avoidance relationships refer to culturally structured means by which people in potentially stressful in-law relationships (particularly between mothers-in-law and their children's spouses) can avoid one another, thereby reducing the stress. This can involve more or less mandatory silence in the presence of the in-law.

13   See Tooker 1967:126 for a discussion of the traditional role of the daughter's mother in this regard in Iroquoian culture.

14   For this sentence to be grammatically consistent, and to make sense, the Huron word here should be *ɩentron* 'she dwells.'

15   In Potier the semireflexive *-at-* is used instead (Potier 1920:353).

5 The Huron and Their Relationship to the Environment

It is difficult to use material from the Huron language to tap into the indigenous knowledge the seventeenth-century Huron had about the land and waters, the flora and fauna about them. Once we have said that they were knowledgeable about their environment, the plants and animals around them, what more can we say? The language can tell us some of the story; however, as the Jesuit missionary linguists were not as interested in botany and biology as they were in religion and politics, a culture-before-nature bias is reflected in the vocabulary they recorded. We can, however, learn some fundamentals: terms for months, community names (which all related to the environment), and names for animals.

The Huron Calendar

In three of our seventeenth-century Huron dictionaries (FHO, FH62, and FH1697) are found names of each month or moon, each named after some natural event or human activity related to nature that occurred during the period in question. These calendars are useful as they tell us something about what the Huron did, observed, and found significant in each month. While all three dictionaries were written after the Huron left the Huronia of southern Ontario, it is fair to say that the calendars reflect the terms used in their old homeland. Jesuit dictionaries were conservative documents. New missionaries would be trained in the Huron language by hand-copying dictionaries. Each "new" version was merely a rewrite, with perhaps a few additions made, and little, if anything, taken away. When Father Pierre Potier wrote his dictionary in the 1740s, for example, he included words not used by the Wyandots he was working with, merely adding "non dict" ('not spoken') or "non aud" ('not heard') after the word or entry. Huron dictionaries from the 1650s to the 1740s are remarkably similar in their entries, the only drastic change coming when the format was changed from French–Huron to Huron–French (with the words presented in a combination of the five Iroquoian conjugations plus alphabetical order). The calendar presented here, then, is a composite of information most likely first recorded in non-surviving dictionaries written during a time when the Jesuits were in Huronia.

Month Entries

Unless otherwise stated, the following entries are from FH1697:244 (exactly as originally written), with other versions included for comparison where significant differences exist References to Potier's dictionary show the noun and verb roots that make up the words or phrases in the entry.

JANUARY
  esk8entesa   le jour cruit un peu
  [day will again become a little longer]   [the day grows a little]
  -ets- (Potier 1920:385); *-ent-* 455

FEBRUARY
  esk8entesk8anne[n]   [les jours] sont plus grands
  [day will again be a lot longer]   [the days are larger]
  -ı8annen- (Potier 1920:253–54); *-ets-* (385); *-ent-* (455)

MARCH
  andatat, anda8atonnen   le debordent des eaux
  [flowing water appears, overflows]   [it overflows, the water]
  -at- (Potier 1920:197–98); *-t-* (277); *-nda8-* (445)

APRIL
  Atsiₗiondi aₗannaₗoha   le poisson d'ore[1] donne
  [walleye, pickerel run]   [the pickerel runs]
  -nnaₗo- (Potier 1920:301)
  ahaon d'aθochingota.   Les grues arrivent
  [cranes or herons arrive]   [the herons arrive]
  -on- (Potier 1920:314); *-aθochingot-* (445)

MAY
  daat endaₗa2a   on seme
  [one plants or sows]   [one plants]
  -ndaₗ- (Potier 1920:274)
  Tichiont 8tsistaraₗi   les fraises en fleur
  [strawberry blossoms open,   [the strawberries are in flower]
  they are in flower]

-ra$_ι$- (Potier 1920:336); *-tsist-* (454); *tichiont* (FH1697:80)

| *Eeront8ten* | on plant l'arbor |
| [one will plant, stand up trees] | [one plants trees] |

-8t-(Potier 1920:437); *-ront-* (453)

JUNE

| *Tichiont a8ahiari /v [tichiont] ahiarista* | temps des fraises |
| [strawberry, its fruit is ripe] | [the time of strawberries] |

-ri- (Potier 1920:345); *-ahi-* (445); *tichiont* (FH1697:80)

JULY

| *Sang8atrannens /v sahies a8ahiari* | temps des framboises ou des meures |
| [raspberries or blackberries are ripe] | [the time of raspberries or blackberries] |

-ri- (Potier 1920:345); *-ahi-* (445); *Sang8atrannens* and *sahies* (FH1697:233)[2]

AUGUST

Onnenhondia.	le bled en lait /v
a8ennenh8t	le ble s'ouvre
[little corn is made]	[the corn is 'in milk'; the corn opens]
[corn stands]	

-ondi-(Potier 1920:410); *-8t-* (437); *-nnenh-* (450)

SEPTEMBER

a8ennenhichien /v ondoiari	le ble meur
/v ondoiaristi	
[corn is completed; corn is ripe]	[the corn matures]

-nnenh- (Potier 1920:450); *-ichi-* (345 and 394); *-ndoi-* (449);*-ri-* (345)

OCTOBER

| *atsihiendo a$_ι$anna$_ι$oha* | la pesche du gr[and] poisson |
| [lake trout run][3] | [the fishing of the large fish] |

-nna$_ι$o- (Potier 1920:301)

| *Annentrata$_ι$on e$_ι$arok* | ... le pesche ... du bord de l'eau |
| [one will cast a net from on the shore (i.e., burbot)][4] | [the fishing on the edge of the water] |

-o- (Potier 1920:402); *-$_ι$ar-* (446) *-nnentrat-* (450)

NOVEMBER

| *chionh8a a$_ι$anna$_ι$oha* | pesche du poisson blanc |
| [whitefish run] | [the fishing of the whitefish] |

-nna$_ι$o- (Potier 1920:301)

DECEMBER

| *Ora$_ι$eniat aratsi ok8etonχ8a* | lorsque l'ours fait ses petits |
| [at the top, peak (?), bear, it gives birth] | [when the bear has its young] |

-ɪenhiat- (Potier 1920:244), -ak8eton- (170); *aratsi* (FH1697:231)

sk8enditiok8ichia2a	On f[ont] les bandes p[ou]r la chasse du cerf
[they again form bands, groups (i.e., to hunt deer)]	[one forms bands for hunting deer]

-*ichi*- (Potier 1920:394); -ɪentiok8- (455)

We have here:

    a) four names related fishing;
    b) three names related to berries;
    c) three names related to horticulture and horticultural activities;
    d) only one term that relates to hunting.

This reflects well the importance of the various activities among the Huron.

Linguistic Evidence Concerning the Huron Relationship to Animals

Finding the Burbot

So, four month-names refer to fish. In addition, in the second chapter, we saw that one of the member nations of the Huron alliance was named after their role in providing cord for fishing nets. The archaeological record of Iroquoian peoples in Ontario tells us that fish had great significance for these peoples. This was recently revealed in an excellent study of the use of fish by a community in what is now Toronto at the Moatfield site, dated at 1280–1320 CE (Williamson and Pfeiffer 2003). The linguistic evidence is particularly useful in identifying one fish in particular whose nutritional role was significant: the burbot (*Lota lota*).

In the writing of Récollet Brother Gabriel Sagard, we find three references to a fish he termed *Einchataon*. The first two references are found in his journal, and read as follows:

> But the fish, of which they lay in a supply for winter after it is smoked, they store in casks of tree-bark which they call *Acha*,[5] except *Leinchataon*, which is a fish they do not clean and which they hand with cords in the roof of the lodge, because if it were packed in any cask it would smell too bad and become rotten at once ...
>
> Some weeks after the catch of the big fish [Atsihiendo], the savages go to catch the *Einchataon*, which is a fish rather like the barbel [catfish] here, about a foot and a half or a little less. This fish is used to give a taste to their sagamite [corn soup] during the winter, and for this reason they make much

of it, as well as the big fish; and, in order that it may make their soups smell better they do not remove the viscera, and the fish keep hanging in bundles on the poles of their lodges. But I can assure you that in Lent, when the weather begins to warm, it stank and has such a frightfully bad smell that our gorge rose at it, while to them it was musk and civet [i.e., a good perfume]. (Sagard 1939:95)

The third reference to the fish is in Sagard's dictionary or phrasebook, under the heading of "Poissons": "Autre comme barbeau. [Another [fish], like a catfish] *Einchataon*" (Sagard 1866).

The French–Huron–Onondaga dictionary of the mid 1650s (FHO) contains two entries that appear to refer to *Einchataon*. The first is in the list of fish names : "du bord de l'eau [on the edge of the water] *Annentrataₗon*" (FHO:17). The second in the two-word phrase that appears as an alternative name for October: "du bord de l'eau. *Annentrataₗon eₗarok*" (FHO; also FH62 and FH1697:244). I believe that this *Annentrataₗon* is the *Einchataon* of Sagard's writing. If one has a sense of how Sagard's writing compares with the Jesuit missionary linguists of later times, this point is fairly clear. First, Sagard often dropped the first syllable of Huron words. Second, he wrote in two dialects, one of which would sometimes not have the sound represented by the -ₗ-. Thirdly, Sagard often used -ein- (or -ain-) where the Jesuit missionary linguists wrote -en-. Finally, he sometimes used -ch- to represent what the Jesuits wrote as -tr-. Consider the following:

ENGLISH	SAGARD	JESUITS
you cry	*sareinta*[6]	*sarenta*[7]
he lives	*hainchontaque*[8]	*hentrontak*[9]

Try taking *Annentrataₗon*, removing the first syllable, changing the -ein- to an -en-, removing the -ₗ-, and changing the -tr- to a -ch-. The result is remarkable similar to Sagard's word.

What does the two-word month name literally mean? The first word, *Annentrataₗon*, comprises the noun root -*nnentrat*- 'shore' (Potier 1920:450), and the verb root -*aₗon*- 'to be inside' (163). The combined meaning is 'on the shore.' The second word, *eₗarok*, consists of the noun root -*ar*- 'net' (446), and the verb root -*o*- 'to be (in) water' (401). The combination means 'one will put or cast a net in the water' (see 402). The whole phrase can thus be interpreted as 'one will put a net in the water from the shore.'

This would seem more to describe how the fish is caught than to name the fish itself. But a clue to what the fish was called comes from the list of different species found in the FH1697 dictionary. In this list, the term *Annentrataₗon* was absent. However, two other fish names appear in this source that were not found in the earlier FHO. It would seem reasonable that one of these names might apply to the fish caught by putting a net in the water from the shore. These two new terms are:

Morue [cod]   *Sanguietsia.*
Saumon [salmon]   *honn'hionch* (FH1697:232)

We can eliminate the possibility that salmon was this mystery fish, as both Sagard and the Jesuits would have recognized it and named it in French.

Could *Sanguietsia*[10] have been the name for the fish earlier referred to as *Annentrata₁on?* The French word 'morue' refers to cod. The burbot is a member of the cod family, and is sometimes referred to as the freshwater cod (Scott and Crossman 1973:645). Its range includes the waters of historic Huronia.

Evidence Relating Annentrata₁on *to the Burbot*

How does the rest of the evidence support the suggestion that *annentrata₁on* was the burbot? We can answer this question by grouping the evidence into five basic points gleaned from the quotations given above. The fish we are looking for:

(a) is caught some weeks after *atsihiendo*, the lake trout;
(b) is something like a catfish;
(c) is typically a foot and a half or slightly less in length when caught;
(d) is not eviscerated after it is caught;
(e) is caught by a net that is cast or stretched out from shore.

A fish that is caught some weeks after *atsihiendo*,
the lake trout

As we have seen concerning the Huron calendar, a term for October that appears in all Huron month lists is *atsihiendo a₁anna₁oha*, a phrase that can be translated as 'the *atsihiendo* come or run.' When Sagard went fishing with the Huron in 1623 to catch *atsihiendo*, the group left in October and stayed until some time in November (Sagard 1939:185–86). If the mystery fish was caught some weeks afterwards, it would have been caught either in late October or November. The burbot is unusual among Ontario fish in being a winter spawner. Scott and Crossman tell us that "It spawns from November to May over the whole of its whole distribution, but mainly from January to March in Canada" (Scott and Crossman 1973:643).

The only other local fish that spawns around that time is the whitefish, which is probably why other authors believe this to be the mystery fish. However, the whitefish has another name in Huron. The usual term for November was "*chionh8a aₗannaₗoha*. pesche du poisson blanc" (FH1697:244), meaning 'whitefish come or run.'

A fish that is something like a catfish

It is useful here to look at exactly what was written in the original French. The exact phrase was: "vn poisson quelque peu approchant aux Barbeaux de par deca" (Sagard 1939:230). The expression "quelque peu" is better translated as 'slightly, to a slight extent' than as the 'rather like' of the published English translation. With its long slender barbel on the top of its chin and the similar barbel-like extensions from its nostril openings (Scott and Crossman 1973:641), the burbot is slightly like a catfish. Bullheads (black, yellow, or brown) are too much like catfish to qualify according to a strict reading of this translation. In addition, they are early summer spawners, and are too short to answer to the description in Sagard (Sagard 1939:591, 595, and 598).

A fish that is typically a foot and a half or slightly less in length when caught

The evidence here again points to the burbot. The average length of the burbot is fifteen inches (381 mm) (Scott and Crossman 1973:641). They reach sexual maturity, thus being involved with spawning, during their third or fourth year (643). At that time, the female is between 11.0 to 18.9 inches (280–480 mm) long. In a 1954 study of Lake Simcoe burbot, the fish were recorded as reaching an average of 432 mm at age three, only slightly less than "the foot and a half" (about 460 mm) that Sagard reported.

A fish that is not eviscerated after it is caught

Why would the Huron not eviscerate a fish after it was caught? There is a good reason not to eviscerate a burbot—its liver has a high nutritional value. Scott and Crossman write:

> The vitamin A potency of burbot liver oil is stated to be about 500 units or more per gram and analyses of the vitamin D potency of the oil obtained from the large liver have shown it to be as good as that obtained from cod liver. (645)

Unfortunately for archaeologists, the way the non-eviscerated fish was processed by the Huron makes it difficult for the significance of the burbot to show up clearly in the archaeological record. When Samuel de Champlain wrote of the corn soup of the Huron, he claimed the following:

When it is all cooked they take out the fish, and crush it very fine, not caring whether they take out the bones, scales or entrails as we do, but putting it together into the same pot, which usually gives it its bad taste. (1929:127)

A fish that is caught by a net that is cast or stretched out from shore

The burbot spawns in shallow water, so it would appear that it could get caught by this method. Scott and Crossman tell us that "the spawning site is usually in 1–4 feet of water over sand or gravel bottom in shallow bays, or on gravel shoals 5–10 feet deep" (1973:643).

Conclusion

I think this evidence is enough to conclude that the burbot is the *Einchataon* of Sagard's writing, and the *Annentrata₍on e₍arok* of the Jesuit dictionaries. The reason I have given so much attention to this point is that it teaches us to respect the Huron people's knowledge of the fish that they caught and the resources that they used. Anthropologists, historians, and other scholars would do well to respect this kind of indigenous knowledge.

Raccoons and Black Squirrels

It is not just fish that are sometimes misidentified from the written record. Occasionally, the same problem occurs with mammals. In what follows, we will clarify references to two mammals using linguistic evidence.

Récollet Brother Gabriel Sagard, when writing about the different animals he encountered during his stay in Huronia in 1623–24, wrote of one whose pelt was valuable. After speaking of wolf pelts, he described how the Huron:

> value the skin highly, likewise that of a kind of leopard or wild-cat, which they call *Tiron*. There is a district in these wide provinces the inhabitants of which they call the Cat tribe [i.e., the Erie[11]]; I think the name was given because of these wild-cats, small wolves or leopards, which are found in their territory. From [the skins of] these wild-cats they make robes or blankets in which they introduce for embellishment a number of animals' tails, sewing them all around the edge and at the top of the back. These wild-cats are scarcely bigger than a large fox, but their coat is quite like that of a full-grown wolf, so that a piece of wild-cat skin and a piece of wolf's skin are almost indistinguishable, and I was mistaken once in making a choice. (Sagard 1939:224)

Unfortunately, several usually reliable scholars dealing with this period have taken Sagard's confused (and confusing) guess at the animal's identity at face value. They have accepted his "espece de Leopard ou Chat sauuage" (Sagard 1939:382) as actually referring to a wild feline. Elizabeth Tooker, in her valuable work, *Ethnography of the Huron Indians*, merely transcribed the translation, referring to *Tiron* as "a kind of leopard or wildcat" (Tooker 1964:158). Conrad Heidenreich, too, led astray by the reference to the "Cat-tribe" concluded that the cougar was being described (Heidenreich 1971:203).

The Huron linguistic evidence is conclusive, but not well known. Sagard's *Tiron* is written in the Jesuit Huron dictionaries as *entiron*. The following is a typical entry:

Chat Sauvage *Entiron* (FH1697: 34; c.f. 231)

"Chat Sauvage," of course, is a French term that refers to the raccoon (see Trigger 1976:441 fn39). Such is the meaning of *entiron*, not only in Huron, but in Mohawk and Oneida as well (Mithun 1984:266). Interestingly, in Tuscarora, the southernmost of the Northern Iroquoian languages, and Cherokee, the only living member of the Southern Iroquoian languages, the term referred to the skunk (Mithun 1984:265).

Another animal, which the Huron called *8ta$_l$i* or *ota$_l$i* had fur treasured above all others in the making of robes. Unfortunately, the early written sources talk about this valuable fur without identifying the fur-bearer. For example, in his description of the animals of Huronia, Sagard wrote:

They have another kind of animal named *Otay*, as large as a small rabbit, with fur very black and so soft, smooth and handsome that it seems to be made of cloth. They set great store by these skins, and make them into robes, and around the edge they put all the heads and tails. (Sagard 1939:224)

In 1639, the pelts, named '*outay*,' were described as the product of Neutral country (JR17:165). It might have been the trip taken in 1640–41 by Jesuit Fathers Jean de Brébeuf and Pierre Chaumonot to visit the Neutral that gave the French the opportunity to learn what the animal was. In 1648, we get the only reference that identifies it (although this does not give its Huron name). Later dictionaries favour the term "bete noire" (FH1697:231; but see Potier 1920:445 for an exception). Father Paul Ragueneau, writing of the practice of shamans seeking in vision the unfulfilled desires or wishes of the guardian spirits of sick Huron in order to cure them, reported the following:

Some look into a basin full of water, and say that they see various things pass over it, as over the surface of a mirror—a fine collar of Porcelain; a robe of black squirrel skins, which are here considered the most valuable ... (JR33:193)

The valued pelt belonged to the black phase of the grey squirrel (Sciureus carolinensis). We can learn something of the northern limits of this animal's range at the time by the fact that Sagard did not identify the animal, even though he wrote about squirrels. In his Grand Voyage (Sagard 1990:307–8), he wrote of three kinds of squirrels in Huronia:

(a) *"sahouesquanta"* (i.e., *ta8ask8ant* (FH1697:59);
(b) *"Ohihoin"* (i.e., *"ohio₁en"* (Potier 1920:445);
(c) *"aroussen"* (i.e., *"ar8sen"* (Potier 1920:445).

The first of these was the flying squirrel, the second was the chipmunk, and the third probably referred to grey squirrels in their grey phase, as Sagard said that they reminded him of the squirrels back in France (1990:308).

The word for the black squirrel is derived from the verb *ata₁i*, which in Potier's dictionary was translated as "etre coloré (couleur brillante eclatante) [to be coloured, brightly]" (Potier 1920: 180). The Mohawk cognate is translated as 'to be dark-coloured' (Michelson 1973:30), so I suspect that the meaning of the Huron verb is 'to be dark and shiny coloured.' Interestingly, the same verb is used for the main term of reference in Huron for beaver (Sagard 1990:318 and FH1697:231). A -*ts*- is placed at the beginning of the verb, adding the sense of "very" to the word, i.e., 'it is very dark and shiny coloured.' Cognates also refer to the beaver in Tuscarora (Mithun 1984:266), and, without the -*ts*- to either muskrat or beaver in St. Lawrence Iroquoian.[12] For the Seneca and Cayuga, the same term refers to mink (Mithun 1984:266 and Chafe 1963:54; although not the Cayuga in Froman et al. 2002:200).

Tsa8enhohi: *It's a Bird, It's a Vulture, It's ... an Eagle*

Interpreting the interaction between Huron and the French Jesuits involves understanding how two different peoples saw the world. There are several traps into which the modern researcher can fall. I fell into one with *tsa8enhohi*. In 1994, I published an article "Tsa8enhohi:The Vulture Seen through Huron Eyes" (Steckley 1994). I followed the French Jesuit perception uncritically, and that led me astray. Like them, I confused Old World vultures with New World vultures. Old World vultures belong to the family *Accipitridae*, whose members include eagles and hawks. New World vultures belong to the family *Cathartidae*, and recently have been connected genetically with storks. Their superficial similarity comes from what is termed "convergent evolution," that is, when two species of different ancestry take on similar forms and perform similar functions: at a gross level think of bats, birds, and pterodactyls and their wings.

We first find reference to *tsa8enhohi* in the *Jesuit Relation* of 1636. Being described is the home of a sacred bird spirit that the Huron passed on their way to and from Huronia along the French River, following the trade route that connected them with the St. Lawrence:

> On the way by which the Hurons go to Kebec, there are some Rocks that they particularly reverence and to which they never fail, when they go down to trade, to offer Tobacco ... the most celebrated is the one they call *Tsanhohi Arasta*, "the home of Tsanhohi" which is a species of bird of prey. They tell marvels of this Rock. According to their story, it was formerly a man who was, I know not how, changed into a stone. At all events, they distinguish still the head, the arms, and the body; but he must have been extraordinarily powerful, for this mass is so vast and so high that their arrows cannot reach it. Besides, they hold that in the hollow of this Rock there is a Demon, who is capable of making their journey successful; that is why they stop as they pass, and offer it Tobacco, which they simply put into one of the clefts, ... (JR10:165–67)

Tsanhohi is a version of the Huron name, *tsa8enhoh(8)i*, a name that appears in the written record in many forms: e.g., *A8enhohk8i*, *Saouhenhohi*, *Thaouenhohoui*, *Thaouonhohoui*, *Tsanhohy*, *Tsaouenhohoui*, and *Tsa8enhohi*. *Arasta* appears to be derived from the verb root *-arat-* 'to sleep' with the causative-instrumental *-st-* meaning 'it uses it to sleep (on)' (Potier 1920:172).

Not only was this bird's name used to refer to a sacred location, but it also appeared as a personal name. One of the most revered Huron names from the seventeenth to the nineteenth century was *Tsa8enhohi*. We can see that in the following brief history of references to bearers of the name.

The name first appears as *A8enhok8i* in the *Relation* of 1641 (JR21:212–13). It is briefly mentioned again, as *Aoenhokoui*, in a later *Relation* (JR34:172–73). It was the name of a young man, the nephew of a leading political figure in Huronia. As sister's son to a leader, he would have been the potential heir to the authority possessed by a prominent lineage. He had been delegated to speak against the Jesuits in Neutral country when the fathers came to visit those people. This would have been a significant role, as the Huron seem to have feared the extension of the French trade to the Neutral.

From Neutral country again we hear of a *Tsa8enhohi* (JR36:140–41) reporting what was going on in that area during the early 1650s. Neither rank nor lineage association is mentioned, so it is difficult to tell whether or not this is the same man.

This is followed by a series of references to an important man, Ignace Tsa8enhoh(8)i, who may or may not have been the same person (or persons) mentioned above. Names were transferred shortly after the death of the previous holder. A letter from Marie de L'Incarnation to her son, dated June 25, 1660, contains references to two people known by the same Huron name: "Eustache Thaouonhohoui" (Marshall 1967:248) and "Ignace Thaouenhohoui" (250), each referred to as a "Huron chief" who addressed his fellow Huron captured by the Iroquois at Long Sault earlier that year. I believe both to have been the same man.

Next, we read of "Tsanhohy, an escaped Huron" mentioned in the *Jesuit Journal* of October of that same year (JR45:162–63). Finally, in the "Account of the Most Christian Death of Ignace Saouhenhohi" (JR55:50–51), we are told of one who had been a prisoner of the Iroquois, and who eventually became the "chief" of the Huron for three years (up until his death in February 1670). His significance can be seen in Jesuit Father Pierre Chaumonot's heartfelt "Account of the Most Christian Death of Ignace Saouhenhohi" in the *Relation* of 1670 (JR53:96–123).

In the Huron community of Lorette, from 1685 to 1844 (with a brief hiatus in the mid-eighteenth century), the chief's name was consistently *Tsa8enhohi* (Vincent 1984:81–82). The name may have been traditionally associated with the Deer clan, as it was connected with the Vincent and Picard families during that time, both Deer clan families. This could be significant, because the chief of the Wyandot, Sastaretsi, was also the leader of the Deer clan and the Deer phratry of his people. This could reflect the connection to authority outlined earlier concerning the name in Huronia.

What did this name refer to? List of animals in Huron dictionaries consistently translate the word as "vautour" (FH0, FH67:17;FH1697:232). But there were no vultures in Ontario in the seventeenth century. For this piece of information, I thank James R. Cowan of the Canadian Raptor Conservancy and Mark Peck, Collections Manager, Ornithology, Royal Ontario Museum (both personal communications). What could the bird be? There is a tradition in the Wendake community at Lorette, Quebec, going at least as far back as the Abbe Prosper Vincent, a Huron priest, that it refers to a hawk. In 1915, Marius Barbeau, working with the last speakers of Wyandot, had the Wyandot cognate mean 'eagle' (Barbeau 1915:99). A Cayuga stem for eagle is *-(a)węhe?-* (Froman et al 2002: 99). Because Old World vultures are more closely related to eagles might lead them to confuse the two from a distance. That the bird in the Jesuit Relations was found on a cliff suggests that it might have been a golden eagle, but because the Old World vultures that the missionaries knew about had bald heads, it might also have been a bald eagle. Translating the term is very difficult, but here is an educated guess. If, judging from the Cayuga word, there is an old Iroquoian noun root something like *-awenh-* meaning 'eagle,' and if the *-ohi-* is a form of the verb root *-o-* 'to be in water' (Potier 1920:401), then perhaps we have a word referring to a raptor that goes into the water to fish. This could be either a bald eagle or an osprey, another large raptor that fishes and has white on its head.

Linguistic Evidence Concerning the Huron Relationship to Plants

The Huron would obviously have made good use of the plants around them, but the Jesuit missionary dictionaries are very selective in their records of this topic. Apart from a few rather random pieces of information, such as a brief discussion of *otrah8ita*, 'sumach' as "Racine a a teindre en rouge, item ad pre aborton [root for dying in red, also for abortion]" (FH1697:167), most of the mention of plants relates to corn and to tobacco.

Corn

The fact that languages develop vocabulary according to the cultural needs of the speakers has been overused and abused a number of times. The most famous example involves the "x" number (usually 20, 32 or 52) of terms for snow in Inuktitut. As an agglutinative or polysynthetic language, Inuktitut constructs many terms from a relatively small number of noun and verb roots that relate primarily or solely to snow, only a few more than English has. Still, it is worthwhile noting the relationship between the Huron language and corn, their main food crop.

The seventeenth-century Huron were farmers whose main crop was corn. Consequently, they had a corn vocabulary that was more developed than that of English. I will present in this section seventeen Wendat terms from French Jesuit missionary dictionaries. Where there are other meanings or references they will be given. Keep in mind that the missionaries were not corn growers, and were much more interested in Huron religious vocabulary. That means that there were possibly other corn terms that never found their way into the dictionaries.

Corn in General

We do not know when the Huron first grew corn. This point is linked to the perennial problem experienced by Ontario archaeologists trying to determine when the Huron first came north of the lake that today bears the Huron name *Ontario* (meaning 'it is a large lake'). We can make a few guesses concerning their acquisition of corn, however, and relate it to their separation from other Northern Iroquoian speakers.

The general Wendat term for corn was *onnenha*, from the noun root *-nnenh-* (Potier 1920:450). Marianne Mithun noted that this term was shared by Onondaga (see Woodbury 2003:1458), Cayuga (see Froman et al. 2002:70), Seneca, and Tuscarora, but not by Mohawk and Oneida, who instead use this root for 'seed' (Mithun 1984:272; for Oneida, see Michelson and Doxtator 2002:576). They use another term for corn. This led Mithun to comment that corn probably arrived in northeast North America "after the initial breakup of the Iroquoian family" (1984:272). She also suggests that both terms for corn probably meant 'seed.' This all makes sense to me.

Ear of Corn

The term for an ear of corn, in most dialects of Wendat, was *-nd8ts-* (Potier 1920:450 and FH1697:67). In the Rock dialect it was *-ndots-* (Sagard 1866), a term also used to describe a kind of bead. But not all ears of corn are the same, so the Huron had several different names for them. There were two names for small ears of corn: *oionk8enda* (Potier 1920:448) and *oronenda* (Potier 1920:453). I am not sure what the difference was supposed to be, but the latter term is often translated in the dictionaries with the word "chetifs" ('puny'; HF59:146 and HF62). Perhaps this relates to ears that have failed to grow large, rather than ones that have yet to grow large. Then there is *iochiea* "epi qui en porte vn autre [an ear that carries another [ear]" (FH1697:67).

Parts of an Ear of Corn

The noun root *-nnraɩenhi-* is translated as "tronçon d'epi [stump or stalk of an ear of corn]" (Potier 1920:452 and FH1697:213) or "trognon d'epi [core of the ear]"(HF59:121 and FHO). That could mean that it referred to the corncob. However, the rarely occurring noun *ongok8a* (Potier 1920:273) is translated as "tuyau" ['pipe, tube, tip'], which may be cognate with the term used in Mohawk, Onondaga, Cayuga and Seneca (Mithun 1984:273) for corncob. Perhaps there was a dialect difference here. The noun root *-ndist-* has generic reference to the "queue d'epi de blé, de fruit, de citrouille [stem of an ear of corn, of a fruit, or a squash]"(Potier 1920:449

and FH1697:166). Interestingly, this appears to be cognate with the Seneca term for "ear without husk but with kernels" (Chafe 1963:50). Then there is *-iontsend-* which is the "bout de l'epi non garni de blé [end of the ear that is not covered with corn]" (Potier 1920:448). A row of kernels is called *oia* (Potier 1920:448). The term also refers to a row of beads on a wampum collar (HF62:42).

Kernels were given two names. The ones that were not yet germinated were called *a8enienta* (Potier 1920:452 and FH1697:85). Germinated kernels used for seed were called *onniona* or *onnion8a* in Wyandot (Potier 12920:451 and FH1697:23). When the ear itself is "en lait" ['in milk'], not quite fully developed it was *8cha* (FH1697:67 and FHO). Interestingly, the Huron distinguished cornbread made from corn that was not fully ripened— *onnonh8encha* (Potier 1920:451)—from that made from more ripe corn, *ase8ena* "Pain de blé d'automne" (Potier 1920:453).

If the skin of the kernels of corn was soft, it was called *oecha*, the same term that was used for human skin (Potier 1920:446 and FH1697:142). If it was hard, it was called *08hista*, a term that had also a broader application (see chapter 6).

The shucks or leaves that cover the corn were referred to with the noun root *-os-*, as seen in the following entry from Potier "*ıaosa* feuilles vertes qui couvrent l'epi de blé [green leaves that cover the ear of corn]" (1920:452).

The Rest of the Corn Plant
A branch of the corn plant was called *oiachia* (Potier 1920:448 and HF62:42). Interestingly, this term had lost currency by Potier's time. The term stalk was *ohe'ra* (Potier 1920:447 and FH1697:201), which appears to be cognate with the Onondaga term (Woodbury 2003:1458). The flower of the corn was called *ıang8ika* or *ıang8ira* (HF59:108 and Potier 1920:450) or *ıang8icha* (HF62:73).

Summary
We can conclude a few things from this list. First, of course, is the fact that the Wendat language did indeed have many terms for corn. Second, we can note how some terms were shared with humans (semen and skin) and with beads (ear and row). Thirdly, and perhaps surprisingly, the Huron do not seem to have used corn images as a productive source of metaphors.

Tobacco
Tobacco was an important element in Huron culture, said to "calm the mind" of both humans and spirits. It lessened hunger on a long trip (Sagard

1939:63), helped people deal with the death of a loved one (JR10:219), and facilitated peace negotiations with enemies (JR27:285 and 301). In the *Jesuit Relation* of 1636, we read of the Huron's belief that:

> there is nothing as suitable as Tobacco to appease the passions; that is why they never attend a council without a pipe or calumet in their mouths. The smoke, they say, gives them intelligence, and enables them to see clearly through the most intricate matters. (JR10:255–57)

Offerings of "pains" (translated as 'cakes' in the *Relations*) of tobacco, put into a fire or sometimes thrown into the water, were used to influence the spirits into helping the Huron with fishing (Sagard 1939:189), curing (JR10:173; 13: 259–61), corn-growing (JR23:53), and travelling the long treacherous canoe path of Quebec (Sagard 1939:171). The *Jesuit Relations* contains an example of the last-named situation, with tobacco being offered at the home of a spirit vulture (see discussion above) on the Ottawa River (JR10:165–67). The gift was presented with the words *Oki ca ichithon condayee aenwaen ondayee d'aonstaancwasi*, which can be translated as 'Spirit, you who live here, here is some tobacco. It is a present I give you to make you peaceful (lit. 'to make you like a field').[13]

While the dictionaries contain no Huron term that translates into French as pain(s), we find two terms for different forms in which tobacco came: ˌ*entsa* and ˌ*andiˌa'ta*. The former term is found as follows:

> Morceau, ou bout de petun. [small piece or end of tobacco]
> *Hense, Deheinsa.* (Sagard 1866)
> *Entsa.* le circle d'un pain de petun, ou bout xxxx[14] partie,
>   le morceau de dedans xxxx poche
>   [the circle of a cake of tobacco, or the end of xxxx, the piece inside.
>   ... pocket] (FH1697)

The second term appears as follows:
> Rouleau de Tab[ac] ˌ*andiˌa'ta*
> [roll (i.e., a twist) of tobacco] (FH1697:204)

The Huron root (either noun or verb) for pipe was -*nnonda8an*- (Potier 1920:451). Mithun claimed that there are cognates in the languages of both Southern and Northern Iroquoians (1984:276). I have found cognates in the following languages, which shows that the same term is shared broadly:

-*nvnawa*-	Cherokee[15]
-*nųnawę'd*-	Onondaga (Woodbury 2003:731)
-*nętawętyanę*-	Tuscarora (Rudes 1987:230)
-*nvnawv*-	Mohawk (Michelson 1973:79)

The Huron main noun root for tobacco is *-enₜ8-* (Potier 1920:446). Cognates exist in the Northern Iroquoian languages of Seneca, Cayuga, Onondaga, Oneida, Mohawk, even Susquehannock (Mithun 1984:274), and probably the language(s) of the Laurentian Iroquoians (in their term for 'to smoke'; Barbeau 1961:196) too, but not Tuscarora or the Southern Iroquoian language of Cherokee. Typical examples are Oneida *-yu?kw-* (Michelson and Doxtator 2002:845), Cayuga *-yę'g(wa)-* (Froman et al. 2002:597), and Onondaga *-yę'g(wa)-* (Woodbury 2003:930).

The word is possibly derived from the Uto-Aztecan **pipa*[16] (a language family that includes Nahuatl, the language of the Aztecs), diffusing north from Mexico along with tobacco itself, until both entered Iroquoian culture. This change of a /p/ sound to a /kw/ sound is not unusual in language change, impelled in this case as the Iroquoian languages do not have a *-p-*. Even the Uto-Aztecan language Pima has the term *wihwi* for tobacco (Swadesh 1964:549).

Another term referred to tobacco in the Huron language: *-tsar-* (Potier 1920:454). The use of the Latin term 'inusitatus' beside its entry in some of the dictionaries (HF62:134, HF59, and HF65) indicates that it was rarely used. In a seventeenth-century dictionary of Mohawk it is seen as the noun root *-tsiar-* incorporated into the verb 'to give' in "*Gatsiara8i* ... donner du petun" (Bruyas 1970:105). The other two languages that have this term are the ones that do not have a cognate for *-enₜ8-:* Tuscarora, which has *-čárhu'-* (Rudes 1987:77), and Cherokee, which has *-tsola-* or *-tsalu-*.[17]

How can we interpret this distribution of the two nouns for tobacco? It is a generally accepted idea in historical linguistics that if forms are found in geographically separated, socially isolated (from each other) languages of the same family, then those forms are probably conservative, and are likely to be older than words that have a less widespread distribution (Anttila 1972:294–97). According to Mithun, the Huron term *-nda8end-*, for potato-like tubers (Potier 1920:448) has cognates in Cherokee (*nuna*) and Northern Iroquoian languages other than Huron: Mohawk *-hnvat-;* Oneida *-hnana?t-;* Onondaga *-nęnohg(w)-;* Cayuga *-(h)ōna'd-* for potato (Michelson 1973:52, Michelson and Doxtator 2002:1131, Woodbury 2003:701, and Froman et al. 2002:240, respectively). From this, we can infer that this food source which was gathered rather than cultivated, pre-dates the splitting up of the Iroquoian languages into Northern and Southern. Contrast that with the Huron word *-ₜares-* (FH1697:76) for cultivated 'beans,' which archaeologically we know came relatively late to the Huron's territory in Ontario. The terms for beans in other Northern Iroquoian languages are not cognate with the Huron term (Mithun 1984:272).

The fact that *-tsar-* extends to the isolated (from Northern Iroquoian) Cherokee and includes the Tuscarora, something that *-en₁8-* does not do, suggests that the former is an older term in Iroquoian languages. This can be interpreted in several ways. One interpretation of this could be that two different sorts of tobacco came north to the territory of the Iroquoians at two different times, the first before the north–south split and the separation of the Tuscarora from the other Northern Iroquoians.

Huron Expressions with *-en₁8-*

We have already come some way in learning about what the Huron thought of tobacco. We can walk even further along this path by seeing how the noun root *-en₁8-* appeared in composition with verbs in Huron expressions. The following are typical examples.

The noun root was used with the verb root *-o-* 'to be wet, in water,' plus a transitive suffix *-h8-* adding the sense of 'put,' to refer to putting tobacco into a pipe. Why they used a verb relating to water, I do not know (they did not use hookahs). Perhaps there was some sense that, like objects put in water, tobacco dissolves when smoked. The following example seems to suggest that in the French translation:

> *₁a₁en₁oh8indi* [to put tobacco in water for someone]
> mettre a q. du tabac dans son calumet pour fumer le reduire en vapeur,
> en eau qui monte au cerveau
> [to put for someone some tobacco in his pipe for smoking, to reduce it
> in vapour, in water that rises to the brain] (Potier 1920:403)

Another example gives advice, but it is not clear whether it is Huron or Jesuit advice:

> Attens a petuner q. tu aies mal aux dents
> [Wait before smoking when you have toothaches]
>
> *Seh8en echien₁ok d'etsisando₁aia*
> [Wait before you put tobacco in (your pipe) when you have a toothache]
> (FH1693:275)

The next example is an obvious specimen of Jesuit advice concerning smoking and Christian rituals:

> ne fume pas avant le communion
> [do not smoke before communion]
>
> *ennonchien ehien₁ok d'ason tesakaristiannonhonχ8i*
> [Do not put tobacco (in your pipe) when still you have the eucharist wafer
> in your mouth] (FH1697:82)

The noun *-en₁8-* combines with the verb root *-ι-* meaning 'to eat or chew' (Potier 1920:252). While this could be metaphorical, it probably does refer to the practice of actually chewing tobacco.[18] The following are examples:

> Tu ne manges point de petun [You do not eat tobacco].
> *Techeche houanhouan* [You will not eat tobacco] (Sagard 1866)
>
> *hoen₁8ach* il mange du petun [he eats tobacco] (FH1697:145)

The noun root could also be used with the verb root *-ιast-* 'to consume, use up' (Potier 1920:240). Interestingly, the three Huron dictionaries whose entries for *-en₁8-* contain this verb, also added the dative suffix, meaning 'for the benefit or loss of someone,' as in the following:

> *a₁atien₁8a₁astandi.* Mon tabac s'est use a moy [my tobacco is used up for me] (HF59:54)

It is especially interesting that each entry includes the following accusation:

askien8a₁asten	tu m'as mange mon petun
[you have consumed my tobacco]	[you have eaten, my tobacco]
(HF62:17)	

Perhaps this was a common complaint among the Huron.

Another problem for the Huron was in trying to grow tobacco in a place too far north for its easy cultivation. In one dictionary, we have the following entry using the verb root *-chia-* 'to finish' (Potier 1920:211):

> *a₁atien₁8ichiatandi* mon petun est mort pour moy [my tobacco is dead on me] (HF65:65)

The noun also appears with the verb root *-nnona-* 'to desire' (Potier 1920:308). This verb could be used to express desire for food, sex, urination and defecation—basic urges. The following are typical dictionary entries; the second example uses the term 'to be with long breath,' which usually referred to starvation or famine:

j'ai envie de petun	[I desire some tobacco]
ιien₁8annonach	[I desire some tobacco]
n'as tu point faim de petun?	[Are you not famished for tobacco?]
te chiatonrichesθa d'8en8a	[Are you not with long breath, starving for tobacco?] (FH1693:274)

Huron has no adjectives. Their function belonged to verbs that incorporated the noun being modified. When the Huron spoke positively about tobacco, they would describe it with -ₜa8- 'to taste or smell good' (Potier 1920:236), or -8ast- 'to be beautiful' (318), as in the following entries:

> oen8aₜa8i [it is good-tasting, good-smelling tobacco]
> oen8a8asti [it is beautiful tobacco] bon petun [good tobacco] (HF62:17)

Trees and Huron Village Names

One way in which ethnolinguistics can prove useful to archaeologists is through an analysis of the names of historic Native communities. Such names can help locate the communities in question, connecting them with archaeological sites. They also can lend insight into the cultural perceptions of the people that did the naming. In this part of the chapter, I will be look-ing at thirty-three village names of the seventeenth-century Huron. I hope that my analysis of these names will prove useful in both locating Huron villages and in understanding how the people saw the land around them.

Before I begin my analysis, I should make a few points about the nature of the translation process. There are two essential qualities that exist for a good translation, as I see it. One is that the translation must fit linguisti-cally, not breaking the rules of Huron grammar and sound combinations. This is a quality that is greatly lacking in a number of the translations given by a predecessor of mine, Father Arthur E. Jones (1908). He had access to grammatical and dictionary material on the Huron language through the manuscripts copied by Father Pierre Potier of the Detroit Wyandot mission during the mid-eighteenth century (later published in an Ontario Archive Report; Potier 1920). However, this did not keep him from violating some basic rules of Huron verb morphology. There are three kinds of words in Huron: verbs (the majority of words), nouns, and particles. Only two roots can appear in a Huron verb. Typically, that involves a noun root and a verb root. The only time two verb roots can appear in a verb is if the first appear-ing one is followed by a nominalizer (almost always -ch-). Particles cannot be incorporated into a verb. The translations of Father Jones often contain two (or more) verb roots, without the presence of a nominalizer. They also sometimes involved incorporating particles into a verb. He was also too quick to delete sounds if they blocked him in his translation path.

The other quality that a good translation must have is that it must "make sense" culturally. This is more difficult to achieve, and to judge. And yet, something of this cultural sense can be seen in the analysis that appears below. As we will see, for a Huron village name to contain refer-ence to trees or poles makes cultural sense. For such a name to make ref-erence to an individual does not.

I must add a disclaimer to this description of the quality of good translation: The translations I am suggesting have varying degrees of certainty.
Some, I am sure about; others are educated, even wild guesses.

Huron Village Names

The single greatest source of Huron village names is trees. If one includes
reference to poles, they make up roughly one-third of the names analyzed
here. We will look at evergreens first. There are two different terms that
refer to more than one kind of evergreen: -nnent- and -ɩenr-.

The noun root -nnent- could be used in Huron to refer to the balsam fir
or "sapin" in French (Abies balsamea) (FHO, FH1693:18 and FH1697:233).
In a dictionary entry, Récollet Brother Gabriel Sagard gave the name as:
"Genieure. Aneinta" (Sagard 1866), referring probably to the juniper or
red cedar (Juniperus virginiana). Potier stated that the noun root could be
used for "tout bois gommeux, tout arbre qui ne fletrit [all gum-producing
trees, all trees that do not wither (i.e., lose their leaves)]" (Potier 1920:450;
see also FH1697:233). In other Iroquoian languages, the noun root applies
to cedar, juniper, tamarack, hemlock, and for evergreens in general (Mithun
1984:270; see also Rudes 1987:233).

The noun root -ɩenr- referred to groves or stands of balsam fir or cedar,
but was not extended to either pine or hemlock. This can be seen in the following entries from seventeenth-century French–Huron–Onondaga (FHO)
dictionary. With pine or hemlock, the term for grove or stand involves using
the noun for the tree plus the verb root -ra- 'to be with' (Potier 1920:325):

Cedre [Cedar] *Ask8ata oɩenraɩon onennion*
              [Cedar, inside an *oɩenra*, we passed by it]
              nous avons passe par un sapiniere
              [We passed by a balsam fir/cedar grove]

Pin [Pine] *Ande'ta. Ande'tara θo*
              [We pass through pine with pine there]

Prusse [Hemlock] *Asatenta. Asatentara θo [o]nennion*
              [We pass through hemlock, with hemlock there]

Sapin.[Balsam] *onnenta. oɩenraɩon* [balsam, in an *oɩenra]*
sapiniere [balsam grove] (FHO)

Given the range of meanings of the two noun roots, I suspect that when
-nnent- is used in a Huron village name it would refer to a mixed evergreen
forest, whereas -ɩenr- refers to a grove or stand of cedar or balsam.

Onnentisati

One Huron village name contains the noun root *-nnent-*. It is the village that is variously written as *On(n)entis(s)at(i/j)* (JR8:139; 13:13, 15, 37–9, 131, 195, 211, 245, and 259; 14:23, 49–51 and 97; 15:25). The verb form *-isati-* is composed of the verb root *-is-* 'to knock or press against' (Potier 1920:397), the causative root suffix *-t-* and the stative aspect *-i-*. When used with a noun, this combination typically refers to being in the corner of something (e.g., a house, lake, or palisade). In this case, the translation would be 'In the corner of an evergreen forest.'

O(u)enrio

The one Huron village name containing the noun root *-ₜenr-* is recorded as '*O(u)enrio*.'[19] The word is constructed with the verb root *-io-* 'to be large, great' (Potier 1920:396), giving the meaning 'it is a large stand of balsam fir or cedar.'

Ang8tens

The noun root *-ng8at-* (sometimes written as *-ngoat-* or *-ngot-*) refers specifically to the white cedar. There is a good chance that it is an element in the village name that appears as *Ang8iens* (JR10:203), *Angoutenc* (JR13:237, 14:73, 15:23–27; 17:165) and *Angouteus* (JR14:33 and 69). I believe that the word being represented is *Ang8tens*, with the *-i-* in the first form and the *-u-* before the *-s-* in the last form being misprints for *-t-* and *-n-* respectively. The most likely verb root is *-en-* 'to fall' (Potier 1920:375). This verb sometimes takes *-s-* with the habitual aspect form, and sometimes *-ch-* (probably what was represented by the final *-c-* in Angoutenc), which could explain why the village name appears with both those endings. The meaning of the word would then be, 'white cedar falls' referring to a place where that tree's falling is a common sight.

The noun root *-rh-* generally refers to a forest (Potier 1920:452), but perhaps also a deciduous forest in particular with some combination of maple, ash, basswood, beech, and elm, a common combination in Southern Ontario. The evidence for this is that in the FHO entries for these trees, we see that a stand or group term was developed using *-rh-*.

ormeau.	*araₜ8at*	*Arak8at ₜarha'ra θo [o]nennion*
[elm]	[elm]	[We passed through elm with forest there]
bois blanc.	*Ati*	*Atie [ₜ]arhaen θo [o]nennion*
[basswood]	[basswood]	[We passed through basswood (with) forest lying]

bois dur	*hachachen*	*achachendachon orha'ra*
[beech]	[beech]	[beech with forest]
Erable.	[o'ata]	*o'ata ₍arha₍e*
[maple]	[maple]	[maple in forest]
Fresne.	[*sakares*]	*Sakares (₍arha₍e)*
[ash]	[ash]	[ash in forest] (FHO)

Excluded from the *-rh-* collection are paper birch and trembling aspen or poplar, as can be seen in the following entries. Perhaps this is because they tend to appear more often in pure stands rather than in association with other trees:

Bouleau.	*Andatsek8a.*	*ondatse'k8a'ra*
[birch]	[birch]	[with the birch]
le tremble.	*ondeand.*	*ondeata'cha₍e*
[trembling aspen,poplar]	[trembling aspen]	[at the trembling aspen]
(FHO)		

The point of this discussion of stands or groves is to suggest that if a Huron village name has *-rh-* in it, it could quite possibly be referring not just to any forest, but to the specific mixture of maple, ash, basswood, beech, and elm.

At least two, possibly four Huron village names contain *-rh-*.

Arhetsi

This village name appears as *Arhetsi* in the *Jesuit Relation* of 1651 (JR36:141), as *Arethsi* in the *Corographie* and *Chorographia*, and as *Aretsi* in the *Description*. Father Jones gives two translations of this name, "The Long Clearing" and "The Struggling Village" (Jones 1908:152), both of which are developed upon the ungrammatical premise that two Huron verb roots can combine in one word. The verb root actually involved is *-es-* 'to be long' (Potier 1920:385). The translation of the combination is 'It is a long forest,' perhaps referring to a narrow strip of deciduous forest against a background that is less forested or has a different combination of trees.

Carmaron

This village name appears solely in Champlain (1929:47). Jones mistakenly claims that the word contains the noun root *-renh-* 'treetops, branches' (Potier 1920:452), compounding his error by going on to associate this village with *Karenhassa*, which does contain this noun root, saying that the two names refer to the same village (see Heidenreich 1971:34 and 303).

The *-m-* in this word is most likely a misprint, there being no *-m-* in the Rock dialect in which Champlain's Huron words were written, nor in the dialect of the Northern Bear, the people in whose territory the village was located (Steckley 1991). The word being represented was probably then something like *Karharon*. For me, the most likely verb root going with -*rh*- in this case would be -*ron*- 'to cross' (Potier 1920:348). A translation for this name would be 'where a (deciduous) forest crosses,' possibly referring to it crossing water, a non-forested area, or an area of a different mix of trees.

Carhagouha

A third village name that could possibly include the noun root -*rh*- is written as *Carhagouha* (Champlain 1929:48) or *Garhagouha* (*Description*). If the noun root is -*rh*-, the only verb root I can see as being in combination with it is -ₜ*aon*- 'to be old, used up' (Potier 1920:235), rendering a meaning of 'where the forest is old, used up.' This would mean that the proper form was *Karhaₜaonha*. This would require that the printer produced -*u*- when -*n*- was in the original writing, not an unusual mistake in the early Huron language literature, and that the writer missed an -*a*-, which is also possible. If this is correct, it would give a resource-based explanation why the community was not around when the Jesuits went to stay in Huronia.

It is also possible that -*rh*- is not involved, but that a term for elm is: *araₜ8at*, giving us 'where there are elms.' For this to be true, the writer of Champlain's *Works* would have to have missed a final -*t*- and added a non-existent -*h*- after a -*u*- sound, both mistakes that Gabriel Sagard made in his phrasebook.

Arent

There is a slight chance that the community named *Arenté* (JR13:233 and 235), *Arrente* (JR24:113), *Arentet* (JR34:217), *Arenta* (Latinized in *Chorographia*) and *Arent* (*Corographie*) could possibly have the noun root -*rh*-. The problem is that no verb root that I can come up with makes an easy fit with such an interpretation.

A number of Huron village names make reference to trees and treetops.

Arontaen

The noun root -*ront*- generally means 'tree' (Potier 1920:453). It appears in the Huron village name *Arontaen* (JR10:285; 13:49, 57, 79, and 151; and 14:47). The verb root used with this noun root appears to be -*en*- 'to lie' (Potier 1920:221), giving the combined meaning 'it is a lying tree, log.' It is worth noting that a slight variation of this name, *Karontaen*, 'where there is a lying tree, log' was the Wyandot word in the eighteenth century for Detroit (Toupin 1996:232).

Karenhassa

The noun root -*renh*- refers to 'treetops, branches' (Potier 1920:452). The village name this noun root appears in is Karenhassa, found in *Chorographia* and *Corographie*. The final -*assa*- appears to involve the verb root -*a*- 'to be of a size, magnitude,' with a diminutive suffix taking the form -*asa*- (Potier 1920:161). This would give a translation of 'where there are small treetops, small branches.'

With a significant number of tree and forest terms being used in the formation of Huron village names, it should not be too surprising to find that terms for poles are also used. The poles that went into the construction of the palisades that surrounded the communities and the longhouses within the communities would also "stick out" as the trees would.

Taentoaton

Two village names that appear in maps, the Latinized *Taruentutunum* in *Chorographia* and *Taentoaton* in *Description*, seem to me to represent the same village, the one with the mission name of "St. Cecile." The noun root plausibly in both terms is -*ent*-, which refers to 'posts, poles, sticks, or stakes' (Potier 1920:446). In Huron dictionary entries discussing the construction of longhouses, this noun root is used as follows:

> *Aentontiek* [poles that continue]   les poutres [the beams]
> (FHO; c.f. FH1697:234)

In my discussion of Huron longhouse construction (Steckley 1987b:27), I suggest that this term was used to refer to the poles that extended from the support poles of the longhouse.

My guess is that the terms that appear in *Chorographia* and *Description* are relatively bad representations of *Ekaent8ton*,[20] meaning 'where there are many (extension) poles standing up,' a term that would employ the verb root -*8t*-'to stand, rise above' (Potier 1920:437).

In his dictionary of the mid-eighteenth century, Potier gave the noun root -*ɩenh*- as meaning "perches qui servent à commencer la cab[ane] [poles that are used to begin the house]" (1920:447). Does this mean that these poles may have performed a scaffolding function, keeping the longhouse up while it was being erected, only to be withdrawn later? There is insufficient evidence. No mention is made of the noun root in the seventeenth-century dictionary lists of longhouse parts (see chapter 6).

While the traditional function of this type of pole is unclear, evidence demonstrates that during the time the Jesuit missionaries lived in Huronia, the noun root was used to refer to the thick poles used to build palisades, influenced by French construction methods. This evidence comes in the form of two Huron village names: *Iahenhouton* and *Taenhatentaron/Tahen-tentaron*.

Iahenhouton

The name *Iahenhouton* appears once, in 1637 (JR14:15–17). The community was reported as being populated by people from *Ossossane*, the main village of the Bear nation. Earlier evidence suggests that *Ossossane* was relocated and reconstructed (JR8:101 and JR10:53). Jesuit Father Charles Garnier, writing in 1637, described the fortification, two towers of thirty poles each, at the corners or ramparts (Jones 1908:306; see Trigger 1976:513–15).

I believe that *Iahenhouton* refers to the poles of those towers. It represents the incorporation of *-ˌenh-*[21] into the verb root *-8t-* 'to stand' (Potier 1920:437), which with the distributive suffix *-on-* (see Potier 1920:61, "De verbo multiplicativo") would render a translation of 'several or many standing poles.'

Taenhatentaron/Tahententaron

My hypothesis that *-ˌenh-* is associated with French-influenced palisade construction is reinforced by the fact that a village, said to have been considered impregnable because of its French-style defence (JR39:247), had the noun root in its name. That village was *Taenhatentaron* or *Tahententaron* (JR17:99). The verb involved is *-ten'tra-*, meaning 'to lie flat, stretch out' (Potier 1920:365). With the distributive *-on-* adding the meaning of 'several, many,' we get a translation of 'where several or many poles are lying on the ground, stretched out.' I believe that this refers to palisades constructed horizontally in the French style.

Quieunonascaran/Khinonascarant

One Huron village name seems to refer to a plant other than a tree. The name is written as *Quieunonascaran* in Sagard (Sagard 1939:76 and 99), and *Khinonascarant* in the *Jesuit Relations* (JR13:125). We can see that both words begin with the cislocative prefix (i.e., *Quie-* and *Khi-*) meaning 'where.' The Sagard form then takes the pronominal prefix *-u-*, while the Jesuit form misses it. This leaves us with *-nonascaran(t)-*. The only good linguistic fit (and it is a tight one) I can see for this is a word represented in the Jesuit Huron dictionaries as *-nnon(h8)askaren-*. The noun root involved I believe to be *-nnonh(8)askar-*. The following dictionary entries translations this:

La plante d'icelle.
Onnonhasquara (Sagard 1866; c.f. 1939:240)

> Onnh8askara   chanvre [hemp]
>   onnonh8askara   cotonnier (arbre) [cotton (tree)]
>   onnonh8askara   cotonnier (herbe) [cotton (plant)] (Potier 1920:451)

Chanvre ... onnonh8askara Cottonnier espéce de chanvre [cotton, species of hemp] (FH1697:33)

Chanvre ... onnonh8askara espece de chanvre qui porte un bouquet en sa fleur [species of hemp that bears a clump or cluster in its flowers] (FHO)

Reference to 'hemp' in a Huron village name makes cultural sense. As Heidenreich notes, there are frequent references in the early sources to the Huron gathering hemp or a hemp-like plant:

> Special mention must be made of the gathering of "hemp." This seems to have been a communal activity involving, in one case, about forty women (JR26:203–5). In all, four types of plants seem to have been used. Sagard (1939:240) mentions a type of "hemp" [onnonhasquara] growing in "marshy damp spots" which was probably swamp milkweed (Asclepias incarnata), while Lalemant (JR23:55) wrote that Huron women gathered hemp on "the untilled plains." The latter reference must refer to spreading dogbane (Apocynum androsaemifoliuim) and Indian hemp (Apocynum cannabium). Hemp was collected in the late summer and fabricated into twine and various products during the winter (Sagard 1939:98; JR23:55, 241). "Hemp" was also obtained from the bark of a tree called Atti by the Huron (Sagard 1939:240). The bark was removed in stripes and boiled to separate the fibres. From the description, the tree could have been basswood (Tilia americana). (Heidenreich 1971:200–1)

Whichever plant was being referred to, I believe that -nnonhaskar- was used, appearing in combination with the verb root -en- meaning 'to collect, gather' (Potier 1920:373–74). With the locative prefix added, we would have a word translated as 'where hemp is gathered.'

Seven of the Huron village names are constructed from noun roots referring to other geographical features.

Tequenonquiaye/Téqueunonkiayé

The village name recorded in Champlain as Tequenonquiaye (Champlain 1929:48) and as Téqueunonkiayé in Sagard (1939:70) is constructed with the noun root -nnont-, meaning 'hill, mountain' (Potier 1920:451). Added to the noun root are the dualic and cislocative prefixes and the verb root -ia$_t$- 'to cut, break' (Potier 1920:264), giving the literal meaning of 'where the hill or mountain is cut in two.' In a number of Huron dictionaries, this literal meaning signifies the base or foot of a hill (FH1697:123 and FHO).

Quieuindohian

Sagard refers to another name for the previous village when he wrote of "our town of *Quieuindohian*, otherwise called *Téqueunonkiayé* (1939:60; see also 194). I see two possibilities for translation, with differing degrees of distortion from the word found in Sagard's writings. Both employ the verb root *-oₗen-* 'to be between' (Potier 1920:405). One, with little distortion, has the noun root *-ond-* 'space, place' (Potier 1920:455), as presented in the following example:

> *Te ondoₗen* au milieu de la place [in the middle of the place, space] (Potier 1920:405)

The other possibility, with greater distortion, has the noun root *-nnont-* 'hill, mountain,' making the word *t'etionnontoₗen* (see FH1697:123), meaning 'between two hills,' and referring to a valley.

Scanonaenrat

The Deer nation village was named *Scanonaenrat* (JR8:125; 10:11 and 17:87). The noun root involved in the name, *-nnon-*, was given several translations by Potier:

ₗannona	le fond de l'eau [the bottom or depth of the water] ...
ₗannona	abyme ... précipice [abyss or chasm ... precipice]
ₗannona	tresor, magazain ... une peche [treasure, shop ... catch]
ₗannona	couture, usage [manners or customs]
ₗannona	le dos [the back] (Potier 1920:451)

It is not clear whether Potier is presenting more than one root here; I suspect that some of them can be linked. Potier had a tendency to over-differentiate in his listing of noun roots (i.e., be a 'splitter' rather than a 'lumper'). The 'bottom or depth of the water' may be linked with the 'abyss, chasm or precipice.' Those two may even be connected with 'the back.' Think of the shared shape. I believe the meaning 'precipice or cliff' to be the most likely one for this village name.

The verb root involved is *-ₗenrat-* 'to be white' (Potier 1920:247). This is culturally interesting because the name of the Deer nation, as we have seen, was *Atahontaₗenrat* (JR36:141), meaning 'two white ears.' With the repetitive prefix signified by the *-s-* at the beginning of the word, the translation is 'it is a very white precipice or cliff.' A second possibility, less likely, is that the name might mean 'very white back,' making the analogy between the landscape and an animal or human back.

Anonatea/Aneatea

Probably using the same noun root, but more difficult to translate, is the village name written as *Anonatea* in some sources (JR13:189, 193, 211, 223, 247; 14:11, 15, 47, and 51) and in one source as *Aneatea* (JR14:7). If the verb root -*te*- 'to exist' (Potier 1920:360) is used in this word, then the final -*a*- could be a diminutive final, something that seems to exist in a number of Huron village names (see *Contarea, Teandatetsia, Ihonatiria,* and *Arendaonatia* below). The resulting translation could be something like 'small cliff exists,' but I cannot be too sure.

In the Huron dictionaries of the seventeenth and eighteenth centuries, the noun root -*tar*-, was translated as "argile [clay]" (FH1697:207), "boue [mud]" (FH1697:207), "fange [mire]" (Potier 1920:453), "terre [earth]" (Potier 1920:453), and "terre glaize [loam, clay]" (FH1697:207). It appears in Wyandot names for rivers: "$_t$*atarok8i* *catarak8i[22]" (Potier 1920:154); "$_t$*ataraske* *R[iviere] de la baye" (Potier 1920:155); and "*ts8tara$_t$en* R[iviere]" (Potier 1920:155).

It is important to note that the two village names I am about translate have been linked (see Heidenreich 1971: map 17) with the name of a Huron nation that shares the use of the same noun root (see chapter 2).

Ataratiri

The village name *Ataratiri* appears in *Description* and *Huronum*. This is the village with the mission name St. Louis, situated by the Hogg River. The evidence for this connection is the close proximity of the placement of the two names in the maps, and the fact that the two names exist in complementary distribution in the three of the four maps of Huronia. In the fourth, *Description*, which frequently gave both mission and Huron names, the two names exist side by side. The verb root used is -*atiri*- 'to support' (Potier 1920:191–92), giving the meaning 'it is supported by clay, wet earth.'

Koutarcano

In *Description*, the name *koutarcano* was presented as the Huron term for Sainte-Marie-Among-the-Hurons. While the word is poorly transcribed, making it difficult to be sure of an exact translation, it is possible that the verb root used is -*on$_t$o*- 'to penetrate' (Potier 1920:413). Elsewhere in this map, an -*an*- is written when an -*on*- was required. That appears in the word written by the northwest corner of Lake Simcoe: *Etiaantarisati*. The -*an*- in this case represents the -*on*- of the noun root -*ontar*- 'lake' (Potier 1920:455).

Contarea

The name *Contarea* appears both in reference to a lake (Heidenreich 1971: maps 12, 13, and 14) and a community (JR10:95 and 181). The name is formed from the noun root *-ontar-* 'lake' (Potier 1920:455), with the irregular verb root *-e-* 'to be water' (which appears to take the form *-ache-* when not in combination with a noun; see Potier 1920:162 and 672), plus what appears to be the diminutive suffix *-a-*. With the cislocative prefix (*-c-* representing a *-k-* sound), we have the meaning, 'where there is a little lake.'

The following names have miscellaneous possible origins:

Andiatae

A name that is most likely a physical entity, rather than a social metaphor is *Andiatae* (JR10:179 as *Andiata;* 13:157, 235, 241, and 243; 14:21, 29, 41, and 51). The most obvious translation here involves the noun root *-ndiat-* 'bridge' (Potier 1920:449). With the locative suffix *-e-*, this gives us the translation, 'at the bridge.' The central location of the village (commented on by Hunter; JR10:326 fn18) could possibly have created a metaphorical sense—i.e., that the villages itself was a kind of bridge—but given the dominance of physical feature names, that does not seem very likely.

Another noun root, *-ndiat-,* takes the meaning 'throat' (Potier 1920:449), which could be a description of the area, rather like the name 'Niagara' meaning 'neck' and referring to the Niagara Peninsula (see Steckley 1992b), although this too seems unlikely to me.

Arendaonatia/Anendaonactia

This village name comes in two forms *Arendaonatia* (JR14:13) and *Anendaonactia* (JR14:45). As there is no noun root *-nnend-* in Huron, the more accurate version is the one with *-rend-* which refers to 'rock' (Potier 1920:452). The rest of the word is difficult to determine; possibly it uses the verb root *-ₜonda-* 'to augment,' with the causative suffix *-t-*, the stative aspect *-i-*, and a diminutive suffix *-a-*, giving us 'rock is augmented a little.' Once again, however, I am not convinced.

Cahiagué

The name *Cahiagué* appears solely in Champlain (1929:49). The best interpretation I can come up with is that it is derived from the verb root *-iaₜ-* 'to cut, break' (Potier 1920:263). With the dualic, making it *kaiaₜi*, we get 'it is cut in two' (Potier 1920:264). The changes made in the transcription (dropping the *-h-*, changing the *-e-* to an *-i-*, and *-gu-* to *-ₜ-*) are not problematic. Still, I am not absolutely sure that this is how the word should be translated.

Ekhiondaltsaan

The village name that appears as *Khiondaësahan* (JR12:113), *Ekhiondalt-saan* ((JR14:27) and *ti ondatsae* (*Huronum*) possibly relates to a physical feature in the area. The name includes the noun root *-ndats-* 'pot,'as indicated in the Latin name *Calodaria* (see Heidenreich 1971:44) that appears in *Chorographia* and in the French name "La Chaudiere," which appears in *Corographie*. With the cislocative prefix indicated here variously as *-khi-*, *-ekhi-*, *-ti-*, and the probable verb root *-en-* 'to lie' (Potier 1920:221), we have: 'where the pot(s) lie(s).' I suspect that this name reflects a physical feature, possibly relating to part of the Hog River hollowed out like a pot. It might relate to the community's performing the function of holding feasts, but the literature does not mention the community doing so. Further, it would be uncharacteristic for a Huron village name not to refer to some physical feature.

Etondatra

This community had a good number of versions of its name. It first appears as *Tondakhra* in 1637 (JR13:49). The *-khr-* is a dialect form that occurs exclusively in Northern Bear. It later appears in another dialect form, with *-tr-*. It is *Etondatra* in *Description*, without the initial *-e-* in *Huronum*. In *Chorographia* it takes two forms: the northernmost point on the Penetang Peninsula is labelled with the Latinized *p. Etondatrateus*, while the village itself is termed *Tondakea*.

Etondatra is probably the most accurate form, which would be composed of the noun root *-ndat-* 'village' (Potier 1920:449); one of the two verb roots that take the form *-ra-* is likely involved, although it is difficult to choose which of two. The verb root 'to be with, among' (Potier 1920:325–26) is a possibility because, when it appears with noun roots that end with *-t-*, it drops the *-a-* that typically follows noun roots (i.e., takes *-tra-* rather than *-tara-*). However, it does not make for a readily understandable translation. If the *-et-* represents the cislocative prefix, a translation of 'where a village is among, with' does not make much sense. The other choice, the verb root 'to be on top' (Potier 1920:332) makes more sense, giving 'where the village in on top (i.e., possibly on top of the peninsula or a hill).' However, in the forms found in the Huron dictionaries, this verb root does not drop the *-a-* after noun roots that end with *-t-*.

Ihonatiria

The village name *Ihonatiria* (JR11:11, 19; 13:169 and 215) or *Ihonattiria* (JR13:175, and 247; and 14:105) appears to be constructed around the verb root *-atiri-* 'to support' (Potier 1920:191–92), but the rest of the word then complicates the matter. The *-a-* could be the diminutive that appears in several village names, but the *-ihona-* is more difficult to interpret. It would be nice if the noun root *-hon-* 'canoe' (Potier 1920:447) were involved, as Jones claims in his verb-overloaded translation, "The Little (Hamlet) above the Loaded Canoe" (Jones 1908:187), but that would leave us with no clear pronominal prefix, which is a mandatory part of a Huron verb. It seems to me to be more likely that the pronominal prefix *-hona-* 'they (as agent) with him or his (as patient)' could be involved, giving a meaning 'they give him little support.' However, such a translation does not make any apparent cultural sense, so it is highly questionable.

Ossossane
The mission village of La Conception was written in essentially three different ways:
   Ossossané (JR13:193, 209, 211, 223, 233, 235, 237, 243, and 251; 19:133 (with *-e-* instead of *-é-*), 217, and 219), *Ososané* (JR13:149, 169, and 181; 16:223 and 20:219) and *Ossosandué* (JR12:113). Nothing that I can come up with is even close, linguistically or culturally. The *-osos-* is a strange combination; perhaps the initial *-o-* is added in error. The Jesuits never presented translations of Huron village names in the *Jesuit Relations* or in the dictionaries, no matter how transparent the translation would be. Perhaps accuracy and consistency of representation (achieved in the dictionaries but not in the place names) was not as important to the Jesuits in transcribing place names as it was with regular words, particularly those that would facilitate conversion. Conceivably, the name might relate to a tree or plant not included in the Jesuit dictionary lists.

Otouacha
As we will see below, this village name found in Champlain (1929:46) has been incorrectly associated with *Toanche*. That is about all that can be said, as no noun or verb looks much like it.

Teanaustaye
The name of the Cord village *Teanaustaye* has been recorded in many forms: *Teanosteaé* (JR12:113), *Teanausteaiae* (JR13:27), *Teanaostahé* (JR13:125), *Teanaustaiaé* (JR16:239), *Teanaustayaé* (JR17:11), *Teanaustayé* (JR17:47), *Teanaustay* (JR17:59), *Teanausteiyé* (JR19:133), *Teanaustaiae* (JR21:205), *Teanaostriae* (JR23:241) and *te annaosteiaj* (Potier 1920:661). While the verb root appears to be *-ia$_l$-* 'to cut, break' (Potier 1920:264),

combining with the dualic prefix (*-te-*) 'to cut in two,' this leaves us with a form *-nna(o/u)st-* that no noun root recorded in the Jesuit Huron dictionaries takes.

Teandatetsia

In *Huronum* there is a village named *Teandatetsia*. It would seem that it involves the noun root *-ndat-* 'village' (Potier 1920:448), the verb root *-es-*[23] 'to be long' (Potier 1920:385). Complicating the translation is the presence of the dualic prefix *-te-* and the diminutive suffix *-a-*, which seems to be part of the grammar of Huron village naming (see *Annonatea, Aren-daonatia, Contarea,* and *Ihonatiria*). Combining these elements, we might translate the name as 'slightly long double village,' but this is problematic.

Teandeouiata

Mentioned twice in the *Relation* of 1635 is the village name *Teandeouï(h)ata* (JR8:89 and 95), which was given as an alternative name for *Toanche* (JR8:89). Unfortunately, the only meaning that I can come up with for this name involves the noun root *-ndeh8-* 'beaver pelt.' It would be tempting to say that it includes the verb root *-ia|-* 'to cut, break,' (Potier 1920:263) with the causative suffix *-t-* and the habitual aspect *-ha-*, but 'it cuts the beaver pelt in two as such a place, by such a means,' makes no apparent sense to me.

Te aontiae

In the four maps of Huron villages, four different names are given to what I feel is the same community by the Hog River: *Chantie* (*Description*), *Kaontia* (*Corographie*), *Kaotia* (*Chorographia*) and *Te aontiae* (*Huronum*). This is difficult to translate. It is possible that the noun root *-hont-* 'bush' (Potier 1920:447) is involved, but the verb used is not readily apparent. There is a slight possibility that the verb root is *-ia$_l$-* 'to cut, break' (Potier 1920:263), with an initial dualic 'to cut in two,' making the translation 'bush is cut in two,' but the short ending of most of the forms makes this problematic.

Toanche

When Champlain came to Huronia in 1615, the first village he encountered after landing on the Penetang Peninsula was called *Otouacha* (Champlain 1929:46). On a tour of Huron communities a few days later, Champlain went to *Touaguainchain* (1929:48). It has long been assumed (Jones 1908:61, Heidenreich 1971:34 and Trigger 1976:300) that *Otouacha* was an orthographically different representation of the village that Sagard later visited and recorded variously as *Toenchen*, *Toinchain*, and *Toenchain* (Sagard 1939:91, 141 and 247 respectively), and that was referred to as *Toanché* in the *Jesuit Relations* (JR8:89 and 91). In contrast to that, the name *Touaguainchain* has largely been ignored (Heidenreich 1971:306). This is a mistake, as *Touaguainchain* is much more likely a candidate for being *Toanché*.

Toanché was Northern Bear village, and the dialect in which the Jesuits wrote the name was also Northern Bear. One of the characteristic features of this dialect is an absence of the *-y-* phoneme. Champlain had dealings almost exclusively with the Rock, whose dialect contained the *-y-* phoneme, as recorded in Champlain's works by a *-g(u)-*, as can be seen in *Carhagouha* discussed above, and in the name for the Mascoutens *Assistaguronons* (Champlain's 1616 map, in Heidenreich 1971: map 3) or as *-y-* in the previously discussed *Tequenonquiaye*.

Sagard's writing of *Toanche* is a little problematic. He lived with the Southern Bear, and his writing is a mixture of Southern Bear and Rock dialects. I am not sure why in his writing of the term there is no *-y-*, although Southern Bear did miss *-y-* sometimes. What helps link *Toanche* and *Touaguainchain* is Sagard's use of the nasalizing *-n-* at the end of the word, and his interchangeable use of *-ain-* and *-en-* to represent the resulting nasal vowel. Finally, the remaining difference of *-ou-* versus *-o-* is not a problem as that represents a dialect difference (see Steckley 1992a).

The name could possibly be written as *te 8aₗenchen*, which could be derived from the verb root *-aₗen-* 'to go out,' potentially a reference to *Toanche* being a place from which people went out of Huronia. The *-te-* could be an indicator that it was a double village, but at this point I am not sure.

Conclusions: Village Names

We have seen in this look at Huron village names that certain terms predominate. In particular, terms related to trees, poles, and topographic features are well represented. It is worthwhile noting as well some elements that are not drawn upon for names: individuals' names, animal names, and social or political functions performed by the community. No term uses the noun root for river, *-nda8-* (Potier 1920:448) or for stream, *-ihon-* (FH1697:188).

With the smaller member nations of the Huron, the village names resemble the national names. Two villages of the *Ataronchronnon*, share the noun root *-tar-* with the national name. The one village of the

Atahonta|enrat ('two white ears') also contains the verb root -ₗenrat- 'to be white.' Also, it should be noted that the dualic prefix appears in six village names (*Cahiagué, Teanaustaye, Teandatetsia, Teandeouiata, Te aontiae*, and *Toanche*), possibly suggesting the existence of double or split villages. Five names may include the diminutive suffix -a-, for reasons that are unclear to me.

Chapter Summary

In this chapter we have looked at several aspects of the Huron relationship to the environment. The Huron calendar (i.e., their terms for months of the year) shows that corn, fish and berries are well represented in month terms, reflecting their significance in the Huron diet. Only one term appears in relationship to hunting, suggesting that meat played a small part in their diet.

Some linguistic detective work discovered that the "mystery fish" of the Huron, the one that they did not eviscerate, was the burbot, or freshwater cod, whose liver would have provided the Huron with vitamins A and D to help them survive the winter. Like the generations of non-Huron Canadians who had to take cod-liver oil, the Huron also had to endure the bad taste. This indicates the extensive Huron knowledge about the beneficial properties of their faunal resources.

The highly specific corn terms give a good indication of detailed knowledge relating to plants. The prominence of trees in village names helps us to see the landscape as the Huron did.

Notes

1 "Dore" is Canadian French for walleye or pickerel. When presented separately, the first word, *atsiₗiondi*, is given as "Poisson d'ore" (FHO:17 and FH1697:232).
2 The reference to blackberries is not found in FHO.
3 Sagard identified this fish as the most important food fish of the Huron (Sagard 1939:185–90). It has been misidentified by some writers as 'whitefish' (Sagard 1939:185, Kinietz 1940:25, Tooker 1967:63, Heidenreich 1971:208–12 and Trigger 1976:41), but, as we see from the November entry, that fish went by another name.
4 Below, an analysis concludes that this refers to burbot.
5 The word here is probably that which Potier represents as "ₗaâchia ... caisse, boisseau ... baril" (Potier 1920:446), and as "ₗahâchra casseau ... caisse &" (Potier 1920:447).
6 Sagard 1866 "Pleurer."
7 Potier 1920:173.
8 Sagard 1866 "Demeurer, ne bouger."
10 Potier 1920:392.
11 This word is difficult to translate. It is quite likely that the verb root is -ets- 'to be long' (Potier 1920:385), with the diminutive -a- following, possibly with the sense of 'a little long.'

The noun root is more difficult to determine. Is the -ngui- the Southern Bear dialect version of the noun for 'finger'? If so, then 'little long finger' might refer to the barbels characteristic of the burbot. This translations need more work or insight.

12 The name 'Erie' comes from an Iroquoian word meaning 'long tail,' and referring to the cougar or mountain lion.

13 "Rats, smelling of musk ... hoatthe" (Barbeau 1961:168).

14 The translation for this Huron sentence in the *Jesuit Relations* adds to the French translation words that covered more than the Huron words stated.

15 Whenever xxxx appears, that means that the omitted word is illegible in the original text.

16 The -v- here (as in the Mohawk cognate) represents a nasal vowel. This word is listed on the website www.wehali.com/tsalagi/index.cfm.

17 The asterisk here shows that the word is a hypothetical construct of the "original" form of the term in Uto-Aztecan, a construct that comes from comparing members of the language family.

18 See the website at www.wehali.com/tsalagi/index.cfm.

19 Linguistic evidence for the long-term practice in the area of chewing tobacco comes from Algonquian languages. According to John Hewson, there is a Proto-Algonquian term for chewing tobacco, based in part on a root for 'mouth' (Hewson 1993:12).

20 The absence of the -ı- is due to the fact that the term was written in the Northern Bear dialect, which does not have this phoneme. The evidence for this place name is in JR8:105–7 and 141; 10:201; 13:177, 207 and 227; *Corographie du Pays des Hurons*, Heidenreich 1971:map 14, hereafter *Corographie; Description dv pais des hvrons*, Heidenreich 1971:map 15, hereafter *Description;* Bressani's *Huronum Explicate Tabula*, 1657, Heidenreich 1971:map 13, hereafter *Huronum;* and Du Creux's *Chorographia Regionis Huronum*, 1660, Heidenreich 1971:map 12, hereafter *Chorographia*.

21 This term was used to refer to Manitoulin Island in *Chorographia*.

22 The use of the -h- here rather than -ı- is because the name is written in Northern Bear.

23 This is a Mohawk version of the name, now associated with the area.

24 It takes the form -ets- rather than -es- before -i-.

6 Material Culture of the Huron

The material culture of the Huron is of great interest to archaeologists. It is the form of evidence they work with and analyze. But their knowledge of material culture can only be partial. Only certain materials tend to survive and show up in the archaeological record. Stones, bones, and potsherds are first on the list; wood only sometimes. And the evidence that survives often forms only part of the original objects. When Huron longhouses are studied, the post molds (small, dark, circular, organic stains) left by the supporting poles are over-represented in the archaeological record. The other parts of the house—the bark roof and walls, and horizontal poles—are much harder to uncover archaeologically.

Further, the way the Huron classified or conceptualized their material culture is not readily found in the archaeological record. Archaeologists are usually then left to the early written record, with all its flaws and biases. The Wendat language can be a great help. It can, to a certain extent, allow the Huron people themselves to speak about the material items that were familiar to them.

In what follows, we will see how the Wendat language can teach archaeologists, historians, teachers, students, and other interested people about Huron material culture by looking at several key items: Huron longhouses, armour, war-bundles, beads, pots, canoes, and also some items that can be called *oh8ista*. We will begin with the most dominant physical component of Huron traditional culture: the longhouse.[1]

The Huron Longhouse

The Huron longhouse is the subject of a great deal of study, both by archae-ologists, and by elementary teachers and students Ontario (as well as else-where in Canada and in the U.S.). As Aboriginal housing is a part of their curriculum, elementary school textbooks regularly feature Iroquoian long-houses (see Arnold and Gibbs 1999:52, 56, 58; and Francis 2000:1 and 11). Reconstructions can be found in Ontario at Sainte-Marie-Among-the-Hurons and at the Huron Village, both in Midland, at the Simcoe County Museum in Barrie, and at Crawford Lake Conservation Area, near Milton. Iroquoian longhouses are a regular part of museum culture in the state of New York as well, in museums run both by Six Nations peo-ple and by non-Aboriginal people. Longhouse bearing websites intended as educational locations for elementary school students can be readily found.[2] The Iroquoian longhouse, then, forms an important part of our rep-resentation and understanding of traditional Iroquoian life. A look at all these representations will show a diversity of opinion on how the buildings were structured.

Presented here are Huron terms for parts of the longhouse, and for material objects associated with the longhouse (e.g., hearths and mats for sleeping). Most of the terms are nouns, and will be looked at in terms of how they are typically incorporated into particular verbs. Most of these examples come from lengthy dictionary entries under the French word 'cabane' in FHO and FH1697.

-nnonchi-/-nnons- 'house'

The Huron noun root for 'house' was *-nnonchi-* (see Potier 1920: 162, 183, 201, and 236), which would take the form *-nnons-* in certain linguistic envi-ronments (see Potier 1920: 241, 267, and 281). In the dictionary entry in FHO, this noun was used in two different ways:

> *Annonste$_l$encha'ra*
> *onatennonste$_l$encha'ra*[3]
> le ciel

[the canopy]   nous avons mis[4] des escorces au dessus
                [we have put (?) some bark on top]

The word *onatennonste$_l$encha'ra* is composed of the noun root *-nnons-*, with the verb root *-te$_l$en-*, a form of *-nde$_l$en-* 'to join' (Potier 1920:281–82), along with the nominalizer *-ch-* (66), and the verb root *-'ra-* 'to be put or be above' (332). The combined meaning is 'we are joined in the longhouse, one above the other.' This could refer to a two-level seating/sleeping practice as described in the following quotation from a 1639 discussion on Huron gambling:

> They have no sooner arrived at the appointed place than the two parties take their places on opposite sides of the cabin and fill it from top to bottom, above and below the Andichons ['platform'; see discussion below] which are sheets of bark making a sort of canopy for a bed, or shelter, which corresponds to that below, which rests upon the ground, upon which they sleep at night. It is placed upon poles laid and suspended the whole length of the cabin. (JR17:203–5)

The other part of the FHO entry to have the noun -*nnonchi*- is the following:

le milieu   *ₗannonchiahenk*
            le milieu de la cabane [the middle of the house]

Unfortunately, the verb used here has neither been identified nor translated.

Four verb combinations with -*nnonchi*- that appear outside the FHO are of anthropological interest. One is the following:

ₗannonchiaₗenristi   Changer la cabane, le transporter ailleurs
                         [to change house, transport it elsewhere]

ₗannonskenristi ...   transporter une cabane ailleurs
                         [to transport a house somewhere else]

(Potier 1920:248)

These combinations are with the verb root -*ₗenrist*- 'to change the place or position of something' (Potier 1920:248). What could be referred to here is literally moving a longhouse, or at least the major poles used in its construction, to a new location. This would be a strategy that would save a lot of tree-cutting, trimming labour, and wood seasoning. However, to the best of my knowledge, such a practice is not referred to in the standard ethnohistorical literature, so can only be suggested at this point. It would be an interesting hypothesis for archaeologists to test out.

The following entry, using the verb root -*ₗon*- 'to be empty' (Potier 1920:163), has some implications concerning Huron notions of social structure, suggesting greater ideas of hierarchy than are usually found in the ethnohistorical literature:

elle e[st] vuide.   *onnonchiaₗon*
[It is empty.]   [it is an empty house]
                      ce que e[st] q[uel]que fois une injure, c'est reprocher
                      q[ue]1 [qu'un]s sont pauvr[es] ou foibles
                      [This is sometimes an insult. It reproaches someone with being poor or weak.] (FH1697:234)

This seems to suggest that, in terms of the number of people and/or possessions found in a longhouse, there was some form of invidious comparison of dwellings and the status of their owners. However, until this is found in sources earlier than 1697, we cannot be absolutely certain whether this existed at the time of first contact or was at least in part the result of Huron contact with the French, who were far conscious of possessions and status.

A potentially opposing term exists: *ₗannonchi* 'it is a full house,' with the noun root incorporated into the verb *-i-* 'to be full' (Potier 1920:393). It appears twice in the Jesuit-written text of *De Religione*, as follows:

sk8arih8ateri ti aonesk8at d'aiontatrihondat ₗannonchiₗe
You know that it causes one to be pleased, that one would be praised, augmented in reputation in a full house. (Steckley 2004:106–7, line 1)

aiotonnen te honderinnen aiaχingat d'aₗote8annen aₗondatontionnen te ₗaent[a]k aat atendacha a te ₗannonske ₗannonchichonk: oₗaresa ₗannenhenta8i, onnionchia a8eti,
It would have been possible [to do it], if they had wished, 'We should go after those who fled and left their villages' where great provisions were lying in every house, full houses with beans, buried corn, and squash. (136–37, line 15)

It would seem from this that the connotations of "full house" included having a great supply of food and a reputation that went along with that.

When *-nnonchi-* is incorporated into the verb *-ohare-* 'to wash' (Potier 1920:405), we have the following Huron ceremonial metaphor:

ₗannonchiohare
[to wash a house]   ... laver la cabane (metap.) faire festin a son entree
                          dans une nouvelle maison ou l'on demeurer.
                          [to wash a house (metaphorically), to hold a ceremony at the entrance of a new house where people are going to live] (Potier 1920: 405)

Similar metaphors exist with *-ohare-* and other nouns. With the noun root *-chiend-* 'name,' we get an expression for the resuscitation of a name (Potier 1920:406 and 446), the ceremony through which a person acquires a new name. With *-ask8a-* 'scaffold' (see also the entry for *ask8atonk8i* for use of this noun), we get a term for a ceremony involving the presenting of gifts during the Feast of the Dead (Potier 1290:406 and 445; FH1697:107). Also see below for a similar Mohawk metaphor with the cognate for the Huron noun root *-ndât-* 'mat' and with a Wyandot expression with the word for 'pot.'

In the political sphere, we have the following use of -*nnonchi*- incorporated into the verb -*io*- 'to be large, great' (Potier 1920:396):

maistre de la cabane.   *honnonchio*
[master of the house]   [he is great in the house] (FH1697:234)

I could not find any examples of the feminine pronominal prefix, giving 'she is great in the house.' This could be noteworthy or not; it might be explained by the distinct pro-male bias in the Jesuit writing.

te ₁anda₁en 'the vestibule or porch'

There are several references in the ethnohistorical literature to the vestibules or porches at the ends of Iroquoian longhouses (see Latta 1985, for an insightful discussion). Sagard, for example, tells us the following:

> At each end there is a porch, and the principal use of these porches is to hold the large vats or casks of tree-bark in which they store their Indian corn after it has been well dried and shelled. (Sagard 1939:95)

In giving a Huron term for the porch, Sagard seems to have been mistaking the tree-bark casks for the porches. In the following entries, he appears to have used the term for the vats or casks, ₁*ahak* (Potier 1920:156 and 447), to refer to the porch:

> Le porche
> *Aque* (Sagard 1866:31)
>
> [B]ut as to the great trunks or logs called *Aneincuny*, which are used for keeping the fire in by being lifted a little at one end, they pile these in front of their lodges or store them in the porches, which they call *Aque*. (Sagard 1939:94)

Sagard often used -*que*- to refer to what the Jesuits wrote as -*k*-, and it was not unusual for him to miss the first syllable of a Huron word (see the section on the noun root -₁*onar*- below). Sagard may have been misreading an earlier source that was providing the information for this passage.

The best description of the porches that appears in the standard ethnohistorical literature is in the writing of Father Joseph-Francois Lafitau about the Mohawk longhouses near Montreal in 1724:

> The Iroquois lodges have exits at the two ends. At each end there is a lobby or small apartment and an outer vestibule.
>
> Their outer vestibule is closed with sheets of bark in winter and serves as a woodshed for the heavy wood. In summer, however, they put their mats on the flat roof of these vestibules which is not raised as high as their lodges. They lie thus in the open air without minding the dew. (Lafitau 1974, vol. 2:21–22)

The most detailed information comes from the Huron linguistic sources. The Huron term for these porches was *te ₗandaₗen*. In the dictionary entries, the term seems to apply to two slightly different places: (a) the space between the two doors at one end of a longhouse; and (b) a space close to the doors at either end of the longhouse.

In chronological order, we have the following entries:

l'entree   *Te ₗandaₗen* [entrance]
                L'espace qui est entre les portes
                [the space that is between the doors]

                item. la place qui est proche de la porte
                [also, the place that is close to the door]

                chi te kandaₗen ihentron
                [he is at the porch at the other side]

                Il est a l'au[tre] bout de cabane ...
                [he is at the other end of the house]

                ₗaro te ₗandaₗen.
                [the porch on this side] (FHO)

L'entre[e] des portes de la cab[ane]. *te ₗandaₗen*
[the entranceway of the doors to the house]
ce n'est pas bien q[uand] les fille y couche(nt)
[it is not good when girls sleep there]
te ₗandeiaa d'aionrat te ₗandaₗen d'e8itsonnha
[it is not good when those who are girls sleep on the porch (i.e., making themselves sexually available at night)] (FH1693:46)

L'espace entre les portes, ou la place qui e[s]t proche des portes. *te ₗandaₗen*
[the space between the doors, or the place that is close to the doors] (FH1697:234)

Kandaₗen ...   (etre devant la porte de la cabane & P.)
                [to be in front of the door of a house]
                item. l'espace mitoyen entre la port de dehors et celle de la cabane
                [also, the dividing space between the outside door and the house door] (Potier 1920:274)

Vis a Vis *te 8andaₗenₗ te sandaₗen ...*   Vis a vis porte de la maison
[opposite the door of the house]

te sk8andaₗen vis a vis de votre porte   [opposite your door]
(Potier 1920:76)

One area of confusion remains. Was the porch inside the longhouse structure, or was it just a roofed vestibule without doors? Evidence presented below concerning the *-endich-* or platforms would suggest that it was outside.

-ndh8- 'the door'

The Huron noun root for door was *-ndh8-*(Potier 1920:450).[5] As we have just seen, Huron longhouses could have two doors at one end. We can learn more about the nature of these two doors by looking at the following entries taken from the Huron dictionaries:

as'e ekandh8ate	la porte de dehors
	[the outside door] (Potier 1920:360)
Onie andhont	la porte de dedans.
	[the inside door] (FHO; cf. FH1697:234)

In the first example, we have the verb root *-te-* 'to be present, exist' (Potier 1920:360) incorporating *-ndh8-* and the locative prefix (see Potier 1920:26–27), with the combined meaning 'a door is located there.' With the first word, *as'te* 'outside' (91), we get 'the door that is outside.'

In the second example, *onie* means 'inside' (FHO). The verb incorporating *-ndh8-* is *-ont-*, 'to attach, be attached,' often used with parts of the body (e.g., legs, arms, nose, and face); (see Potier 1920:419–21). The combined meaning is 'the door attached inside' (i.e., to the main body of the house).

The outside door may have been made out of different material than the inside or main door, if the situation was similar to that described by Lafitau for the early eighteenth-century Mohawk:

> The doors of the lodges are of moveable sheets of bark hung from above with neither key nor lock ...
>
> They double their doors to protect themselves from cold and smoke and make a sort of second door of blankets of skin or wool. (Lafitau 1974 vol. 2:22)

Other details about the door, probably most true of the inside door, come from the following dictionary entries. First, the door was opened by lifting it and putting it to one side:

8ta,enhen ...	Soulever, lever q[uelque]. c[hose]. d'une cote, comme une porte
	[to raise, lift something to one side, as a door]
't[6]	
,annh08ta,enk	soulever la porte, l'entr'ouvrir ...
	[to raise the door, to open it]

't
Sennho8ta₁enk   lever la porte, entr'ouvre la
                         [raise the door, open it] (Potier 1920:439)

The door was sometimes held up or kept open with a stick, as can be seen in the following dictionary entry:

't
₁aenta onnh8aiannontati …
[it is used to keep the door open]   un baton tient la porte entr'ouverte
                                       [a stick holds the door open]
(Potier 1920:265)

The last combination has *-ndh8-* incorporated into the verb root *-iannonte-* 'to be open, not joined' (Potier 1920:265).

Knocking on a door had metaphorical meaning:

't
₁annh8ae   frapper a la porte de q[uelqu'un].
[to hit a door]   [knock on someone's door; metaphorically, to call
                         to council] (Potier 1920:163)

The verb root used in this last case is *-ae-* 'to hit' (Potier 1920:163).

te andhia'ronk: crossbeams

Other parts of the longhouse appear to have the noun root *-ndh8-* in them. One involves a part of the door:

les poutres
[the beams]   *Te Andhia'ronk*
                les poutres qui traversent les portes
                [the beams that cross the doors] (FHO; c.f. FH1697:234)

The verb root in this combination appears to be *-'ron-* 'to cross' (Potier 1920:348), giving the whole word the possible meaning of 'it crosses the door.' This would seem to be referring to the crossbeams from which the door, probably the inside one, hangs.

₁andhok8enda 'partitions/headboards'

Another part of the longhouse could be derived from *-ndh8-*. Unfortunately, so far the word has defied all my attempts at analysis:

Le dossier   *₁Andhok8enda*
[headboard]   cloison de dedans la cabane
                  [partition inside the house]
                  item. le dossier de leur lits
                  [also, the headboard of their beds] (FHO)

ₗ*Andho'k8enₗda*   cloison de dedans la cabane
                          [partition inside the house]
                          v. dossier ou l'on appuyer
                          [the headboard or backing that one leans against]
(FH1693)

These headboards/partitions probably resembled what Lafitau was referring to when he wrote that eighteenth-century Mohawk longhouse platforms were "shut in on all sides, except that of the fire" (Lafitau 1974 vol. 2:21). It also conforms to the notion of a family unit as a "maniere d'establie"('stall or stable'), a term that appears in the ethnohistorical literature with reference to the platforms (see Dodd 1984:318–19 for an excellent use of good translation in researching the parts of the longhouse).

-nnre's- 'the end wall'

The noun root *-nnre's-* refers to the gable or end wall of the longhouse. Unfortunately, in the following FHO entry, the section for this noun is extremely difficult to read:

le pignon   ₗ*Annresa.*
                 le pignon de la cabane.
                 [the gable or end wall of the house]
ₗ*Annre'sa'ron.*
                 faire le pignon … ab. *A'ron*, mettre de travers
                 [to make the gable … from *A'ron*, 'to cross]
aste etio(andres)ata
                 au pignon de dehors
                 [at the outside gable] (FHO; see FH1697 and Potier 1920:451)

As in the discussion of the door, the verb *-'ron-* means 'to cross,' and is used with parts of the longhouse that cross the width of the building.

In the last part of the entry, the verb root used appears to be *-ta-* 'to reach or be at the end' (Potier 1920:358). With *aste*, 'outside,' we get: 'gable or end wall that reaches or is on the outside.' This may be referring to the end wall of the porch.

Another incorporation of *-nnre's-* into a verb is the following, with the verb root being *-8eₗ-* 'to close' (Potier 1920:319):

d
ₗ*annresk8aₗi*   pignon ou coste de la cabane etre bouche
                 [the end wall or side of the longhouse is blocked or closed]
(Potier 1920:320)

While it is not clear whether this refers to the wall's end or side being covered with bark, or to its not having doors, I suspect it is the latter.

-endich- 'platform'

One of the most poorly understood aspects of the Huron longhouse is the structures on the side or sides of the building. I am using the word 'platform' to refer to them, but their function is problematic. One problem in particular has been raised by a number of archaeologists (Noble 1968, Dodd 1984:212, 318–19 and Latta 1985:49–50). While the published sources written in the seventeenth century speak only of platforms that ran the entire length of the longhouse and were on both sides, archaeological evidence suggests a greater variety, with platforms sometimes being shorter, existing only on one side, and even being totally absent from some longhouses.

I think that we can propose to use linguistic evidence to add to the understanding of Huron longhouse platforms. I will focus here on: (a) linguistic evidence supporting the archaeological evidence; (b) platforms at the end of the longhouse; and (c) platforms used as tables or sideboards.

The Huron noun root for platforms was -endich-. The word occurs in the standard ethnohistorical literature twice: first, as *Eindichaguet* in the writings of Sagard; second, as *andichons* in the *Jesuit Relations*.

Sagard copied the following passage almost verbatim from Champlain's *Works*, adding only the Huron term (see Champlain 1929:123):

> At the two sides there is a kind of bench four or five feet high extending from one end of the lodge to the other, on which they sleep in summer to escape the importunity of the fleas ... The whole space underneath these benches, which they call *Garihagueu* and *Eindichaguet*, they fill with dry wood to burn in winter (Sagard 1929:93–94). *Eindachaguet* would have been written in the Jesuit Huron dictionaries as *endichaįe*, 'on or at the platform.' (see Potier 1920:76, "ad. apud")

The *Jesuit Relations* reference was given earlier in the *-nnonchi-* section:

> They had no sooner arrived at the appointed place than the two parties take their places on opposite sites of the cabin and fill it from top to bottom, above and below the *Andichons*, which corresponds to that below, which rests upon the ground, upon which they sleep at night. It is place upon poles laid and suspended the whole length of the cabin. (JR17:203–5)

While both these references describe platforms extending the length of the longhouse, this is not specifically referred to in any of the Huron dictionary entries:

> L'andichon   Endicha ...
> le lieu ou l'on met le xxxx[7], au coste de la cabane
> [the place where one puts xxxx, at the side of the house' (FHO)

Andichon   lieu eleve, ou l'on met q[uelque]. c[hose]
            [elevated place, where one puts something] (FH1697:28)

Other parts of the longhouse that stretched the length of the building were specifically stated as doing so in the French translations of the entries (see *-ask8atonk8i-* and *-ₗonar-* below). However, no such reference is made concerning *-endich-*, nor any specific mention of the platforms being on both sides of the building. Not finding something is usually the weakest form of evidence, but we are dealing with the typically very consistent Jesuit missionary linguists. I believe that the linguistic evidence of non-mention, then, is consistent with suggestions made by archaeologists that not all longhouses had platforms along the length of the building or on both sides.

As with *-ndh8-* 'door' and *-nnre's-* 'end wall,' the noun *-endich-* was incorporated into the verb *-'ron-* 'to cross.' A literal translation of this combination into English would be 'platforms that cross' (i.e., that cross the ends of the longhouse). The translation into French presented in the dictionaries was "le seuil" (FHO and FH1697:224), meaning 'doorstep, threshold.'

A question arises from this. If platforms were placed at ends where doors were as well (as the French term "le seuil" suggests), does this indirectly suggest that the *te ₗandaₗen* (porches) that were close to the door would be outside, there being not room for both at the same place?

As we have seen, dictionary entries for *andichon* refer to objects being placed on them. We have also seen the Lafitau quotation concerning the "canopies" over the beds. This point is reinforced by the way that the noun *-endich-* was used by the Huron to refer to items of French material culture:

Andichon.   Lieu eleve, ou l'on met q[uelque] c[hose], table, buffet [elevated place where one puts something, table, sideboard]

Endichatoₗe'ti   Autel [altar] (FH1697:13)
Buffet ...   ou l'on mets les utensiles.
[sideboard]

Endicha   [where one puts utensils] (FH1697:28)

This was probably the main function of the platforms, as *-endich-* was not translated as 'bench' or 'bed.' As we will see below, the term for 'bed' was *-ndat-*. In addition, the Huron translation for the French "banc" ('bench'), "chaise" ('chair'), and "siege" ('seat') was *onkesarak8a* (FH1697:21 and 32), which means 'one sits on it' (Potier 1920:167). See Dodd for a different argument on this point. Further, in Onondaga and Cayuga, the noun root is translated as 'shelf' (Woodbury 2003:408; Froman et al. 2002:439).

-ndât- 'mat'

The Huron noun root *-ndât-*[8] referred to an individual's mat used as a bed or resting place, and by extension one's place or spot in the longhouse:

natte, lit place [mat, bed, place]	*ₜandata*
Tsinnen ondata.	qui est ce qui se met la, se couche la? [who is it that places himself there, that sleeps there?]
onₜendata8eₜindi.	on ma bouche la natte, on ma chasse de la cabane [they close up my mat, they chase me from the house] (FH1697:129)

The verb root in the last Huron word is *-8eₗ-* 'to close.' Among other things, the entries demonstrate that the noun root has a high potential for metaphor in the Wendat language, and other Northern Iroquoian languages. In Mohawk, the cognate term *-nakt-* (see Michelson 1973:76), when incorporated into the verb *-ohare-* 'to wash,' gives us the following metaphor:

Gannaktohare ...	laver la natte, dit quand on jette de la porcelaine sur un corps mort [to wash the mat, said when one throws wampum onto a dead body] (Bruyas 1970:67)

Father Pierre Potier's "Termes et expressions des Sauvages" offers a number of different metaphorical expressions apparently relating to this word for 'mat':

arriver sur La natte de Q ... c'est arriver chez lui
[to arrive on the mat of someone ... it is to arrive at someone's place]

Une natte teinte de sang ... c'est avoir eu des personnes tuées à la guerre
[a mat tainted with blood, that is (to say) to have had people killed in war]

Nettoyer une Natte teinte de Sang ... c'est appaiser La douleur que L'on a des personnes tuées a la guerre
[to wash a mat tainted with blood, that is to say to sooth or appease the pain of one who had people killed in war]

Preparer La natte pour Q ... c'est etre prêt de la recevoir chez soi
[to prepare the mat for someone ... it is to be ready to receive someone at one's place]

fumer sur La natte ... c'est jouir d'une profonde paix
[to smoke on the mat ... that is to enjoy a profound peace]
(Toupin 1996:285)

garder Le Sac des Colliers sur La natte … c'est attendre Le moment favor-
able pour deliberer d'affaires
[to keep the bag [of wampum] necklaces on the mat … is to wait for a
favourable moment for deliberating on matters] (286)

-tsenh- 'hearth'

The standard ethnohistorical literature refers to there being two families
per hearth in a Huron longhouse. In Champlain's *Works*, we have: "In one
such cabin there will be twelve fires, which made twenty-four households"
(1929:122–24). In Sagard's writings, we have:

> In one lodge there are many fires, and at each fire are two families, one on
> one side, the other on the other side; some lodges will have as many as
> twenty-four families … (Sagard 1939:93–95)

In the *Jesuit Relations* we read that "In each cabin there are five fireplaces,
and two families at each" (JR15:153).

There is support for this position in the Huron dictionaries. The noun
root for 'hearth' is *-tsenh-* (Potier 1920: 454; FH1697:80 and 234). One of
the most common uses of this noun in these dictionaries is the following:

Le foyer	*te onatsanhiaj*
[the hearth]	nous sommes au mesme feu vis a vis l'un de l'autre …
	[we are of the same fire, opposite one another]
(FHO)	
katsenhia$_l$i	diviser le foyer, les uns d'un coste, les autres de l'autre
[to cut the hearth in two]	[to divide the hearth, with some at one side, the others at the other]
te on$_l$itsenhia$_l$i	nous sommes vis a vis l'un de l'autre
[we cut the hearth in two]	[we are opposite one another]
(FH62; c.f. Potier 1920:73)	

The verb root here is *-ia$_l$-*, which with the dualic prefix (represented by
-te- or *-k-*) gives the meaning of 'to cut or divide in two' (Potier 1920:264).
With the noun root for 'hearth,' we get the translation: 'to divide a hearth
in two.'

-nda$_l$ar- 'support poles'

The noun root *-nda$_l$ar-* 'pole' had two main uses with respect to longhouses,
as can be seen in the following dictionary entry:

les pilons   *ₗAndaₗar8t*
[the piles]   pieu qui soustien les pieu[x]
                [post that supports the poles]

                Andaₗara
                ou pend le bled ...
                [where corn is hung] (FHO)

The first part of this entry has *-ndaₗar-* incorporated into the verb *-8t-* 'to stand, rise above' (Potier 1920:437; see also FH1697:234). The combined meaning is 'standing pole,' referring to the vertical support poles of the longhouse. As the entry heading for both uses of *-ndaₗar-* is "les pilons," this would seem to be the main use of the noun.

In Potier's writings, we find a slightly different form, possibly coming from a different dialect of Huron:

ₗandaₗarara   grande perches dans la cabane a pendre q.c.
                 [large poles in the house for hanging things]
(Potier 1920:448)

The second use, as an isolated standing pole from which things could be hung, is seen in the following two examples. The first comes from the *Jesuit Relations*, in Father Jean de Brébeuf's discussion of the gifts received by a murder victim's family. In a special ceremony, the murderer's family provided gifts that were "put on a pole which [is] raised above the head of the murderer, and are called *Andaerraehaan*, that is to say, 'what is hung upon a pole'" (JR10:217). *Andaerraehaan* is probably *ₗandaₗarenhaon*, using the verb *-enhao-* 'to bring, take' (Potier 1920:258). With this noun we have the meaning 'it is brought on a pole.'

The noun was also used for poles possibly employed either in poling canoes, the reference isn't quite clear:

ₗandaₗara   perches qu'on met dans le canot
                 [poles that one puts in the canoe] (FH1697:235)

-ent- 'extension poles'

Another term for "perche" ('pole') in the FHO entry is based on the noun root *-ent-* (Potier 1920:446). In that entry, it comes between the two *-ndaₗar-* examples given above. In all the dictionaries it is a commonly found noun, usually translated into French as "baton" [a 'stick' or 'pole'] or "buche" ['log']; sometimes it is "perche," and sometimes "bois" ['wood']. The root appears in the place name for Manitoulin Island, *ekaentouton* (JR55:132, 136, 140, 170, and 174; JR59:216), with the verb

-*8t*- 'to stand'(Potier 1920:437), meaning 'where there are many standing poles.'

In the FHO entry it appears as follows:

Aentontiek   les poutres
[the beams] (FHO, c.f. FH1697:234)

The verb used is -*ontion*- 'to continue' (Potier 1920:424), giving a combined meaning of 'poles that continue.' This probably refers to continuing or extending from where the vertical poles leave off. This could be either a general term for other poles or for vertical extension poles specifically.

-*ask8atonk8i*- 'longitudinal poles'

The FHO entry for longitudinal poles (i.e., poles that run the length of the longhouse) is unfortunately a blurred one, as is indicated by xxxx and the bracketed terms below:

les perches   *Asak8aton'k8i*   les longues pieux ou perches qui regnent de la cabane qui (ti)ennent les (ceintures) xxxx
[the long poles that run the length of the house, and that (hold up) the (arches)]

(tous) celles de dehors que celles de dedans
[(all) those of the outside and the inside]

(FHO)

A similar, but more limited entry is the following:

longues pieces qui regnent le long de la cab[ane]   *ask8aton'k8i*
[long pieces that run the length of the house] (FH1697:234)

The poles were mentioned as being both on the outside and the inside of the building. These were probably longitudinal poles on both sides of the bark wall.

The word cannot be a noun by itself. It is either a verb or, more likely, a noun incorporated into a verb. It might well contain the noun root -*ask8*- 'scaffold, bridge' (Potier 1920:445). This noun root in Cayuga means 'roof, bridge' (Froman et al. 2002:411), and with different verbs is used to denote a bridge, overpass, porch, roof or ceiling. It holds similar meanings in Onondaga (Woodbury 2003:249–50). What the verb might be is not yet clear to me.

-ndent8tr- 'second row of longitudinal poles'

In the FHO entry following the one for the longitudinal poles, and also under the heading of "les perches," we have the noun root -ndent8tr-:

ˌAndent8tra	les perches qui sont au second rang
	[the poles that make up the second row]
te kandent8tra	celles qui sont au 3e rang.
	[those that make up the third row] (FHO)

So far, this term has defied analysis. It could be related to the noun root -ndend8ar-, generally referring to the poles and paddles used to propel canoes (FH1697:235). The entry for the third row of longitudinal poles adds the dualic prefix, adding the sense of 'the second' to the term for the second row. It is the second additional row.

-ˌonar- 'central suspended poles'

As we have seen above, -ndaˌar- could be used when speaking about poles from which objects could be hung. Another term, -ˌonar-, was used to refer to such poles when they were suspended from the centre of the longhouse, over the fires. Unfortunately, the FHO entry is blurred, but is still useful:

ˌaˌonara	les perches ou plustot longues pieux (debris) qui regnent le long de cabane
	xxxx au milieu le long de feux pour pendre la chaudiere.
	[the poles or (the remains of) long beams that run the length of the house
	xxxx in the middle of the line of fires for hanging the pots]
ˌAˌona'rontak	perches pendues du haut de la cabane pour xxxx
	[poles hung from the top of the house for xxxx] (FHO)

The latter part of the entry has -ˌonar- incorporated in the verb root -ont- 'to attach, be attached,' the verb used in the word for the inside door. The combined meaning is 'attached pole.' This term appears twice in the writings of Sagard, albeit somewhat disguised:

In the midst of the lodge are suspended two big poles which they call *Ouaronta*; on them they hang their pots and put their clothing, provisions and other things, for fear of mice and to keep their things dry. (Sagard 1939:95)

Perches suspendues au dessus du feu.
[poles suspended over the fire]
Ouaronta. (Sagard 1866)

Although *ₗAₗona'rontak* and *Ouaronta* look somewhat different, it should be kept in mind that in Sagard's Huron writing:

(a) *-u-* was sometimes printed when *-n-* should have been used. The noun meaning 'gums,' for example, appears in Potier as *ₗannonacha* (1920:451); Sagard gives:

> Les gencives. *Anouacha*
> [gums] (Sagard 1866)

(b) the first syllable was often missing. What Potier rendered as *ₗarenda8ahe* (1920:316 and 452), Sagard gave as *Reindahohet* (Sagard 1866).

(c) a final *-k-* was sometimes omitted. For the number 'three,' written as *achienk* in Potier (1920:106), Sagard gives *Hachin* (Sagard 1866).

(d) sometimes in Southern Bear dialect forms, the *-ₗ-* was missing. For the term for nose, Potier gave *ₗaₗondia*,[9] while Sagard gave *Aongya* (Sagard 1866).

-ndast- 'rafter poles'

The noun root *-ndast-* means 'rafters' in a good number of Northern Iroquoian languages (Mithun 1984:277; for Onondaga, see Woodbury 2003:1278). In Huron, it seems to have been used to refer to the curved posts that formed the roof:

les ceintres
> *Andasta*   les perches qui font la voute de la cabane fichees en haut
> [the poles that make the vault of the house, attached above]
>
> *ₗAndasta8ak8i*   les courbes
> [the curves, arches] (FHO)

The term *ₗAndastak8ai* involves the verb root *-8aP8-* 'to curve' (FH1697:42). The curve aspect is stressed in a seventeenth-century Mohawk dictionary:

> *Gannasta,*   perches a faire cabane, celle de dedans que l'on courbe pour servir de moule a la cabane
> [poles for making a house, those inside poles that are curved to make the mould or shape of the house] (Bruyas 1970:68)

Another reference to this term is slightly different:

> *ahanda'st8ten*   il fiche les perches de lit
> [he is attaching, has attached the bed poles] (FH1693)

As the verb used here is -8t- 'to stand, rise above' (Potier 1920:437), it probably refers to the purely vertical poles set inside the longhouse to support the platforms or canopies referred to above.

-nde'torak- 'roofing poles'

On the outside of the roof were sticks or poles used to join the sheets of bark that formed the roof. This can be seen in the following entry:

perches de dehors	*Ande'to'raka*
[outside poles]	petites perches qui se mettent sur les escorces en voute pour les faire joindre
	[small poles that are placed on the sheets of bark on the vault in order to join them] (FHO)

The following entry, from another dictionary, stresses this function of holding the roofing bark together:

petites perches p[ou]r tenir les escorces   *ₗande'to'rak.*
[small poles for holding the sheets of bark] (FH1697:234)

The construction of this term is instructive. It appears to be made up of the noun root -nde't- 'pine' (FH1697:233) and the verb root -ora- 'to attach, haft' (e.g., an axe or an arrowhead) (Potier 1920:426). The combined meaning could be 'pine that attaches, hafts.'

-st- 'bark'

The word for the bark covering a longhouse was just the generic term for bark—the noun root -st- (Potier 1920:453):

les escorces	*ₗAsta, ₗask8ata, Arak8at aionastonti*
[the barks]	*ce que xxxx les escorces pour couvrir la cab[ane]*
	Ab. *ₗAstontion*
	[that which xxxx the bark for covering the house] (FHO)

The verb in *ₗAstontion* is -ontion- 'to continue' (Potier 1920:424).

The two Huron nouns following -st- are the terms for cedar and elm respectively (Potier 1920:453 and 452). This suggests that they were the two kinds of bark used most often in the making of Huron longhouses in the early contact period. The *Jesuit Relations* reported that cedar was considered the best covering (JR8:105;13:45; and 14:43).

The process of preparing the bark for the roof seems to have involved heating, probably steaming or boiling the sheets to make them pliable. Consider the following reference in Potier:

sestanda8ant   amollis cette ecorce dans l'eau
              [soften this bark in water] (Potier 1920:277)

The verb root used with *-st-* here is *-nda8a-* 'to warm, to be warm' (277). The literal meaning of the combination would be 'warm this bark.'

-ronk8- 'smoke hole'

There are a number of references in the standard ethnohistorical literature to 'smoke holes' in the roofs of Huron longhouses (Champlain 1929:124, Sagard 1939, and JR8:107). The Huron term for a smoke hole is the noun *-ronk8-* (Potier 1920:453), possibly derived (with the addition of the instrumental suffix *-k8-*) from the verb root *-ron-* 'to pierce, be pierced, opened' (Potier 1920:349).

In the FHO, we have the following taken from a very blurred entry:

trou   xxxx*ronk8aharent* ...

        ndio tsironk8are8ha
        fermez le trou de la ...
        [shut the hole of the ...]

    tsironk8are8haska
        xxxx le cheminee
        [xxxx the chimney] (FHO)

The first Huron word in this entry has *-ronk8-* incorporated in the verb *-haren-* 'to have holes, openings' (Potier 1920:259). The next two words containing *-ronk8-* have the verb *-re8h-* 'to darken, have darkness' (342). The following two entries from Potier offer a better picture of this combination:

ɩaronk8arehi ...   fermer le trou de la cheminee
              [to close the (smoke) hole of the chimney]

tseronk8are8ha   ferme le trou de la cheminee
              [close the (smoke) hole of the chimney] (Potier 1920:342)

The next entry adds the suffix that has the effect of "undoing" the semantic content of the verb, so instead of referring to closing the hole, the reference is to opening it:

ɩare8haska8an ...   ouvrir, donner ouverture a q.c. qui faisoit jour par
              q. ouverture
              [to open, create an opening in something that lets
              in the light of day by some opening]

oronk8are8haska8an   ouvrir le trou de la cheminee (on oter l'ombre)
              [to open the smoke hole, (to remove the shade)]

tsironk8are8haska   ouvre le trou de la cheminee
                           [open the smoke hole] (Potier 1920:342)

The Changing Face of Huron Material Culture: Beads and *Oh8ista*

The French fur trade brought with it a tremendous change in the material culture of the Huron. Novelties such as glass and metal items became highly desirable. The people extended the meaning of an old word, *-8hist-* to refer to a range of objects made from these materials. We will turn to *-8hist-* in a moment, but first let us examine the topic of beads. Shells and shell beads were tremendously valued items in traditional Huron culture. Too often this has been perceived as a sign of their primitiveness. The principles by which they came to be valued are the same ones that made items such as gold and diamonds expensive in Europe; primarily, if something is difficult to come by, it is expensive. This follows the logic of the Huron verb root *-ndoron-*, which, you may remember means both means 'to be difficult (e.g. to obtain)' and 'to be valuable' (Potier 1920:295).

Beads

The significance of beads in Iroquoian culture cannot be overestimated. As wampum belts, they were tokens and documents of peace (e.g., between Aboriginal nations and between Aboriginal and European nations). As necklaces and bracelets, they were valued jewellery. While good work has been done by archaeologists on the subject of the beads used by Ontario Iroquoians, linguistics has contributed little to the subject. The only important study in this regard is Gunther Michelson's "Iroquoian Terms for Wampum" (1991). He identified three categories and twelve roots and stems of significance. The third category, "descriptive terms for specific wampum belts or wampum strings" will not be presented here as it has no parallels in Huron, but the first two bear fruitful discussion.

Category A: "terms which could mean nothing but wampum"

-nkorh- or *-nko?r-*[10]

This form is shared by the Iroquois languages of Mohawk, Oneida, Onondaga, Cayuga, and Seneca, and also by the Susquehannock, who spoke a related Northern Iroquoian language (Michelson 1991:109; see also Michelson and Doxtator 2002:1257 for Oneida and Woodbury 2003:807 for Onondaga).[11]

*-nōkwir-

This form was used in Mohawk, Tuscarora, and in St. Lawrence Iroquoian (Michelson 1991:109).

*-nōkhwarot- or -nōkhwarōt-

Michelson only finds this in Huron (Michelson 1991:110), but I would argue that it also occurred in Tuscarora, as -θkwaruT- 'bead'[12] (Rudes 1987:263). Michelson found the term in Sagard and Potier. I can add information from the dictionary sources I have, in which it takes two forms, -nnonk8arot- (FH0159 and FH67:160) and -nnonk8ar8t- (FH1693:285, FH1697:153, and Potier 1920:451, reflecting the Cord and Wyandot dialects respectively).

One of the most interesting uses of this word in Huron relates to political dealings:

il porte dedans son sein la porcel. des iroquois, p[ou]r n[ou]s trahir
[he carries inside his robe the wampum of the Iroquois, for betraying us]

onnonk8ar8ta ihondet d'hotinnonchiondi hoti8en
[wampum, he bears it (secretly) in his robe, that which belongs to the Iroquois] (FH1693:285)

The wampum does not even have to be mentioned for the notion of betrayal to be expressed, as can be seen in the following:

N. son₁8aarenh8a.

[N. bears our bag, sack]	N. nous trahit pprie porter a nos Ennemis le sac de porcelaine [N. betrays us, properly, to bear to our enemies the bag of porcelain.] (FH1697:212)

atrih8andet (etre porteur d'affaires secrettes p[otier]) avoir dans son sein q. collier, q present d'affaire … [(to be a bearer of secret affairs, Potier) to have in one's robe some necklace, some political present]

*otrih8andet	il tient dans son sein, un collier d'affaires [he bears in his robe a political necklace]
(Potier 1920:287)	
oki itsondiak onnonk8ar8ta	*vous estimez extraordinairement la porcelaine [You esteem or value porcelain extraordinarily] (Potier 1920:167)

Unfortunately, it is difficult to know where the betrayal theme comes from originally. Did it come from the Huron, the French Jesuits, or from their shared discussions?

*-ęrhar-
This comes from Jesuit Father Jacques Bruyas's 1670s Mohawk dictionary, where it means "canons de porcelaine' [shell tubes] (Michelson 1991:110).

*-nyo?ask-
This is the Huron term for 'white wampum.' Michelson cites Potier, but it is also included in other Wendat language sources:

ondioaskon	Porcelaine blanche (HF62:68; c.f. HF65:109)
onnonk8ar8ta ondih8askon	Porcel. Blanche (FH1693:285)
ondih8askon	Porcelaine ... blanche (FH1697:153)
ιandioaskon	porcelaine blanche (Potier 1920:449)

There is an interesting contrast between the presentation of this colour of wampum with one word, with the two-word phrase used to signify dark wampum. The one presentation of the word for dark wampum that I have found is:

onnonk8ar8ta ιatsihenstatsi	Porcel. noire (FH1693:285; c.f. FH1697:153)

The word for 'noire' used here is 'it is called charcoal,' the term used to refer to anything black. It was the primary term of reference to the Jesuits, because of their black robes. Since there is no special term for this dark wampum, can we conclude that dark wampum was newer to the culture, something considered other than the ordinary? Or is it better to say that dark was the default colour, so needed no special term?

-swęht-
This is a term used by the Onondaga and the Seneca to refer to 'wampum belts' (Michelson 1991:110). Following Rudes, Michelson suggests that this term came from Algonquian (114), coming from the same source as the word *Sewant*, used in colonial writings in New York to refer to wampum.

-yōw-
This is one of two Mohawks term for wampum belt (110).

-yōni-

This is the other Mohawk term for wampum belt (Michelson 1991:110).

There are Huron terms related to wampum not found in other Iroquoian languages:

-enst- 'beads'

The noun that gave generic reference to beads was -enst-. The following are typical dictionary entries, presented in chronological order:

Canons de porcelaine.	*Einsta*
[tubes of porcelain] (Sagard 1866)	
canon ... de pierre ...	*ensθa*
[tube ... of stone] (FH1697:30)	
canon de porcelaine.	*ensta*
3 canons de porc.	*achink i8ensta ennensta*
[three stems of porcelain]	[three, such a number of beads, they (are) beads] (FH1693:285)
ensta	Canon de pierre, tuyau, ce qu'e(?) creux
Taₗenston	donne moy un canon de porcelaine &
(FH67:38)	

ensta ... canon de porcelaine ou de verre
[tube of porcelain or of glass] (Potier 1920:454)

Two points can be made from these entries. First, the French word 'canon' suggests a tubular shape for these beads, and possibly a historical priority for that shape (i.e., the term represents the first used shape of shell beads). Second, the different materials cited point to the general applicability of the term. Interestingly, none of the modern Northern Iroquoian dictionaries contain readily perceived cognates.

In an entry concerning money, the related noun root -ents- was used twice for two different values:

20 S[ou]. *tso8insat*	[it is one -ents-]
40 S. *Skarentsat*	[it is one -rents-, see discussion below]
4 francs *skandeh8at*	[it is one beaver pelt][13]
un ecu. *achink i8entsaₗe*	[it numberes three -ents-] (FH1697:123)

-re'ns-

In the Wendat language, a string of beads worn around the neck is named with the noun root -re'ns-, a term also referring to a bowstring. This can be seen in the following entries, presented in a rough chronological order:

Corde, ligne [cord, line]	ɩAre'nsa
Collier … ɩare'nsa [necklace or cord] (FH62)	collier ou corde
ɩaren'sa	Corde de rassade ou de porcelaine, chapellet [cord of glassware or of porcelain, string of beads]
taren'saon	donne moy un chapellet [give me a string of beads]
chrensenh8a?	porte tu ton chapellet [are you carrying/wearing your string of beads?]
horen'ske'te	il porte un chapelet ou un collier au col [he is wearing a string of beads or a necklace on the neck]
sarenske'tat	porte ce collier [wear this necklace]
ahonarenske'taska	on luy a enleve son collier [they removed his necklace] (HF65:160)
Corde … ɩarensa	corde d'un arc, ou du chapellet [cord of a bow, or of the chaplet, rosary or string of beads] (FH67)
grain. ɩarensa [grain, bean]	item une file de grains & [also, a row of grains etc]

donne moi des grains p[ou]r me faite un chapelet
[give to me the grains for me to make a necklace of beads]

tannont o{ɩ}a'k8enda d'a{ɩ}atrensonnia
[give it to me, an eye, that which made a string] (FH1693:168; see also 57)

ɩarensa … corde … corde d'arc & … branche de porcelaine, de & … [cord … bowstring … 'branch' of porcelain] (Potier 1920:452)

It seems to refer in the traditional Huron context to a bead necklace whose primary use was for show, as an ornament:

Collier d'usage. ɩacharo. [customary or usually used necklace]	de parade, ɩarensa [for show] (FH1697:37; see also 41, 87 and 153)

ɩarenske'te … porter un collier d'ornement ou un chapelet [to bear an ornamental collar or a chaplet or rosary] (Potier 1920:250)

It should come as no surprise that it came to be used to refer to a rosary, as in the following expressions relating to counting or saying one's rosary:

ₗarensañienton[14]   dire son chapelet, le parcourir grain à grain
                [to say one's rosary, to go over it grain by grain]

chapelet   ₗarensa   le dire ₗarensotrah8i[15]
[rosary]   [to say it] (Potier 1920:25 and FH67)

*Ta8atrendaenhas de sk8arenserrak 8arie orensa 8en eetsiatrendaenhas
d'en8anensotrak endi*
[Put -ren- for us, when you say your string of Mary's beads. We will put -ren-
for you when we go from one end to the other of our strings]

Priez pour nous quand vous direz vos chapelet, nouns prierõs pour vous,
disans les nostres
[Pray for us when you say your rosary; we will pray for you when we say ours]
(JR41:166 and 172)

-char-

Another necklace was called *-char-* (FH62, FH67:48, FH1697:37 and Potier
1920:446). We have seen it above as the everyday necklace "d'usage" rather
than the more showy ₗarensa "de parade." This one has a cognate in Oneida,
-stal- (see Michelson and Doxtator 2002:669).

Category B: "terms that were used as a designation for wampum but whose basic meaning refers to something other than wampum"

Michelson identifies two noun roots and one verb stem in this category:

-nahs-

This refers to a string of wampum in Mohawk, Onondaga, and Cayuga.
Michelson discusses its primary meaning as follows:

> One root is *-nahs-* 'a strand or string of strung-up objects, including quills'
> (Woodbury, personal communication). Hewitt, in his discussion of terms for
> 'wampum,' listed the form *Kaná's* as 'a braid or plated object' (Hodge
> 1910:908). (Michelson 1991:111)

There is no cognate in Huron.

-rõkwahs-

The noun root here is referred to as 'wampum belt, string of wampum and
chain' in various Mohawk sources. Michelson emphasizes 'chain' as the
primary meaning (1991:112). While no Huron cognate relates to wampum,
there is the noun root *-ron(8)achi-* that refers to a braid or sheaf (Potier
1920:453), which could be a cognate.

*-hnitshe:ts-
This is found in Tuscarora and, according to Rudes (in a personal communication to Michelson), "may originally have had the meaning 'long-hipped' or 'long-kneed.'" There is no apparent Huron cognate.

Bead Names Based on Other Names

- ₁a'k8enda- **glass beads**

The following passage is often quoted in the literature on the Huron. It is the best known metaphor for a glass bead in the Huron language and is taken from a discussion of Huron dream or vision guessing, in which people guess what object someone saw in a dream, and then give it to that person:

> "What I ask for is seen in my eyes—it will be marked with various colours" and because the same Huron word that signifies 'eye' also signifies 'glass bead,' this is a clue to divine what he desires—namely, some kind of beads of this material, and of different colours ... (JR17:189)

The shared noun root was -₁ak8end-, meaning 'eye.' The following are typical dictionary entries, again in chronological order:

Rassade. *Acoinna*
Les yeux. *Acoina, Acoinda*. (Sagard 1866)

Rassade
o₁a'k8enda   2ae [second or consonant stem conjugation]
ondaie d'(a₁a)tsichatsi   [it is called 'red']
ondaie d'otsingoratsi   [it is called 'blue, green'] (FHO)

grain de rassade. *o₁ak8enda* (FH1697:87)

oeil ... *o₁ak8enda* (FH1697:133)

o₁ak8enda ... oeil ... rassade. (Potier 1920:446)

₁annontatsi **'it is called leg'**

The term *₁annontatsi* appears in the following dictionary entries:

Canons de verre.   *Annontatse*.
[tubes of glass]   [it is called leg]

Pour mettre, pour serrer des   *Anontatsehoirhousta*,[16] *Outerousta*
canons (se sont des longues
patrinotres a se parer)
[for making, for clasping the tubes
(they are for adorning long 'our
fathers' (rosaries)] (Sagard 1866)

Canon ... de pierre ...   *annontatsi*
[stem of stone]   [it is called leg] (FH1697:30)

The verb root used here is *-as-* 'to name, be called' (Potier 1920:208). We saw it earlier in identifying similarities for colour terms (e.g., *atsihenstatsi* 'it is called charcoal' for the colour black (FH1697:239)). It probably performs a similar function performed here, referring to the shape rather than the colour.

While the noun root is clearly *-nnont-*, a little difficulty stems from the fact that two different nouns take that form, and either meaning would work—'leg' and 'the pit or stone of a fruit.' As the beads are 'longue,' and as body-part analogies were common in bead names, 'leg' seems the most likely.

Bead Shapes

Sagard's phrasebook contains two terms for beads that appear in no other source. Perhaps he was recording Huron at a productive time for naming, with the new glass beads coming in from the trade:

Canons grands & gros de pourceleine.   *Ondosa*
[large and wide tubes of porcelain] (Sagard 1866)

The noun root most likely related to this is the noun root *-nd8ts-* or *-ndots-*'ear of corn' (Potier 1920:450). Sagard does write this as *-ndotsa-* elsewhere (Sagard 1866), so it might seem odd that he would present it as *-ondosa-* here, but his work is littered with examples of using *-s-* where the Jesuits used *-ts-*, so it is worth considering that it might be the same word.

The other term found only in Sagard's dictionary appears in the following entry:

Canons gros & quarrez que les filles mettent deuant elles.   *Scouta.*
[wide and (?) tubes that girls put in front of themselves] (Sagard 1866)

This is probably from the noun root *-skot-* 'head' (Potier 1920:453), which also appears in Sagard's dictionary as *scouta* (Sagard 1866).

Wendat Words and Pots

Given the archaeological interest in Huron pots, it is important to have a look at how the Wendat language was used in speaking of pots and pottery. According to Marianne Mithun's work on "The Proto-Iroquoians," the Wendat noun root for 'pot,' *-ndats-* is cognate with the Mohawk, Oneida, Onondaga, Cayuga, and Seneca word for 'pail' (Mithun 1984:277). This word seems generally to refer to 'vessels' in Northern Iroquoian languages; in the case of Onondaga and Oneida, this noun root also refers to pots and kettles (Woodbury 2003:1420). The Northern Iroquoian verb that refers to pots (Mithun 1984:276), which appears as *ú:ta*[17] in Mohawk, and *u:ták* in Oneida, could be cognate with the Huron verb root *-nnao-*, although I have never seen another example of an old form in Northern Iroquoian having a *-t-* in other languages, but an *-n-* in Wendat. That happens with Tuscarora, not Huron.

Terms for pots were used metaphorically concerning the Huron Feast of the Dead, as was recorded in the *Jesuit Relation* of 1636:

> This feast abounds in ceremonies, but you might say that the principal ceremony is that of the kettle; this latter overshadows all the rest, and the feast of the Dead is hardly mentioned, even in the most important Councils, except under the name of "the kettle" [i.e., chaudiere or pot]. They appropriate to it all the terms of cookery, so that, in speaking of hastening or of putting off the feast of the Dead, they will speak of scattering or of stirring up the fire beneath the kettle; and employing this way of speaking, one who should say "the kettle is overturned," would mean that there would be no feast of the Dead. (JR10:279)

Unfortunately, I can find no references to such metaphors using the noun root *-ndats-* in the Jesuit missionary dictionaries; instead the terms that I have found are quite concrete and pedestrian. They refer to such things as pots being big (Potier 1920:161), broken (231), loaded (251), enlarged (253), covered (301), suspended (307), under (332), broken (337), too small (354), poured into or out of (365), and thin (365).

The only useful Jesuit source concerning pot metaphors comes from Potier, when he was recording Wyandot figures of speech during the mideighteenth century. Unfortunately, these were written only in French, not in Wendat. What it does demonstrate is a close connection between war and pots:

Mettre La Chaudiere sur le feu	[to put the pot in the fire]
... declarer La guerre	[to declare war]
Suspendre La Chaudiere sur Le feu	[to suspend the pot over the fire]
... declarer La guerre	[to declare war]
Renverser La chaudiere	[to turn over the pot]
... cesser Les hostilités	[to cease the hostilities]
(Toupin 1996:283)	
Proposer une Chaudiere	[to propose a pot]
... c'est proposer une entreprise militaire	[to propose a military enterprise]

Mettre à La chaudiere	[to put in the pot]
... c'est bruler un hom[me]	[to burn a man]
faire Chaudiere	[to make a pot]
... c'est vivre ensemble de bonne [union]	[to live together in good union]
Tirer un hom: de La Chaudiere	[to take a man from the pot]
... c'est lui donn[r] la vie	[to give him his life]
Rompre La Chaudiere	[to break the pot]
... c'est se brouiller tout à fait	[to quarrel] (Toupin 1996:286)

The New 08hista

Europeans brought to the New World a good number of items of material culture that the Huron had not seen before. Even the substances these items were made of were new. With the exception of unsmelted copper, metal was unknown to the Huron prior to contact. Glass, the material from which the most-desired beads were made, was a mystery. What did the Huron think of metal and glass, and of the artifacts made from these foreign materials? Looking at the application of the noun root -8hist- can give a partial answer to these questions.

-8hist- before Contact

What did the noun root -8hist- mean prior to contact? One traditional use of -8hist- referred to fish scales.

Escailles [fish scales]. *Ohuista*. (Sagard 1866)

Ecaille de poisson. *08hista*. (FH1697:59; c.f. HF59:128, HF62, HF65:140, FH67:86, and Potier 1920:452)

The following are two typical dictionary entries using the noun root with this meaning:

ho8istore[18]
il est couvert d'ecailles [he is covered with scales] (HF62; c.f. FH67:86 and Potier 1920:431)

sek8istenk[19]
ecale le poisson [scale the fish] (Potier 1920:431)

Another meaning that seems to have existed prior to contact is the hard shell or hull of a kernel of flint corn:

o8hista	... ecorce de ble d'inde [bark or shell of corn]

(Potier 1920:452; c.f. FH1697:23)

Bled ... dinde ... l'ecorce	*o8hista.*
le casser entre 2 pierres [to break between two stones]	*kah8istia,i*[20] [to break with two -*8hist*-]
Bled ramoli d[e] l'eau p[ou]r f[air]e du pain [corn softened by water in order to make bread]	*o8histanda8an*[21] [it is warmed -*8hist*-]

(FH1697:23)

We can see from dictionary entries such as the following that -*8hist*- was used to refer generally to metal:

O8hista ... tout sorte de metaux [all kinds of metals]
(FH1697:15; c.f. FHO, HF59, HF65, FH67:97, and Potier 1920:452)

The noun root -*8hist*- was most often used to refer to iron, the metal that the seventeenth-century French imported to New France in the greatest amounts. When -*8hist*- was used to translate the word 'iron,' it was not qualified or additionally described by being incorporated into a descriptive verb. This indicates that it was the basic, standard variety of -*8hist*-:

fer [iron] *o8hista* (FH1697:75; c.f. FHO, FH62 and FH67:97)

This can be contrasted with silver and gold, which the Huron encountered much less often, and which, when referred to, had the noun root incorporated into verbs that added description:

Monnoye [money] ... d'argent [of silver] *o8hista,enrat*, d'or [of gold]
O8histandoron (FH1697)

In the former case, we have the noun root incorporated in the verb -*,enrat*- 'to be white' (Potier 1920: 247). The same combination appears in Mohawk (Michelson 1973:58) and Oneida (Michelson and Doxtator 2002:636). In the latter case, the verb is -*ndoron*- 'to be valuable, difficult' (Potier 1920:295), which also appears in Mohawk (Michelson 1973:48), Oneida (Michelson and Doxtator 2002:636), Cayuga (Froman et al. 2002:138) and Onondaga (Woodbury 2003:1142). This was a term that also referred to any precious metal, or to money in general, as follows:

θo i8a d'ok8istandoron?	[There is how much valuable -*8hist*-?]
Combien y a t'il argent?	[How much money is there?]

(Potier 1920:161)

There are numerous references in the Huron dictionaries to metal-working, almost exclusively to working with iron. The following is a representative sample, taken from two dictionaries (FH1697: 75 and 79; Potier 1920:262, 290, and 347):

₎a8histae	forger
[to hit -8hist-]	[to forge, bear iron]
ha8histondiak	forgeron
[he makes -8hist-]	[blacksmith]
₎a8histannenaj	ferrer
[to attach -8hist-]	[to iron, add iron to]
₎a8histandie	fourbir du fer
[to rub -8hist-]	[to polish iron]
ote8hista8aχ8i	fer courbe
[it is bent -8hist-]	[curved iron]
₎a8histari₎i	etendre le fer·
[to press -8hist-]	to spread out, extend iron

Goldsmithing is given at least one reference. With the verb root -o'ka- 'to spread on or coat' (Potier 1920:406), we get combinations such as the following:

aha8istoka	[he has spread -8hist-]
il a dore cela	[he gilds that] (Potier 1920:406)

While the Huron referred to a number of metal objects as -8hist-, the one most often found in the dictionaries was 'bell.' This is not unique to Huron, as the noun root is also used that way in Onondaga (Woodbury 2003:1009). The following is a typical entry:

cloche sonner [bell to ring]
₎a8histontati (with -ontati- 'to swing'; see Potier 1920:423)
₎a8histoiannon (with -o(r)i- 'to move'; see Potier 1920:432)
clocher [steeple]
etio8histandiont [it is where the -8hist- is suspended]; (with -ndiont- 'to hang'; see Potier 1920:307) (FH1697:37)

The bell was said by the Huron to have a voice, as in the following:

a te 8a₎ek asken sk8a8eti atsatrendaendeska d'o8histato₎eti e8atatiahaj
je vous prie tous prier toutes les fois que la cloche sonnera
[Come, I ask of you, all pray every time the bell will ring] (Potier 1920:242)

The word o8histato₎eti uses the verb root -to₎e(n)- 'to be true, to know, or be certain' (Potier 1920:366) which came to be associated in Jesuit and

Huron thinking with the Christian notion of holiness. As we will see below, the combination could be used to refer to a sacred medal as well as the church bell.

Here is another example in which *-8hist-* is said to have a voice:

ska8endarati etie8histontaθa	ils sonnent la cloche d'une seule cote ... ils tintent
[it has a single voice when they swing the *-8hist-*] (Potier 1920:337)	[they ring the bell on one side ... they toll]

Another metal object sometimes referred to with *-8hist-* was a medal, as can be seen in the following entries:

aₗe8histaterendinnen[22]	J'avois oublie un medaille
[I would have forgotten my *-8hist-*] (Potier 1920:187)	[I would have forgotten a medal]
o8histatoₗe'ti	medaille
[it is 'true' *-8hist-*]	[medal]
o8histaₗaon[23]	medaille antique
[it is old *-8hist-*]	[old medal] (FH1697:117)

The noun root was also used to signify glass. This seems to have been only a limited use in the Huron dictionaries, however, confined to a few references to mirrors and windows (HF59 and HF65). The latter we can see in the following passage from the Huron writings of Jesuit Father Philippe Pierson, recorded sometime early in the 1670s. I have put the *-8hist-* words in bold:

*ₗannonskon achiatatia desa, ontaₗannonchiara'k8at de chie8enda; d' onn' achiak8endondat, aste ona'ti achie8ennonₗok, ta ti te stoncharaχend aₗarak8taha, te ₗannonchiaharen **o8hista etio8histarah8i**, stante orak8aes d'**o8hista**, ontaₗarak8innion ak8atiatonₗotak iθochien n'ondechon; de t'a8erhon ataₗatondechonₗotak iθochien n'ondechon; de t'a8erhon ataₗatondechonₗontak. stante oataechend etiondecha, chieₗannen ondechatentsi*

[When you speak in a house your voice penetrates through it. When you speak loudly your voice penetrates even though you do not. A sunray does not pierce the house **when glass is inserted**. The **glass** does not stop the sunray, even when it is not damaged. That is like a spirit entering the earth, wishing to penetrate the earth. It would not be stopped by the great thickness of the earth.] (Potier 1920:632)

Chapter Summary

I have made a number of suggestions as to the nature of Huron longhouses at the time of early contact. First of all, as a labour-saving device, the Huron may have transported parts of their houses, some of the big poles perhaps, when they moved location. Secondly, the "emptiness" or "fullness" of a longhouse, in terms of people or possessions, was a potential source of invidious comparison. Thirdly, the longhouses had vestibules, roofed structures either between two doors at the end, or just outside of a single door. The ends of a longhouse also could be closed in, and it appears that the end walls had at least one set of cross beams, from which the inside doors hung. Fourthly, the longhouses had platforms that were not necessarily on both sides, nor did they always extend the length of the building. These platforms could cross the width of the ends of the longhouse,. People kept utensils on these platforms, and at least occasionally put canopies overhead to provide space for other people on a second level.

Inside a longhouse, family household spaces may have been partitioned, possibly with dividers resembling Huron doors, creating something like stalls or stables. Further, a person's mat that served as a bed possibly acted to define symbolically that person's space, physically and socially, in the longhouse. The hearths used by the households were shared by at least two families.

The Huron had a number of different nouns for the poles used in the construction of the longhouse. The entries for these nouns give us a good idea of the structure of these buildings. One of the nouns, *-nda₁ar-*, was for vertical poles. Incorporated into one particular verb, it signified the supports that could have other poles (with another name) extended from them. Incorporated into another verb or by itself, the term refers to poles from which things were hung. Another noun for vertical poles, when incorporated into a particular verb, referred to curved rafters that formed a vaulted roof; when incorporated into another, it denoted bed poles.

Two different terms were used for longitudinal poles, one for those at the first level, and another for those at the second or third level. Another term applied to poles suspended from the centre of the longhouse, poles from which the Huron hung corn and other objects.

Three features of the roofs were discussed in the linguistic sources. Sticks on the outside of the roof were used for joining the sheets of roofing bark. These sticks appear to have been pine. The bark seems to have been primarily cedar and elm, and to have been heated in hot water or steam to be made pliable. Finally, there is mention of smoke holes that could be opened or closed.

Concerning beads, two of the Northern Iroquoian terms for wampum presented by Michelson, one for white and one primarily for dark found in the Wendat language. This plus the extensive unique vocabulary in Wendat suggests that much of their wampum-related cultural forms were developed after they split from the other Northern Iroquoian peoples and moved to southern Ontario.

The Jesuit missionary dictionaries turn out to be a bit of a disappointment concerning terms for pots. While we know from the *Jesuit Relations* that the metaphor of the pot was used extensively in talking about the Feast of the Dead, and we know from Potier's list in French that the pot was used metaphorically to talk about war, dictionary entries fail to reflect either of these two semantic areas.

Finally, in the noun root *-8hist-*, we see a term originally used to refer to hard objects, such as flint corn skin and fishscales, expanding to refer to iron, metal, and glass, which were new to the Huron at the time of contact, and objects made out of these materials.

Notes

1 Another building of significance, the sweatlodge, is discussed in chapter 9.
2 See, for example, www2.sfu.ca/archaeology/museum/danielle_longhouse/keepers/housing.html.
3 The *-ona-* is a Northern Bear form for the pronominal prefix meaning 'we.'
4 I cannot be sure of the "mist" here. The writing is severely blurred.
5 There were several dialect forms of this noun root: *-nnh8-*, *-ndh8-*, and *-n'th8-*.
6 The superscript -*'t*- is Potier's addition, reflecting his experience with the Wyandot dialect of Huron. The Wyandot noun root for door would be *-n'th8-*, with other dialects having *-nnh8-* and *-ndh8-*.
7 This word is so blurred that I cannot read it. This is true of the other passages marked with "xxxx."
8 The Onondaga cognate *-nakd-* has virtually the same meaning (Woodbury 2003:677).
9 The -*g*- here is a superscript entry by Potier in which he is adding what he heard from the Wyandot, instead of the -*d*- in the dictionary that he was copying.
10 The '*' here and elsewhere refers to the word being a hypothesized form.
11 It is also found in the early French–Huron–Onondaga dictionary as *otkora* (FHO:159).
12 The -*T*- here represents a phoneme in Tuscarora that can take sounds other than just -*t*-.
13 This noun root appears in Potier as "ₗandeh8a … peau de castor … de chat &" (449); also, we have "Peau … de castor, de chien & ₗandeh8a" (FH1697:142).
14 The -*ñ*- here represents a -*ny*- sound.
15 The verb root used here is -*otra*- 'to go over, traverse' (Potier 1920:435).
16 This is two words, the first being *Annontatse*. I have not yet translated the second word.
17 The colon here refers to the vowel being long.
18 This uses the verb root -*ore*- 'to cover, be covered' (Potier 1920:431).

19 This probably uses the verb root -en- 'to collect, gather' (Potier 1920:375).
20 This uses the verb root -ia_ι- 'to break, cut' (Potier 1920:263).
21 This uses the verb root -nda8a- 'to be warm' (Potier 1920:277).
22 This uses the verb -aterendi- 'to forget' (Potier 1920:187).
23 This uses -ιaon- 'to be old' (Potier 1920:235).

7 Huron Ceremonial Culture

In the *Jesuit Relation* of 1636, Father Jean de Brébeuf discusses the "festins" or ceremonies of the Huron. According to Brébeuf: "All their feasts ["festins"] may be reduced to four kinds. *Athataion* is the feast of farewells. *Enditeuhwa*, or thanksgiving or gratitude. *Atouront aochien* is a feast for singing, as well as for eating. *Awataerohi*, is the fourth kind, and is made for deliverance from a sickness thus named" (JR10:177–79).

In this first section of this chapter, we will investigate through translation something of the nature of these ceremonies. Brébeuf's list, of course, was not exhaustive. Four other ceremonies of great significance to the Huron need to be mentioned. It appears that Brébeuf was only mentioning in this list ceremonies that the Jesuits felt were relatively innocuous. The four significant ceremonies not included are ones that can readily be seen as posing a threat to the missionaries. One is the war ceremony mentioned in chapter 8 and referred to in the following quotation from Potier:

iihotrens ond8ta₁e'te
[he (habitually) benefits from invoking spiritual power in ceremony, one carries the war bundle]

il fait un festin de guerre, il leve du monde pour un part de guerre
[he held a war ceremony; he raised the country for a raid]

ondaie ihotren ond8ta₁e'te
[he, he benefits, has benefitted from invoking spiritual power in ceremony, one carries the war bundle] (Potier 1940:203)

c'est lui qui fait le festin (metap) q[u]i est le chef.
[it is he who holds the ceremony, (metaphorically) who is the chief]

Another centres around the key Iroquoian religious concept of *orenda*, which relates to medicine. This will be discussed in chapter 9 on medicine and disease. The third significant ceremony conspicuous by its absence from this list is the *endak8andet*, related to sex; the fourth is *onnonh8aroria*, which seems to have entailed a type of vision state connected mainly to the death song. They will be discussed below. First, we return to the ceremonies Brébeuf felt comfortable mentioning, beginning in alphabetic order with *Athataion*.

Athataion

The word is actually *Atsataion*. FHO presents the ceremony as follows:

> *Atsata₁ion* festin d'adieu, au depart v.g., allant au guerre, en traittexxxx[1] [ceremony of farewell, of departing; for example, going to war, to trade xxxx] (FHO; c.f. FH1697:237 and FH62)

The literal meaning of this name can be seen in the following:

> *atsatanion* ... prendre son repas [to have one's meal]
>
> *onn-ahatsatanion*   voila qui prends son repas (fait son dernier repas ...)
>   [behold, one who had his meal (makes his last meal)
> (Potier 1920:204; c.f. HF62:43, HF59:37 and HF65:45)

The last phrase captures the essence of the meaning and significance of the ceremony: i.e., that the meal one is having could be the last one together with family and friends. The noun root involved is the rarely used *-atsat-* 'meal' (HF62:93 and Potier 1920:446),[2] but the verb used is unclear. (One possibility is that it is *-on-* 'to arrive' (Potier 1920:314).) The key point here is that the ceremony is named after something that actually takes place, a kind of personal last supper. The people eat together before one, some, or all of them go off and engage in something dangerous. Goodbyes are said, as if the meal were the last shared with the community.

Atouront Aochien

The first word in this phrase is more accurately rendered as *atonront*. The printing error of *-u-* for *-n-* was not uncommon when recording words in Aboriginal languages, in this publication and in other volumes of the *Jesuit Relations*. (We will see this when we come to *Enditeuhwa* as well.) The meaning of *atonront* is given in the following entry from Potier's dictionary:

> *atonront* ... chanter en guerrier une chanson laquelle l'assemblee repond par les hen, hen, reiterer, et qui l'accordent en cadence

[to sing a war song, to which the assembly responds with a hen, hen, that is repeated and according to a particular cadence or rhythm] (Potier 1920:200; c.f. HF59:35 and HF65:40)

Earlier dictionaries support the notion that this singing related to warfare (FH1693:56, FH1697:32, and HF59:35) and that there was a hen, hen response (HF59:35 and HF65:40), although the passage from *Relation* presented at the beginning of the chapter (along with evidence relating this practice to the sweat lodge; see chapter 9) leads me to think that the verb *atonront* was not solely used to refer to warfare. Tooker notes that the Mohawk used a cognate of this term in the seventeenth and eighteenth century (1978:457, citing Bruyas 1863:40 and Lafitau 1724, 1:521, and 2:190), and the Seneca had a twentieth-century cognate in a verb meaning 'to sing a personal chant' (Tooker 1978:457).

It should be noted as well that the "hen, hen" response was not confined to songs of war, but was used in other socially important songs.[3] The expression for this response was *atonrichenti* containing the noun *-atonrich-* 'breath' and an as-yet-undetermined verb root. The following shows its use:

Atonrichenti   faire le he he he a celuy qui chant
                    [to make a "he, he" response to one who sings] (FHO)

A close association existed between song and ceremony, with a complex vocabulary to match. Before continuing with the analysis of this term, I will outline briefly some distinctions made in the language regarding song.

The Huron term for 'beginning a song' is a noun-and-verb combination *karih8ak8an*, which literally means 'to seize or grab a matter, affair.' Potier presented it as meaning 'to lift up one's voice or begin a song' (1920:272).

The verb *ₗaatsi* meant 'to sing,' seeming to have a social purpose such as for dancing or medicine, as follows:

Taₗ8asen d'aₗ8andra8a.   Chante nous un air a danse
[sing it for us, we dance]   [sing for us a song to dance to] (HF59:62)

taₗiasen   ... chante moy, pour moy dit un malade
[sing for me]   [sing to me, for me, says a sick person] (FHO)

Such a personal association existed between individuals and song that there was a verb form, *ₗaa8ist* which meant 'to imitate someone's song':

ₗAa8ist   ... imiter la chanson de q[uel'qu'un]
                 [to imitate the song of someone]

hetsa8ist   chante sa chanson
                 [sing his song!] (HF62)

Another verb shows how songs tended to be sacred. It specifies singing that was not used in ceremony: "*End8tsihati* ... chanter pour passer le tems [to sing to pass the time]" (Potier 1920:377). The necessity for having such a verb to talk about the unusual tells you what the usual practice was.

The second word in the name of this ceremony, *aochien* (Northern Bear dialect for *aₗochien*), means 'one holds, or they hold a ceremony' (Potier 1920:214), giving a combined meaning for the phrase of 'one is singing a song, one holds a ceremony.' The verb does not denote a war song. We reach this conclusion by a process of elimination. If the singing was generally religious, then the noun root *-rend-* would have been used, which referred to sacred songs, dances, prayers, ceremonies, and spells (see below). If the song were to benefit someone, such as a sick person, then the verb *-as-* would be used (see above).

Awataerohi

This one seems to have been a slightly inaccurately written Northern Bear dialect form for what should be *Ataₗaenraoh8i*. Elsewhere in the *Jesuit Relations*, it was written as *Aoutaerohi* (JR10:183 and 199; 13:189; and 14:59), *Outaerohi* (JR17:197), and, more accurately as *Aoutaenhrohi* (JR21:151). The following passage from the *Relation* of 1637 describes the nature of the ceremony:

> This feast is an *Aoutaerohi*, where we saw a real sabbat. The women sang and danced while the men struck violently against pieces of bark ... They took, to keep time as it were, burning embers and red-hot cinders in their bare hands, then passed their hands over the stomach of the patient—who, as part of the ceremony or for some other reason, tossed about like a maniac, incessantly shaking her head. The feast ended, she became very quiet. (JR13:189)

In one of the French–Huron dictionaries, we have the following entry:

Ataₗaenraoh8i   f[air]e une danse ou l'un mets des cendres chaud sur les malade
                  [to have a dance where one puts hot cinders on the sick]
(FH67)

Contained within this word is the noun root *-ₗenr-*, 'ashes, cinders' (Potier 1920:447). The verb it is incorporated into appears to be *-o-* 'to be in water, wet' (Potier 1920:401–3), giving the combination the meaning of 'putting ashes in or on something' (see the entry for *aₗenroh8indi* in Potier 1920:403).

It should be mentioned that ashes have a ceremonial significance in other Northern Iroquoian ceremonies. In the modern Midwinter Ceremony, as noted by Tooker in 1978 (1978:457–58), messengers are sent, at the beginning of the ceremony, to go through the longhouse stirring ashes with special paddles.

Enditeuhwa

All three ceremonies discussed so far refer to a concrete, physical act: having a meal, singing in refrain, and putting ashes on a person. We have could call this a 'grammar of ceremony names' that would be expected to apply to *enditeuhwa*.

First we need a more accurate rendering of the name for this ceremony. We get that, plus a context for the ceremony, in the following entry from FHO:

Enditen'h8aen	faire festin de remercier xxxx v.g. ho[mm]e nouvellement revenu des Ennemys [to hold a ceremony of thanks; xxxx for example, a man newly returned from the enemy] (FHO; c.f. FH1697:237, and FH62)

Contained within this word is the noun root -*ɩenten'h8*- 'the side of a human or animal' (Potier 1920:455). The following dictionary entry shows this and also contains an example of the use of this noun with the verb involved in the name of the ceremony:

gentenh8a[4].	Le coté [the side].
aɩitenh8aɩe	a mon coté [on my side]
Enditenh8aen.	se mettre sur le coté [to put oneself on one's side]
askati senditenh8aentak	mets toy sur l'autre coté [to put yourself on the other side] (HF59)

Added to the noun in the word for the ceremony is the semir-eflexive prefix -*end*- and the verb root -*en*- 'to put' (Potier 1920:219). Taken together, we get the meaning of 'to put oneself on one's side.'

It is highly likely that, as with the other three ceremonies, this refers to a specific action performed by one or more participants during the course of the ceremony. Being placed on one's side must have had symbolic significance in Huron culture. From an archaeological perspective, this might suggest that the act of burying people on their side, as opposed to their front or back, had meaning for the Huron. It might have been done to express some sort of symbolic message, probably relating to giving thanks.

Two Ceremonies Brébeuf Excluded

Enda'k8andet: Having "Ceremonial" Sex

One of the key ceremonies not included in the Jesuits' "sanitary" list was the *Enda'k8andet*, which involved young people in the community having sex. Typically, it is mentioned as part of someone's vision in terms of effecting a cure, as the last and the longest-lasting aspect of a general curing ceremony (JR17:147 and 179; 34:217). Trigger refers to it only occurring between single people (Trigger 1976:83), which may be true, but the Jesuits said that it involved "many fornications and adulteries" (JR17:179), which suggests that some married people may have participated. In none of the Huron dictionaries, however, is adultery mentioned in the meanings or connotations of the ceremony.

The word for the ceremony appears in the *Jesuit Relations* as *andac8ander* (JR17:146; the final *-r-* being a misprint), *Andac8andet* (JR17:178), and *Endak8andet* (JR34:216). The noun root involved, *-nda'k8-*, meant both 'sex' and 'marriage' (HF59:86, HF65:104, FH1697:98 and 115). The main two contexts in which the Jesuits used the former sense were in terms of this ceremony, and regarding being a virgin, e.g., *te ₍anda'k8ateri* e.g., 'she has not known, experienced sexual intercourse'(FH1697:223); with the verb *-(en)te-* 'to know, experience' (Potier 1920:225). In terms of marriage, with the verb *-i-* it meant 'to take or have as wife (FH1697:75 and HF59:86). In other Northern Iroquoian languages it seems to refer just to marriage and wife (Mohawk, Michelson 1973:76 and Cayuga 2002:193).

With the verb root *-ndet-* 'to envelop' (Potier 1920:287), the noun root only referred to sex outside of wedlock, typically translated using some form of the Latin *fornicari* (FH1697:79, FH62, HF65:104, FH67:101, and Potier 1920:287). (When the Jesuits thought a word was obscene, they translated it into Latin rather than French.)[5] This occurred with the translation of *-nnenh-*, 'corn,' as "semen huum [human semen]" (Potier 1920:450), *-nnhonchi-*, usually translated as 'egg,' as "testiculi [testicles]" (Potier 1920:450) and *-8innonch-*, usually translated as an adolescent girl, as "verenda mulieri [female external genitalia]" (Potier 1920:452). In the dictionaries, the ceremony name has a dative suffix, giving the sense of 'for' (someone) rather than with (someone)':

Enda'k8andetaiondi ... f[ai]r[e] festin d'imp[ureté] p[ou]r q[ue]lq[ue]
[to make a ceremony of impurity for someone]
(HF59:86; c.f. HF65:104)

| *ende'k8andetandi* | R. fornicari pro aliquo [to fornicate for someone] |
| *ta₁endak8andeten* | [have sex for me!] (Potier 1920:287) |

This last line would probably be uttered by the one who desires curing. Although he did not use the word, Récollet Brother Gabriel Sagard appears to have been writing about at least one form of *Enda'k8andet* in his *Long Journey to the Country of the Huron*. The more earthy Récollet appears to have been less afraid to talk about the particulars of the ceremony. His description seems to have made it a "ladies' choice" type of curing ceremony (at least when a woman was being cured), as in the following passage:

> In the Huron country there are also assemblies of all the girls in a town at a sick woman's couch, either at her request according to an imagination or dream she may have had, or by order of the Oki for her health and recovery. When the girls are thus assembled they are all asked, one after another, which of the young men of the town they would like to sleep with them the next night. Each names one, and these are immediately notified by the masters of the ceremony and all come in the evening to sleep with those who have chosen them, in the presence of the sick woman, from one end of the lodge to the other, and they pass the whole night thus, while the two chiefs at the two ends of the house sing and rattle their tortoise-shells from evening till the following morning, when the ceremony is concluded. (Sagard 1939:120)

Onnonh8aroria: The Death Song

The Huron word *onnonh8aroria* is made up of the noun root *-nnonh8ar-* 'head, brains' (Potier 1920:451) and *-o(r)i-* 'to move, disturb' (Potier 1920:432). Putting them together, we get a meaning something like 'it disturbs the brain, moves the brain.'

There are a good number of references to this term in the *Jesuit Relations*, referring to its presence as a Huron ceremony from 1636 to 1646 (JR10:175–77, and 183; 17:167–87; 20:29–31, 39, and 263; 23:53, and 103–5; and JR30:101), and at the Onondaga mission from 1656 to 1670 (JR 42:155–69 and 195–97; and 54:41). It is typically depicted as a wild affair in which people run around from house to house as if crazy, with other people guessing what it is that they or their familiar spirits desire. The following example will illustrate:

The *ononhara* is for the sake of mad persons, when someone says that they must go through the Cabins to tell what they have dreamed. Then, as soon as it is evening, a band of maniacs goes about among the Cabins and upsets everything; on the morrow they return, crying in a loud voice, "We have dreamed," without what. Those of the Cabin guess what it is, and present it to the band, who refuse nothing until the right thing is guessed. You see them come out with Hatchets, Kettles, Porcelain, and like presents hung around their necks, after their fashion. When they have found what they sought, they thank him who has given it to them; and, after having received further additions to this mysterious present—as some leather or a shoe-maker's awl, if it were a shoe—they go away in a body to the woods, and there outside the Village, cast out, they say, their madness; and the sick man beings to get better. (JR10:175–77)

The situation is different in the Huron dictionaries, although we do have matching references under the noun *onnonh8ara* 'head, brains' itself:

Onnonh8ara   superstition ou ils font les fous
                  [superstition in which they play the fool]
(HF62:82; c.f. HF59:118, HF65:130 and Potier 1920:451)

Further, another term refers specifically to the act of running from place to place in this way: *atrentinnon*. This is composed of the noun root *-rent-* 'leg' (HF59:140) and the verb root *-inde-* (as *innon* with the stative aspect) 'to drag, crawl' (Potier 1920:323), to give a meaning something like 'one drags one's leg.' The translations in the dictionaries are as follows:

atrentinnon   aller courant ca et la co[mm]e on fait en chantant la
                   chanson de mort *lonnonh8aroia*
                   [to go running here and there as one does in singing
                   the death song *onnonh8aroia*] (HF59:140)

atrentinnon   aller en courant ca et la comme on fait dans
                   l'*onnonh8aroia*.
                   [to go running here and there as one does in
                   onnonh8aroia] (HF65:160)

atrentinnon   ... courir d'un bord et d'un autre, de cabane en
                   cabane ...
                   [to run from one side to another, from house to house]

Chatrentindend   tu courrois de cabane en cabane
                   [you ran from house to house] (Potier 1920:323)

In the lead-in to the first two quotations, immediately after the repre-sentation of the noun *ₗarenta*, is written *inusit*,[6] a short form for the Latin term *inusitatus* 'unusual, strange, uncommon.' The usual noun root for leg is -nnont- (Potier 1920:451). The -rent- might relate to the calf of the leg (see chapter 8, the discussion of Huron armour), there being no other Huron term that does. So perhaps the running around somehow involved periodic dragging of the calf.

The first quotation above refers to the death song, which is significant because this is how onnonh8aroria is usually translated in the Huron dictionaries (HF62:82, FH1693:56, HF59:118, HF65:130, and FH67:42). A broader discussion is mentioned in the following three dictionary entries:

₁Annonh8arori	proprie du chant dont vn hoe chanter faisant xxxx, item faisant suerie, item un captif d(e) guerre cantus solitarius chant sans music
	[properly of the song of a man who sings while ... xxxx ... also while holding a sweat, also a prisoner of war singing alone, without music] (FHO)
₁annonh8arori ...	Chanter la chanson de mort, en branslant la tete et comme [courre] en chemin faisant
	[to sing the song of death, while shaking the head and while running on a path] (FH1697:33)
₁annonh8arori ...	chanter une chanson de suerie ... de voiage ... la chanson de mort
	[to sing a song of the sweat lodge ... of the voyage ... of death] (Potier 1920:432)

A good description of a death song comes from Luther Standing Bear, a Lakota man born in the mid-1860s. Referring to it as a "brave song," he wrote in 1933:

Sometimes during the night or stillness of day, a voice could be heard singing the brave song. This meant that sorrow was present—either a brave was going on the warpath and expected to die, or else a family was looking for the death of some member of it. The brave song was to fortify one to meet any ordeal bravely and to keep up faltering spirits. I remember, when we children were on our way to Carlisle School,[7] thinking that we were on our way to meet death at the hands of the white people, the older boys sang brave songs so that we would all meet death according to the code of the Lakota—fearlessly. Then when Buffalo Bill took a number of us to England, the ocean became very rough, and it being our first sea voyage we thought death was staring us in the face. The ship seemed very small and helpless in the middle of that vast expanse of tossing, tumbling waves, so when death seemed imminent we sang our brave songs and had anything happened we would have gone down singing. (Standing Bear 1978: 217–18)

Tooker reported in 1978 (457) that a cognate term survived in modern Mohawk (see also Michelson 1973:83), Onondaga, and Cayuga, referring to the important Midwinter Ceremony. Another recent Cayuga reference (Froman et al. 2002:630) also refers to it and mentions "dream guessing" as a traditional part of the ceremony.

Summary

We have seen in this chapter that the seventeenth-century Huron had a rich ceremonial culture, a culture that prominently featured songs. In his early discussion of Huron culture, Brébeuf mentioned four ceremonies, but did not refer to four other ceremonies, apparently those that he did not want to mention to the audience of the *Jesuit Relations,* people who supported the missionaries financially and politically. The two of these not featured in this chapter will be discussed in the chapters on war and medicine.

Notes

1 This signifies a blurred passage that I cannot read.
2 The rarity is indicated in the Potier entry by his use of the Latin short form "inus" after the noun.
3 In 1999, when the various remnant groups of the Huron (including me as a newly adopted Wyandot) got together to re-bury the ancestors from the 1636 Feast of the Dead, we chanted "hen hen" when the bodies were brought to the site of the re-burial.
4 The -g- that begins this word is usually represented as -ɩ-.
5 That the Jesuits used a Latin rather than a French word here to translate a word they considered 'sexual' or 'dirty' is not unusual.
6 Potier uses this as well in the dictionary entry for -rent- (Potier 1920:452).
7 The Carlisle School was an early residential school that had Aboriginal students from all over the United States.

8 Warfare

A linguistic analysis of Huron warfare can contribute to our understanding of the people. For example, certain objects provided rich sources of metaphor for speaking in council about war. In the chapter on material culture, for example, we saw various war-related terms using the noun root *-ndats-* 'pot.' The same is true for the number of metaphorical statements that included the words for 'axe' (the noun root *-ach-*, and the verb root *-ato₁en-*,'to be an axe' (Potier 1920:445). The noun *-acha-* was used with eleven different verbs in the fifty-three-page text *De Religione*, written by Jesuit Father Philippe Pierson in the early 1670s, making it one of the most productive nouns in that work. Later, Jesuit Father Pierre Potier recorded a long list of axe images of war, which I present here (the translation from French into English is my own):

LITERAL EXPRESSION	METAPHORICAL MEANING
to tie up the axe	to suspend warfare
to sharpen the axe	to wish to commence war
to throw the axe into the depths of the earth	to no longer listen to talk of war
to fish the axe out of the river	to recommence war
to take away the axe	to cause a cessation in the hostilities
to throw the axe to the sky	to cause open warfare
to drop the axe	to cause a cessation of arms
to retake the axe	to recommence war
to attach the axe to the door	to issue a challenge (Toupin 1996:284)

An important link between ethnolinguistics and other fields of study exists when the ethnolinguist gives meaning to physical objects, which a historian may read about in a recorded speech, or an archaeologist might uncover from the ground. Scholars can then be speaking the same language when they discuss the object in question.

The Huron Mat of War

In what follows, I want to establish that mats made from rushes, used to form war bundles or sacks of sacred items (which can be likened to portable altars), had connotations of warfare. This differed from when rush mats were called -ndât- and referred to an individual's mat used as a bed or resting place, and by extension one's place or spot in the longhouse (see chapter 6) and, more significantly, from rush mats called -ien(d)-, which referred to a mat as an image of peace (see below). I feel that this latter distinction between 'mats of war' and 'mats of peace' was part of the dualism of Huron thought (see chapter 1 regarding the dualic). More importantly, in terms of material that archaeologists are more likely to uncover, it is suggested that parts of ravens, especially their beaks, had war-related significance.

To discover the multiple meanings of these war bundles, we need to look at the use made of the word *ond8ta_ie'te*. Mention is made twice, plus once without the actual word (JR10:183), of a warrior spirit or 'god of war' called *Ondoutae(h)te*. In 1642, Father Jerome Lalemant wrote that:

> *Ondoutaehte*, whom they recognize as the God of War, often appears to them—but never without inspiring fright, for he is terrible. Sometimes he assumes the countenance of a man mad with rage; again, that of a woman whose features are only those of fury. (JR23:153)

Father Paul Ragueneau, writing in 1648, also uses this word in a discussion of how the Huron demonstrated some knowledge or a perception of the Christian God in some of their traditional beliefs:

> In war, and in the midst of their battles, they give him the name of *Ondoutaete* and believe that he alone awards the victory. (JR33:225)

The Huron dictionaries do not mention this word as being the name of a war god, but present it as relating to a person who holds a feast or ceremony of war, and who goes on to lead the subsequent war party (see entries for FHO "festin" and "guerre"; also FH62, FH65:43, FH1693:145, and FH1697:75). These entries typically employ the verb stem -atren- 'to invoke spiritual power in ceremony (see chapter 9). The following example from Potier's dictionary will illustrate:

ihotrens ond8ta₁e'te
[he (habitually) benefits from
invoking spiritual power in ceremony,
one carries the war bundle]

il fait un festin de guerre, il leve du
monde pour un part de guerre
[he held a war ceremony; he raised
the country for a raid]

ondaie ihotren ond8ta₁e'te
[he benefits, has benefitted from
invoking spiritual power in ceremony
one carries the war bundle]
(Potier 1940:203)

c'est lui qui fait le festin (metap)
q[u]i est le chef
[It is he who holds the ceremony,
(metaphorically), who is the chief],

References also exist to the war leader without specifically making the
connection with the ceremony. The earliest occurs in Sagard's dictionary:

capitaine pour le guerre. *Garihou doutagueta* (Sagard 1866, "armes")[1]

The word *Garihou* here comes from the noun root *-rih8-* 'matter, affair'
(Potier 19209:453). The combination of this noun and *ond8ta₁e'te* was used
in contrast to the name for 'peace chief' or civil leader, "*Garihou andionxra*"
(Sagard 1866 "armes" and 1939:149). The noun *andionxra* is derived from
the root *-nd₁ionr-* 'mind, thoughts' (Potier 1920:449).

It could be that the Huron were employing a simplified or pidgin Huron
when communicating first with Sagard (or whoever was the first to record
these terms). When terms for 'war leader' are presented in later dictionaries, this form is not found. Instead we find *-rih8-* incorporated into the
verb root *-ont-* 'to attach, be attached' (Potier 1920:418). Typical examples
are the following:

Capitaine … *hotrihonta'k8i n'ond8ta₁e'te*
[he has the matter attached to him, the one who carries the
mat]
il e[st] ch[ef] de guerre
[he is the war chief] (FH1697:30; c.f., FHO)

ennonchien ond8ta₁e'te esk8arihontak, ₁andi₁onra i8ochien ta₁8arihontak
[do not make it a matter attached to me, it carries the mat; make it a matter attached to me, the mind]
ne faites pas chef de guerre, mais seulement chef de conseil.
[do not make me the war chief, but only the council chief] (Potier 1920:420)

There is also a reference to the ceremony without a connection being
made to a war leader. It is somewhat hidden by the absence of the first syllable. The quotation is from the *Relation* of 1649, in the then largely Christian community of Ossossane:

Among others, there was a desire of a *Doutetha* Dance—to which the Magician, who had come from another village, wished to annex a feast of *Endakwandet*.[2] (JR34:217)

Two more uses of *ond8ta₁e'te* exist. They are for speaking of the ordinary warriors, and of war itself. An example of the former is the following:

ond8ta₁e'te soldat, guerrier [soldier, warrior] (HF59; c.f. HF65)

Frequently in the Huron dictionaries, the term signifies 'war' (Sagard 1866 "armes" (the word appears as "*Outtaguete*");" FHO, FH1693, FH1697:89, and JR64, facing page 58; and Steckley 2004:114, line 7).

I would argue that the main embodiment or personification of *ond8ta₁e'te* was the leader of the feast of war and subsequent raid, rather than any god or warrior. This interpretation sees warfare as a parallel sphere to civil affairs, in which people spoke of the leaders when they wished to refer to a particular Huron nation (JR10:231 and 257–59). The only evidence suggesting that my supposition is correct is relative prevalence in the Huron dictionaries. Of the nine Huron dictionaries used in my research, seven refer to the feast leader. Only two refer to ordinary warriors, and just one to a god of war (FH62).

The main term for 'warrior' appears to have been *oskenra₁e'te* (HF59, HF62:121, HF65:177, FH1693, FH1697:196, and Potier 1920: 251), which also appears in Mohawk (Michelson 1973:68). This involves the same verb root plus the noun root -*skenr*-,[3] translated by Potier as "guerre" (1920:453).

Further, I suspect that if the Huron believed in a spirit that was primarily responsible for victory or defeat in warfare, its name would have been something like *Airesk8i* (see *Aireskouy*, in JR33:225 in the Huron context), the name of an Iroquois spirit that had that responsibility (Goddard 1984).

The Literal Meaning of *ond8ta₁e'te*

So far we have just dealt with the contexts in which *ond8ta₁e'te* was used. We have not yet addressed the question of what the word literally meant. This is an important question, as Huron ceremonial names often related to physical actions or elements (e.g., 'having a meal' for the ceremony of farewell, and 'applying ashes' for a curing ceremony). It would be instructive, then, to check for a physical act or object to which *ond8ta₁e'te* might refer. This could enable us to gain some insight into what took place during the feast or ceremony of war.

The word *ond8ta₁e'te* has two main components: a noun root and a verb root. The latter is *-₁e'te-*, which the Jesuits translated as "porter q[uelque] c[hose]," meaning 'to bear or carry something' (Potier 1920:250). Cognates in other Northern Iroquoian languages are *-kehte-* in Mohawk, meaning 'to carry over the shoulder' (Michelson 1980:37), *-keht(e/u)-* in Oneida 'have a burden on one's back'(Michelson and Doxtator 2002:470) and *-gehd-* in Onondaga, meaning "carry on one's back; carry around the body" (Woodbury 2003:1032). The idea of it meaning 'to bear on one's shoulder, neck or back' suits the noun roots with which it was used: nouns for 'robe,' 'wampum necklace,' 'carrying bag,' 'shoulder strap,' 'load of wood,' and 'cradleboard' (Potier 1920:250).

The noun root in this word is *-nd8t-* or *-ndot-*. It has two kinds or levels of meaning, one as raw material, the other as a manufactured product. The first is presented in the following entry:

₁Andota.   le gros bout du jonc, de cane, de bled
                  [the large end of a rush, reed or cornplant]
(FHO; c.f., HF59, HF62, HF65, FH1697:103 and 129, and Potier 1920:450)

The second meaning, possibly derived from the first, meaning of a manufactured product is a 'mat:'

aienda   natte
                  [mat]

₁and8ta … st8tondiak   tu fais une natte
                        [you make a mat] (FH1697:129; c.f. FHO)

The fact that the same noun root referred to both rushes and mats is demonstrated in the following entry:

Ondota gros bout de jonc, canne ou natte [large end of rush, reed or a mat] (HF65; c.f., HF59)

The two terms for mat in the entry from the French–Huron dictionary both appear to refer to mats made out of rushes. We know that the noun root *-(h)i(h)end-* (realized as *-iend-* above) was associated with rushes from the information presented in entries such as the following:

Jonc a faire v.g., des nattes   *₁ahienda*
[rush for making, say, mats] (FH1693:190; c.f. FH1697:103)

What is the difference between the two terms? The difference essentially exists in the use and symbolic meaning of the two mats. The noun root *-(h)i(h)end-* refers to mats used for lying or sitting on. The symbolic meaning was of peace. Both of these points can be seen in this excerpt

from a discussion of the nine principal gifts presented by the family of a murderer to the family of the victim, all of the gifts being laden with heavy
symbolic meaning (see Steckley and Cummins 2001:229–30):

> [T]he ninth [gift] is, as it were, to place and stretch a mat for her [i.e., the
> mother of the victim], on which she may rest herself and sleep during the
> time of her mourning, *condayee onsa*[4] *hohiendaen*. (JR10:221)

The phrase at the end can be translated as 'This is the mat on which he
places her,' with the noun root for mat being *-(h)i(h)end-*. That this generally has a meaning of 'being at peace' (as opposed to 'being at war') is suggested by the meaning given to 'resting on a mat' by the Ottawa, who were
long term neighbours of the Huron, and then the Wyandot. Below is a speech
given by an Ottawa war leader, followed by an interpretation by Antoine de
la Mothe Cadillac, who had lived with these people from 1694 to 1698,
before both moved to the Detroit/Windsor area, along with the Wyandot:

> "My brothers, it is true that I am not a man; nevertheless, you know that I
> have already faced the foe. Our men have been killed. For a long time the
> bones of so-and-so, our brother, have rested in such-and-such a place. It is
> time that we should go and see them. Now you know that he was a brave
> man and worthy to be avenged. *We have rested in peace on our mat.* Today,
> I arise, for the spirit who rules me has promised me broth and fresh meat.
> Take courage,[5] young men, crop your hair, put on your war paint, fill your
> quivers and let us console our dead; let our war songs re-echo through the
> village, awaken our brother who was slain, he will be content when he had
> been avenged."
>
>   It should be observed that the Indians always call one another brothers
> or companions, and that, in this harangue, the term "broth" or "fresh meat"
> means killing men and capturing prisoners; "cropping the hair" means tak-
> ing off the garb of mourning; to "put on war paint" is to dress themselves
> up and adorn themselves; *to "rest on the mat" is to repose and live in peace*.
> (Kinietz 1965:252; emphasis mine)

Potier recorded the following Huron metaphorical expressions using the
French word "natte." in his mid-eighteenth-century recording of "Termes
et expressions des Sauvages." Unfortunately, he did not indicate which of
these expressions in their original Huron used *-(h)i(h)end-* and which
-ndât- (see chapter 6). I suspect that the former was used when the meaning of peace or peace-making was involved; the latter would be employed
when the sense of place was primary:

> arriver sur La natte de Q ... c'est arriver chez lui
> [to arrive on the mat of someone ... it is to arrive at someone's place]

Une natte teinte de sang ... c'est avoir eu des personnes tuées à la guerre
[a mat tainted with blood, that is (to say) to have had people killed in war]

Nettoyer une Natte teinte de Sang ... c'est appaiser La douleur que L'on a
des personnes tuées a la guerre
[to wash a mat tainted with blood, that is to say to soothe or appease the
pain of one who had people killed in war]

Preparer La natte pour Q. ... c'est etre pret de la recevoir chez soi
[to prepare the mat for someone ... it is to be ready to receive someone at
one's place]

fumer sur La natte ... c'est jouir d'une profonde paix
[to smoke on the mat ... that is to enjoy a profound peace]
(Toupin 1996:285)

garder Le Sac des Colliers sur La natte. .c'est attendre Le moment favor-
able pour deliberer d'affaires
[to keep the bag of (wampum) necklaces on the mat ... that is to wait for
a favourable moment for deliberating on matters] (286)

What, then, was the use to which the rush mat termed *-nd8t-/-ndot-* was
put? What was its symbolic significance? An important entry in Potier's
dictionary helps us:

ond8ta₍e'te   porte la natte de guerre (avec tous les manitous enveloppes
                dedans)
                [carrying the mat of war (with all the manitous enveloped
                inside)] (Potier 1920:251; see also 450)

By having a meaning of 'one carries the mat of war,' this entry shows a
distinction between mats of war and mats of peace, just as we saw distinctions between war chiefs and peace chiefs, war longhouses and peace longhouses, and a 'soul of war' (*eiachia*, 'heart' which involved courage, anger
and vengeance), and a 'soul of peace' (₍andi₍onra 'mind,' see chapter 1 on
the dualic).

The War Bundle among Other
Great Lakes Peoples

To the best of my knowledge, there is nothing in the ethnohistorical literature about the seventeenth-century Huron that would readily explain what
the mat of war could be and what the "manitous" they carried were. We
must search farther afield (but not too far) for such explanations among two
Algonquian-speaking peoples, the Miami and the Illinois, who lived not far

south of the Great Lakes. Writing about the Miami of the late seventeenth
and early eighteenth centuries, Kinietz gave this description:

> The war mats or bundles carried by the young men and in which they placed
> their tutelary birds were made by the women. They took round reeds which
> grew in the swamps, dyed them black, yellow, and red and made mats three
> feet long and two feet wide: they folded over one end for about a foot in
> the form of a comb case. (Kinietz 1965:177–78)

In a 1710 account that Kinietz attributes to Antoine Denis Raudot, we
learn how the Illinois used the contents of their mats or bundles of war.
Notice here the association of the mat with the leader of the war party,
and the role of bird manitous or spirit-empowered charms. First, Raudot
refers to the Illinois practice of raiding in parties of fifteen to twenty:

> To form these parties a war chief gives a feast in the month of February ...,
> and tells the warriors that since the time approaches to go to get men, they
> must render their duty to their birds in order that they will be favorable to
> them, for all those who go to war among the savages have, besides their man-
> ito, birds in which they have great confidence. They keep the skins of them
> in a sort of bundle made of reeds. The feast finished they go to fetch it,
> draw out of it their birds, spread them on a skin in the middle of the cabin,
> and sing all night apostrophizing them to the sound of the chichigoue [tur-
> tle shell rattle]. One, addressing himself to the crow, begs it to give him
> the same speed in pursuing the enemy as it has in flying, another speaking
> to the hawk asks for the same force against his enemies that it has in killing
> other birds,... At dawn they take back all their birds, and when the chief of
> the enterprise wishes to leave he holds a second feast and invites all those
> who brought their birds.

Then Raudot quotes the war leader's address to those who would go on the
raid with him:

> "The birds that we have prayed to have assured me of our victory, and their
> protection joined to your courage must make us dare all." *The leader car-
> ries the mat of war*..., in which all those who march place their birds, and a
> good supply of herbs and roots for dressing the wounded ...
>
> When they arrive near the place where they expect to find their ene-
> mies, the chief draws all the birds from his mat immediately, makes them
> a short prayer, and sends out his scouts. They then fall on the enemy, pur-
> sue them while imitating the cries of their birds, and try to take prisoners ...
> (Kinietz 1965:404–6; also see 197–99)

In sum, what we have here is a practice in which the rush mats are used
to hold bird charms. Men invited to a feast of war bring these charms or

amulets[6] to the ceremony and lay them out on their mats. The spirits of these birds are addressed at the feast in order to help bring the war party victory. When the war party embarks on the raid, the leader carries all the bird charms with him in his mat or bundle, to be addressed again when they are near the enemy.

How does this relate to Huron beliefs and practices connected with war? The purely linguistic evidence would appear to support the idea that the feast of war had at least one person, the leader, who had a mat or bundle in which he kept amulets giving access to spirit powers. The "grammar" or rules of ceremony names, as we have seen, suggests that carrying a mat was an integral part of the tradition of the feast. Such names contain reference to a key activity that takes place during the ceremony.

The Huron did have amulets to assist them with spirit power in various areas of life. The name given to them was *aask8andik* (JR17:149, *ascwandies;* 17:203, 207–11 and 215, *Ascwandics;* 21:135, *aaskwandiks;* 33:211–13, *Aaskouandy;* and 39:27, *Aaskuandi*). The term is composed of the verb *-8a-* 'to take' (Potier 1920:315), with a noun root *-at-* 'body' (which sometimes takes the form *-s-* or *-sk-*) (446). With the dative suffix, represented by *-ndi-* here, we have a meaning that Potier gives as "acheter q. person: ou q. animal [to buy some person or some animal] (316). This suggests that the amulets must be faunal. Examples given in Potier mention dogs and fish, but there is no reason to believe that it could not include birds as well.

Father Paul Ragueneau wrote of them in the following way in 1648:

> They believe that these Aaskouandy will make them luck in the chase, in fishing, in trade, or at place; and they say that some have a general virtue for all those things, but that the virtue of the others is limited to a certain thing, and does not extend to another; and that, to know what their virtue is—namely, in what they bring good fortune—one must be told of it in a dream.
>
> Now it is a quite common practice for those who have these Aaskouandy to give them a feast from time to time, as if, by giving a feast in honor of that familiar Demon, they make him more propitious to them. At other times, they will invoke him in their songs, and will beg friends also to join them, and to help them in those prayers. (JR33:213)

While warfare was not specifically mentioned here, I would argue that this does not preclude warfare as an area in which the *aask8andik* were significant. It would be inconsistent for them not to be. I suspect that the Jesuit missionaries who wrote about *aask8andik* were not as knowledgeable in Huron warfare practices as they were in other areas of Huron life. They did not travel with war parties, nor were they particularly welcome guests for much of the mission period at feasts of war. Throughout much of this time these ceremonies were expressions of Huron independence from the Jesuits. During the early years they provided a forum for venting anger at the association between the coming of the missionaries and the coming of diseases; in later years they served as a focus for traditionalists (see reference to the *Doutethy* dance earlier in the chapter).

Ravens and Huron War Bundles

Birds had spiritual significance to the Huron. They played a prominent role in dream visions and in providing *aask8andik* (see JR10:193 and 26:267, for example). Of particular importance were ravens. We see in the *Jesuit Relations* a number of references to "corbeau," a French term that is sometimes translated in the *Relations* as 'raven,' sometimes as 'crow'—both are valid translations in modern French. However, the Jesuits distinguished between "corbeau" meaning 'raven' and "corneille" meaning 'crow' in their Huron dictionaries (FH1697:232 and HF62). I believe that they probably would have done so as well in the *Relations*.

With this interpretation in place, we have the raven represented in the *Relations* as being significant both in visions (JR15:177, 17:153 and 33:193), and its beaks as an *aask8andik* (JR33:211–13 and 39:27). The Huron were not alone in placing importance on the raven. Their neighbours, the Ottawa, also did. Cadillac spoke of Ottawa war leaders having visions of ravens to help them in the feast of war and having raven symbols on their canoes while on a raid (Kinietz 1965:251 and 253). The reference to the crow in the Illinois passage above may have been a translation of "corbeau."

The Wyandot, who were a remnant group of the Petun and Huron, have similar stories. At the beginning of the twentieth century, Marius Barbeau recorded stories of historic warfare in which the Wyandot leader of a raid used the skin of a raven as a spiritual helper. The following is part of a story of a Wyandot raid on the Seneca:

> Then he made another small fire, and while throwing pinches of sacred tobacco on the red embers, he repeated his wishes for a great revenge. He now pulled out the dried skin of a kind of large crow, called *Ko͞rȨ' 'ko͞mȨ'* [a Wyandot version of the Huron word for raven], shook it, and threw it to the ground. The crow became alive and flew around several times. The chief said, "Uncle[7] *Ko͞rȨ' 'ko͞mȨ'*, it is now your turn to follow the trail!" And the crow flew ahead all the night long, croaking from time to time, so that the warriors might follow the right trail. The next morning they stopped

and ate a little. All through the day they followed the crow as they could
see it flying slightly above the ground. They soon became aware that they
were getting near the enemy, as the crow was now often seen flying back
and forth.

At night, they stopped, and the head-chief seized the crow and shook it.
It had now become a mere dried skin, to be put away. (Barbeau 1915:277)

The term used here is the Wyandot cognate for the Huron term for
raven (*onra'k8anne*, FH1697:232; c.f. FH62).

Huron Armour

Written evidence tells us that many Aboriginal peoples used wooden armour
during the period of first contact. This aspect of Aboriginal material culture soon disappeared after the arrival of guns and metal arrowheads, however, so good information about the nature of the armour is scarce. Scholars
of the Huron have traditionally been limited to two sources: a picture published with Champlain's writings, and the following passage from Sagard:

They wear a sort of armour and cuirass, which they call *Aquientor*, on their
back and legs and other parts of the body to get protection from arrow-
shots; for it is made proof against those sharp-pointed stones, yet not against
our Quebec iron heads when the arrows fitted with them are shot by a stout
and powerful arm, such as that of a savage. These cuirasses are made of
white rods cut to the same length and pressed against one another sewn and
interlaced with little cords, very tightly and neatly. Then (they have) a buck-
ler or shield and the ensign or flag, which is (at least those which I have seen
are) a round piece of tree-bark, with the armorial bearings of their town or
province painted upon it, and fastened to the end of a long stick, like a cav-
alry pennant. (Sagard 1939:154)

In the following discussion, I will augment these sources, filling out the
picture with material from several Huron dictionaries. The information
will come primarily from two lists of the names for the various pieces that
constituted Huron armour, one from FHO, and a later one from FH1697.

atient8r 'it covers with sticks'

To begin with, the term for armour that occurs in the passage from Sagard,
Aquientor, is a Southern Bear dialect word primarily made up of two main
parts. The noun root is *-ent-* 'sticks, poles, wood' (Potier 1920:446), and
the verb root is *-or-* 'to cover, be covered' (431; the *-8-* is also Southern
Bear dialect). Taken with the semi-reflexive prefix (which is the *-aqui-* in
Sagard, *-ati-* in the main dialect used in the Jesuit dictionaries), we get 'it

covers with sticks.' The most complete entry in any Huron dictionary presents the combination as follows:

> *atientori*   s'armer ou etre arme ... quasi dicas: se couvrir ou etre couverte de bois
> [to arm, or to be armed ... as if to say to cover oneself or be covered with wood] (Potier 1920:431)

It should be noted that this noun root has a double connection to warfare. The noun root *-ent-* appears in Potier with the translations of "baton, perche ... pieu ... buchette ... promesse ... parole [baton, pole, stake ... stick, promise, word]" (1920:446). Sticks were delivered to invite people to ceremonies, including those of war. The latter connection is seen in the following translation into French of the verb *ɩaentenhaon* 'to take, carry a stick': "porter la buchette, v.g., p[ou]r festin guerre [to carry the stick, for example for the war ceremony]" (FH1697:148).

onnonh8arocha 'head covering'

The first entry in both armour lists starts the armour at the top, with the helmet:

> le casque [the helmet] *onnonh8arocha* (FHO)

This word does not help us much as it was just the generic word for any covering of the head, derived from the noun root *-nnonh8ar-* 'head,' as seen in Potier's dictionary:

> *ɩannonh8ar8cha.*   chapeau, bonnet, tout ce qui couvre la tete.
> [hat, bonnet, all that which covers the head]
> (Potier 1920:451)

oɩachia 'chest'

The French term "le poitral," used to translate this Huron word, seems to be the term that is variously presented in armour-related literature, both in English and French, as "poitrail," "poitrel," and "peytral." It refers to the front armour of a horse, the part that hangs from the horse's neck and its withers. The noun root is typically translated in the Huron dictionaries as "poitrine," meaning 'chest' (FH1697:152, HF65:71, and Potier 1920:446). As we will see, naming a piece of armour after the part of the body protected is a common feature of these names. In the Champlain picture, this piece of armour is depicted as hanging from the shoulders and reading down to just past the hips.

asx8a 'trunk of the body'

The French term used in both dictionaries to translate this piece of armour is "le dossier" (FHO and FH1697:234). This is a little strange, as "la dossiere" was the usual French term for the backplate of a cuirass, while "le dossier" typically refers to the head of a bed or the back of a seat. Perhaps this is a descriptively accurate use of "le dossier," as in Champlain's picture the back piece looks something like the back of a high-backed chair.

The Huron term *asx8a* appears to be a slightly different form of a word that usually is written *ₗask8a* and is used to denote the trunk of the body, as can be seen from the following dictionary entry:

> *ₗask8a*   sein ... ventre ... coffre de l'a[nim]al
>   [bosom, breast, stomach, chest of an animal] (Potier 1920:453)

andie8ara 'attachable shield'

This term is a difficult one to work with. Although both lists have the word as "les fesses," meaning 'buttocks,' that is not a direct translation. In the dictionaries in which the noun root *-ndie8ar-* appears, it is translated either as "bouclier" meaning 'shield' (Potier 1920:449 and FH67) or as "cuirasse" meaning 'armour' (HF59:98). Other dictionaries have what appear to be other dialect forms, *-ndi8ar-* (HF62:70) and *-ndear-* (FH62 and FH1697:25) translated as "bouclier a l'algonquine," i.e., an Algonquin shield. In one source this is set in opposition to the "bouclier a la huronne," named *o[ₗ]are8a* (FH1697:25). Potier contains a contradiction to this; *oₗare8a* is presented as being an Algonquian shield (Potier 1920:447). I suspect that the messy nature of the evidence here reflects the decline in use of this object with the changes brought about by the use of metal arrowheads and guns. The dictionary writers of the late-seventeenth and eighteenth centuries probably hadn't seen one of these shields, making it easy for them to err when recording or copying the word.

We can look to an entry in the early FHO dictionary to discover something about this object:

> les fesses [the buttocks] *andie8ara*
> *ahotindie8arontonj ₗa8eti* (FHO)

The final phrase seems to me to employ the verb root *-ont-* 'to tie, be tied' (Potier 1920:422), giving a translation of 'they would all have their shields tied on.' Perhaps what we have here is a shield that could be attached to protect the buttocks.

andhe'ra 'thigh covers'

The French term for this piece of armour, "les cuissards," was used generally at the time to refer to armour that covered the thighs. The term, in
fact, is related to the French word for thighs, "les cuisses." This Huron
term seems to be a dialect version of the usual word for thighs, which was
ₗandhechia (FH1697:239 and FH62). There seem to have been two sections of this part of the armour. This is suggested by the use of the plural
in French, but is more clearly seen in the use of the dualic prefix -te- in the
following phrase in FHO:

> Les cuissards   *andhe'ra te hotindherontonj ₗa8eti*
>   [they all have two thigh-pieces tied to them] (FHO)

The two parts might be front and back. In the Champlain picture of
Huron armour, the part covering the thighs appears to be joined at the
side to form a kind of wooden skirt. However, the use of the dualic to refer
to actions done with two legs (e.g., *-aratati-* 'to run') (Potier 1920:171), and
-atrat- 'to jump'(202), makes it also possible that the two parts were distinct
pieces for each thigh.

atiocharonk8at 'it reaches the elbow'

The French term used to refer to this piece of armour is "les brassards."
This word is constructed similarly to the previous term, based on the name
for the body part being protected—in this case "le bras" [the arm]. The
French piece of armour usually referred to by this name typically was an
assemblage including one part for the upper arm, one for the elbow, and
another for the lower arm. This is quite different from what appears to
have been the case with the Huron nearest equivalent.

The Huron word appears to contain some form of the noun root for
elbow, *-iochi-* (FH1697:238) and the verb stem *-ron-* 'to be at such a distance'
(Potier 1920:329). The combined meaning could be 'it reaches the elbow.'
Again, in the Huron phrase found in FHO, we have the use of the dualic
prefix indicating "twoness."

> les brassards   *atiocharonk8at*
> *ₗa8eti tehondatiocharonnion* [they all have it reaching their two elbows]
> (FHO)

Curiously, the Champlain picture shows no such pieces, just straps that
appear to connect the *ask8a* to the arms.

atrenchia 'calf of the leg'

The French term here is straightforward: "les jambes" [the legs]. The Huron
word is more difficult. It could be a dialect form (with the semi-reflexive

prefix *-at-*) of the noun root *-rent-* 'leg' (HF62, HF65:160, HF59:140 and Potier 1920:452). This is not the usual word for leg; the dictionaries mark it as "inusitatus" 'uncommon.' I suspect that it referred to the calf.

This object would seem to have been constructed of one piece, because it lacks the dualic:

hondatrenchiaronnion [they have it to the calves of their legs] (FHO)

Guns: Shooting the Tubes

The writings of both the first observers and the later scholars are often affected by an ethnocentric assumption that Aboriginal people were in awe of European culture and technology, with the result that an important part of the early contact story is often told misleadingly, or not told at all. What did the Huron first think of the guns of the French? The standard written sources are mute in addressing this question. A few basic clues come from linguistic material, such as the terms the Huron used for guns and for the shooting action of the guns.

The seventeenth-century French word for 'gun' was "fuzil" or "fusil," represented in Huron by the noun root *-honra8ent-* (Sagard 1866; FH67; FH1693:161; FH1697:15, 82 and 242; HF59:77; HF62:38; HF65:91; and Potier 1920:447). We can see that this term was developed early during the contact period as a first impression. It appeared as *Horahointa* in Sagard's phrasebook, which drew upon his 1623–24 experience, plus that of his predecessors in interacting with the Huron.

Prior to contact, the word had another meaning, which we can see in several dictionary entries that translate it as "tuyau"(HF59:77, HF62:38, and HF65:91), the modern French for 'tube' or 'pipe.' We can learn more about this meaning if we look to how this noun root is used when it refers to a tube. Derived from *-honra8ent-* is the term for a "plante nommée Angelique" (HF65:91): *etsohonra8ent8annen* (HF59:77, HF62:39 and HF65:91). This is likely the Angelica atropurpurea or masterwort, a tall plant with hollow, tube-like stalks. The Huron word can be analyzed as follows:

etsohonra8ent8annen

-ets-	repetitive prefix, in this context meaning 'very'
-o-	'it'
-honra8ent-	'tube'
-8annen-	augmentative suffix, 'large' or 'great' (see Potier 1920:254)

This would give us the meaning of 'very large tube or tubing.'

To discern further the pre-contact meaning of the word one can look for cognates in Huron and related Northern Iroquoian languages. The

Jesuits believed, and I concur, that cognate with -honra8ent- was the shorter
-honr-:

> Fusil à tirer [gun for shooting]
> ohonra8enta ... ab [from] ₁ahonra plume [feather] (FH62)
> ₁ahonra plume, gosier, artere [feather, throat or gullet, artery] hinc [from
> this source]
> ohonra8enta, tuyau, fuzil. (HF59:77, c.f., HF65:91)

Here are the cognates in related Northern Iroquoian languages for the
shorter term:

Mohawk	-hur-	(Michelson 1973:57)
Oneida	-hul-	(Michelson and Doxtator 2002:410)
Onondaga	-hsʉR-	(Woodbury 2003:560)
Cayuga	-(h)o'd(a)-	(Froman et al. 2003:470)

None of these languages uses this shorter term for feather. And Tuscarora, also a Northern Iroquoian language, but one that was separated
from the others at the time of contact (the people not joining the Confederacy until the early eighteenth century), took a different route.

The exact process of derivation here is unclear, because -8ent- does not
have a particular meaning or grammatical function that can be readily dis-
cerned. It could be that the term was borrowed from another Northern
Iroquoian language, possibly with the verb root -ot- 'to stand.' The root is
-8t- in Huron (Potier 1920:437). In Mohawk and Oneida this 'standing
tube' meaning seems possible, with the Mohawk -huro?t- 'tube' (Michelson
1973:57) and the Oneida -?whalot- 'to be hollow' (Michelson and Doxtator 2002:877). The latter authors posit this type of translation for Oneida.
In Cayuga, there is -(h)owe'eḋ(a) meaning 'tube, cylinder, hose' (Froman
et al. 2003:348), which bears a distinct resemblance to the Huron term for
tube. The derivation there is again unclear.

Summary

I am suggesting that the Huron had a war bundle that held physical objects
or amulets that gave access to spiritual power, first in a feast of war, and
later in a raid. Prominent among these objects were the beaks, skins, and
possibly other parts of ravens. The beak might have been thought to give
direction in a raid, as the noun root for beak, -nnionchi-, also referred to
the prow of a canoe (Potier 1920:451).

What are the implications here for archaeologists? Huron councils of
war were held in the house of a war chief (JR13:59). So it is possible that

such a house might be identified by the presence of a mat or mats containing parts of a raven. Likewise, someone buried with raven remains might be identified as a war leader.

A cautionary word: We have seen in this section, and in the discussion of -*ndât*- in the longhouse section, that a single physical object can be "multi-vocal"—it can have strands of meaning that diverge depending on a non-physical context.

In looking at the terms for the different pieces that made up the traditional wooden armour of the Huron, we have seen that most of the terms are slightly unusual forms, ones not generally seen in the Jesuit Huron dictionaries. This has two possible explanations. One is that the dialect in which the terms were recorded was not the dialect of later dictionaries. In not having the -*y*- phoneme, they follow the Northern Bear dialect, so that is a possibility. The other explanation may be linked. With the disappearance of Huron armour, the terms dropped out of common conversation, taking on a life only in the list of words, possibly compiled in the 1630s when the Northern Bear dialect was used by the Jesuits, and just copied from dictionary to dictionary.

Finally, we have looked at the term used for 'gun' in the Wendat language. Rather than the 'thunder stick' of 1950s cowboy and Indian movies (with which the author is very familiar), which depicts Aboriginal awe at the technology of the European, we find a more purely descriptive term, connecting a gun to other long tubular objects, such as feathers and plants.

Notes

1 This conflicts with his calling them "ordinary warriors" in his *Long Journey* (Sagard 1939:149). I believe that in the latter case he made an error. As the words involved are probably in the Rock dialect (as we have seen in the chapter on Huron nations, it was unusual for the Southern Bear words to begin with -*g*-), I suspect that this error occurred because Sagard copied incorrectly what had been written by someone more familiar with the Rock nation.

2 This is the ceremonial sex event described in the previous chapter.

3 This noun root only appears with this verb, and its precise meaning is not known.

4 I believe that the repetitive here, indicated by the -*s*-, has the symbolic meaning of restoration rather than the literal meaning of repetition. A number of other gifts have this form as well.

5 The expression 'take courage' is another expression shared by the Wyandot and the Ottawa.

6 I prefer the word "amulet" to "charm," as the latter has diminished in the English language from something that related to the spiritual, to a mere piece of jewellery.

7 The raven here was being addressed as mother's brother or teacher.

9 Medicine and Disease

Among the hardest words to translate from Aboriginal languages into English are the words for 'medicine.' The Huron were great believers in the idea that dreams and visions could provide important information, communicated by spirits with whom they had close relationships. This extended into their conceptualization of medicine. If a woman felt sick, a shaman would investigate the cause of the sickness in several ways, including her physical state, social relationships, and spiritual life. The shaman would ask the woman about her dreams, looking for messages from protective spirits. A spirit might be telling the woman that a particular dance should be held, or that she should be given a talisman or charm that had a particular appearance.

The Huron referred to the spirit and this communication as *on₁8ennonk8at*, meaning 'our medicine' (see Steckley 2004:33–36). When they spoke of a spiritual message, they would say *ondaie ihaton on₁8ennonk8at* 'that is what our medicine said' (JR10:141). When Jesuit missionaries wanted to translate the Christian concept of the single soul, they used the word *on₁8ennonk8at* (Steckley 2004:48–49, 60–63). Any knowledge of Huron medicine coming from the dictionaries written by the Jesuit missionaries could be partial (in both senses of the word), focused on the spirit aspects, seeing them as the competition, or even the enemy. Still, the linguistic exploration is worthwhile. The Jesuits were good scholars when it came to "knowing thy enemy."

The medicine section of this chapter is confined to two elements: *orenda* and the sweat lodge.

Orenda

Ever since Tuscarora scholar J.N.B. Hewitt's groundbreaking article "Orenda and a Definition of Religion" (1902) and continuing with his work at the Smithsonian, particularly his Bureau of American Ethnology reports *Iroquoian Cosmology*, parts one and two (1903 and 1928 respectively), the Iroquoian term *orenda*, named after its Huron form, has been part of the ethnographic and comparative religious literature relating to the Aboriginal people of North America. It is one, if somewhat a junior member, of the three most prominent terms in the literature: the Algonquian *manitou* and the Siouan *wakan* being the two others.

Hewitt wrote of *orenda* as follows:

> Orenda. The Iroquois name of the fictive force, principle, or magic power which was assumed ... to be inherent in every body and being of nature and in every personified attribute, property, or activity, belonging to each of these and conceived to be the active cause of force, or dynamic energy, involved in every operation or phenomenon of nature, in any manner affecting or controlling the welfare of man. This hypothetic principle was conceived to be immaterial, occult, impersonal, mysterious in mode of action, limited in function and efficiency, and not at all omnipotent, local and not omnipresent, and ever embodied or immanent in some object, although it was believed that it could be transferred, attracted, acquired, increased, suppressed, or enthralled by the orenda of occult ritualistic formulas endowed with more potency. (Hewitt 1928:608 n3)

John Napoleon Brinton Hewitt (1859–1937) was raised on the Tuscarora Indian Reservation by his mother, who was part Tuscarora, and his Scottish father, who had been adopted by the Tuscarora. He was brought up speaking English, and did not learn the Tuscarora language until he was eleven years old. When he was twenty-one, he got a summer job as an assistant for Erminnie A. Smith of the Bureau of American Ethnology (BAE). It turned out to be a long-term job as they worked collecting texts and building a Tuscarora–English dictionary for five years. When she died, he applied for and got a job that lasted the rest of his life. He engaged in some work looking for links between languages, but his most famous and influential publications are his piece on *orenda* and his collection of Iroquois tales.

Hewitt presented a series of ways in which the noun *orenda* was used, but he did not give the source of his examples. Like his contemporary Iroquoianist Marius Barbeau, his etymologies often appear to be more speculative than grounded in the knowledge of a native speaker or modern linguist. He did not place many of his statements in the context in which he heard or learned it. He often comes across as making "just so" statements. This would have been more legitimate had he been an elder, raised in traditional language and culture, but he was not, so his statements are somewhat limited in value. We need other contexts, other social locations, in order to obtain a culturally deep understanding of the *orenda* concept. The seventeenth- and eighteenth-century writings in and about the Huron language by the French Jesuit missionaries can help here. Of course, this source, too, has its failings, its subjective partiality, but it still can add meaningfully to our understanding of this concept.

French Jesuit Missionaries and Orenda

The French Jesuit missionaries set as one of their early goals, the learning of the Huron language. They particularly focused on religious terminology, as that told them what the competition was saying, and gave them the vocabulary necessary for their own religious discourse with the Huron and the Iroquois. The latter is potentially significant here as the Iroquoian religious context from which Hewitt obtained his information would have been influenced by generations of Jesuit–Iroquois dialogue first developed in the Huron context.

To investigate the entries that relate to *orenda*, I will focus primarily on two Huron forms, one a verb root appearing in the Jesuit writing as -*atren*-, the other a noun root, -*ren(d)*-. While I cannot say for certain that these terms shared a common origin in one particular root, I believe that at least by the seventeenth century these two forms were cognitively linked for the Huron. I will refer to them collectively as -*ren*-.

I believe the verb -*atren*- to contain a verb root -*ren*-, with the semireflexive prefix -*at*- added. The resulting verb stem has the subject placed in the patient position. I will be asserting that a reasonable translation for the combination is something like 'to ritually invoke (and be the recipient of) spiritual force or power.' Perhaps because of its relatively explicit, direct ceremonial connections, and perhaps in part because of European bias in favour of nouns, the Jesuits did not use this verb to translate Christian spiritual concepts. Rather, they used the noun root exclusively.

Holding Ceremonies

The verb was recorded in Jesuit dictionaries as meaning "faire festin [to hold a ceremony]" (Potier 1920:203). A typical entry is the following:

ihotrens	il a fait le festin
[he (habitually) benefits from invoking	[he held a ceremony]
spiritual power in ceremony] (HF62:43)	

The habitual aspect suffix is used in the Huron word. As we have seen (in chapter 1), this signifies something that is usual or repeated. The French translation differs in that it appears to refer to a one time occurrence.

When someone provided the gifts or supplies necessary for holding a ceremony, this was expressed with a verb form that added the causative and dative suffixes:

son₁8atrentandi	il nous a donne [dequoy faire festin]
[he makes it so that we can hold a	[he gives to us that which (is needed)
ceremony invoking spiritual power]	to hold a ceremony] (HF62:42)

When this combination is followed by *ond8ta₁e'te* 'one carries the bundle or mat of war,' which you will recall refers both to battle and to those who lead in battle (see chapter eight), we get a reference to a war ceremony in which someone tries to attract others to come on a raid with him. The war leader did this in part by laying out and addressing the mat or bundle in which he carried the sacred objects that help him defeat his enemy.

ihotrens ond8ta₁e'te	il fait un festin de guerre, il leve du
[he (habitually) benefits from	monde pour un part de guerre
invoking spiritual power in ceremony,	[he held a war ceremony; he
one carries the war bundle]	raised the country for a raid]
ondaie ihotren ond8ta₁e'te	c'est lui qui fait le festin (metap)
[He benefits, has benefitted from	q[u]i est le chef.
invoking spiritual power in ceremony,	[It is he who holds the ceremony,
one carries the war bundle]	(metaphorically), who is the chief]
(HF 62:42)	

The Medicine Dance Society

So we know that -ren- relates to invoking spirits and holding ceremonies. In this section I will establish that there is a strong association between -ren- and dance, particularly as used towards spiritual, socia,1 and medicinal ends. Understanding the nature of this connection is especially important in comparative studies, as it gives historical depth to what in some senses can be called a Huron version of the "Midewiwin" of their Ojibwa neighbours.[1] The range of meaning of the medicine dance society is most clearly demonstrated in the entry in Potier's dictionary. In his work with the Wyandot of the Detroit/Windsor area, he had not heard that use of the

verb himself, possibly because of the influence of his predecessors in opposing the society and its ceremonies, but he included what earlier Jesuits had
recorded:

> *atren* ... 1o d'etre d'une certain danse, d'un certain corps, societé, confrerie
> de danse, y etre incorporé, associé ... 2o etre participant de
> q[uelque] c[hose], y avoir part, etre de la parti, ligue, faction; etre
> consentant, d'intelligence, du nombre de la bande (non aud)
>
> [1: ... to be of a certain dance, of a body, society, brotherhood of
> dance, to be incorporated, associated with [such a society] 2: ... to
> be a participant in something, for there to be a share, to be a party,
> league, faction; to be consenting, to be colluding with, to be of the
> number of the band (not heard [by Potier])] (Potier 1920:203)

He was speaking of a group such as the one Brébeuf encountered in
1636, a medicine society of about eighty people, which very much resembled the Ojibwa Midewiwin, a society whose ceremonies prominently featured dance. It was also similar to the False Face Society of the Iroquois.[2]
The subject was introduced through a discussion of one who was sick and
who had experienced a dream of how to be rid of his sickness. In Brébeuf's
words:

> He dreamed ... that there was only one certain dance which would make
> him quite well. They call it *akhrendoiaen*, inasmuch as those who take part
> in this dance give poison to one another. (JR10:205)

The "poison" was apparently more symbolic than actual, although
Brébeuf accused them of occasionally using real poison (JR10:209). The
ceremony consisted of ritually

> killing one another here, they say, by charms which they throw at each
> other, and which are composed of Bears' claws, Wolves' teeth, Eagles'
> talons, certain stones, and Dogs' sinews. Having fallen under the charm
> and been wounded, blood pours from the mouth and nostrils, or it is sim-
> ulated by a red powder they take by stealth ... (JR10:209)

The members of the society were drawn from a number of neighbouring communities. Once they arrived just outside the host community, they
began to sing, with the people of the host community responding in song.
According to Brébeuf:

> From the evening of their arrival, they danced, in order to get an understand-
> ing of the disease; the sick man was in the middle of the Cabin, on a mat.
> The dance being ended, because he had fallen over backward and vom-
> ited, they declared him to belong entirely to the Brotherhood ... and came

to the remedy therefor which is usual in this disease ... It is the dance they call *Otakrendoiae*; the Brethren they call *Atirenda*. (JR10:207)

Sorcery

Two of the words mentioned above, *akhrendoiaen* and *otakrendoaie*, are derived from *-ren-*, with the noun root incorporated into the verb root *-o(r)i-* 'to move, disturb' (Potier 1920:432). The first one uses the reciprocal prefix, typically meaning 'each other.' The suffix is unclear. Both may come from the word represented in a dictionary as "*Atrendoïannon*, mov[ent] sortes [moving spells]" (FH1697:197). In FHO, the following combination of the noun root *-ren-* and the verb root *-o(r)i-* appears:

te ontatrendoiach	qui mouvent sortes, sort de danse
[they move or disturb *-ren-* with each other]	[that which moves spells, a kind of dance] (FHO; "danse")

The term *Atirenda* comes from a verb form not found in Potier, again pointing to a lapse in practice among the Wyandot owing to Jesuit missionary influence. It does, however, appear in a seventeenth century dictionary as follows:

Atrenda faire des sortileges [to make or cast spells] (HF65:43; c.f. HF59:139)

It is not clear whether this is a noun plus an unknown verb or a word derived in some way from the verb stem *-atren-*.

The translation of "un sorcier [a sorcerer]," "un devin [a diviner or soothsayer]" was often recorded when a particular form of the verb root *-ιonda-* 'to augment' (Potier 1920:254), (*-ι8annen-*, sometimes referred to in the literature as the 'augmentative'), was added to the noun *-ren-* (FH1697:54 and HF65:43). This form of the verb was most often used with respect to people to mean 'great, augmented' in a positive sense. This first occurred in Sagard's writing, when he claimed that this was the opinion that the Huron had of the Récollets, as opposed to the rest of the French. As recorded by Sagard, the Huron called them, "*Arondihuanne ... issa*, You are people who understand matters on high and spiritual" (Sagard 1939:138).[3]

While Sagard seemed flattered by this label, the Jesuits would have discouraged any connection between themselves and this name. Brébeuf identified early those bearing this name as being linked to the Devil. In 1635, he wrote:

[T]here are a large number of Doctors whom they call *Arendiouane*. These persons, in my opinion, are true Sorcerers, who have access to the Devil. There are some Soothsayers, whom they call also *Arendiouane* and who undertake to cause the rain to fall or to cease, and to predict future events. The Devil reveals to them some secrets, but with so much obscurity that one is unable to accuse them of falsehood ... (JR8:123–25)

Throughout the Jesuit mission to the Huron, there were frequent references to such sorcerers or diviners, showing a deep Jesuit concern with their satanic competitors (JR10:35, 37, 43, 185, 197, and 199; 13:187 and 241; 14:29 and 59; 15:137; and 33:221). It should not be surprising, then, that the word was not used in any of the Jesuit literature in the Wendat language to indicate anything Christian.

Other Meanings

The dictionaries appear to show another two uses of the verb root *-atren-*. I say "appear" because there is some possibility that this is simply another verb that sounded the same. I doubt it, but there is a possibility. Both uses could fit into the meaning range of the *-ren-* concept with not too great a stretch. One, is the sense of 'to profit' or 'gain from something,' apparently connecting such occurrences with spiritual power. The following is the entry from Potier's dictionary. It should be noted that he had not heard this term himself, perhaps because the missionaries before him had long opposed such connotations:

atren s[4]   ext profiter, tirer du profit, du gain, du fruit de l'utilité, de l'avantage de q[uelque]. c[hose]., y gagner, avoir sa part u profit (non aud: dic *atrondrak8i*)

[to profit, to draw some profit, some gain, some fruit, some utility, some advantage from something, to gain, to have some share of the profit (not hear, say *atrondrak8i*)][5]

taoten ichien aon₁atren?   que gagnerois-je à cela (valet)
[What would I *-ren-*?]   [What would I gain from that? (validated)][6]

taoten esatren?   qu'as tu gagné à cela?
[What will you *-ren-*?]   [What have you gained from that?]
(Potier 1920:203; c.f. HF62:42 and HF65:43)

The other potential use of *-atren-* is 'to blame falsely, for no apparent reason.' Again, it was something that Potier had not heard:

atren   R. s'en prendre à q. sans sujet, le maltraiter à tort lui faisant des querelles d'allemand, lui en vouloir mal a propos (non aud:)

[to blame someone without subject, to maltreat someone for a
wrong, a German quarrel [i.e., a groundless one], to bear a
grudge inappropriately (not heard)]

taoten aₗonatren?   pourquoi t'en voudrois-je, pourquoi m'en
[Why would I *-ren-* you?]   prendrois-je à toi?
                                       [Why would I wish to blame you?]

taot ichien aχeatren   pourquoi m'en prendrois-je à eux (valet)
[Why would I *-ren-* them?]   Why would I blame them? (validated)

asaₗotren d'echiaaha   il s'en est pris aux enfans, mal a propos,
[He *-ren*-ed them, children]   injustement
                                       [He blamed the children inappropriately,
                                       unjustly]

atiaondi ahaₗatren   en verité c'est sans sujet qu'il s'en est prit à
[completely, he *-ren*-ed one]   lui, qu'on l'a battu
                                       [in truth it is without subject, reason that he
                                       blames one, that one fights him]
(Potier 1920:203; c.f. HF62:42, HF65:43)

A possible connection between this latter meaning and *-atren-* in the spiritual sense is the fact that the noun root *-ren-*, when used with the verb
root *-8t-* 'to stand,' had the sense of wishing someone ill, as in the following:

Atrend8tandi   … souhaiter du mal a q
[to make *-ren-* stand for someone]   [to wish ill for someone]

oki onₗ8atrend8tandik   le demon nous souhaite du mal
[it is a spirit, it stands *-ren-* at us] [the demon wishes us ill]
(HF65:43; c.f. FH1693:200 and HF59:139)

Jesuit Christian Use of -ren-

In the Ledesma catechism, the product of his work with the Huron from
1626–28, Brébeuf used this combination with the intended meaning of 'to
bless, to be blessed, to consecrate,' as in the following (see also Brébeuf
1830:7:16–17 and 15:19–21), taken from his translation into Huron of the
Ave Maria:

Ahonakrendotas eoüa chioutonrraè ecochiatè
[They should stand *-ren-* to him, also, at your stomach, where the fruit is]

& benist est le fruict de vostre ventre IESVS
[and blessed is the fruit of your womb, JESUS]

A similar meaning, this time of the consecration of the body of Jesus, occurs elsewhere in the catechism:

akhrendotande ne aot orronè Aiesus Christ Onenguiaenchaens
[one is going to stand -*ren*- at the 'holy' body of Jesus Christ, He saves us][7]

consacre le precieux corps de nostre Sauueur
[consecrate the precious body of our Saviour] (Brébeuf 1830: 15:19–21)

It should not come as much of a surprise that after this catechism, this pattern was not used again by the Jesuits. Brébeuf must have learned about the demonic connotations of what he had said.

The Christian conceptual use to which the Jesuits put the noun -*ren*- was primarily to signify 'prayer,' perhaps at least in part reflecting the traditional association of the word with song in addition to dance (Barbeau 1960:106, HF65:43). The Jesuits seem to have been careful to narrow down the verbs with which the noun could be combined in order to portray a strictly Christian application of this potentially loaded term.

Thus, the only Christian combination you find is with the verb root -*en*- 'to put, place' (Potier 1920:219), referring to praying, sometimes to hoping for something (probably after praying). The following example of the former comes from the *Jesuit Relation* of 1654:

Ta8atrendaenhas de sk8arenserrak 8arie orensa 8en eetsiatrendaenhas d'en8anensotrak endi
[Put -*ren*- for us, when you say your string of Mary's beads. We will put -*ren*- for you when we go from one end to the other of our strings]

Priez pour nous quand vous direz vos chapelet, nouns prierōs pour vous, disans les nostres
[Pray for us when you say your rosary; we will pray for you when we say ours] (JR41:166 and 172)

The following example of the latter use comes from HF62:

Atrendaen ... esperer [to hope]

θo a₁atrendaen ti ka8end8ten d'ies8s d'ihatonk
[there I put my -*ren*-, his word is of such a nature, that which Jesus says]

mon esperance est de la parolle de I[esus] que dit
[my hope is of the word that Jesus says] (HF62:105)

Huron Sweat Lodges

In 1988, Rob MacDonald wrote a comprehensive article called "Ontario Iroquoian Sweat Lodges" (MacDonald 1988:17–26). He effectively drew together several varieties of information—archaeological, historical, and medical (concerning altered states of consciousness). In so doing, he presented a convincing case for his claim that archaeological researchers need to use a breadth of sources to come to terms with what he called "the symbolic and ideological components of culture" (1988:24). In what follows, linguistic material from the Huron language will be added in order to broaden further the base of our understanding of Ontario Iroquoian sweat lodges.

In the Huron dictionaries of the seventeenth and eighteenth centuries, there is a twofold division of terms applied to sweat lodges: (a) words based on the verb root *endeon*, referring to sacred or spiritual contexts; and (b) words not based on *endeon*, referring to more profane or non-spiritual contexts. This can be seen in the following entry:

Endeon	f[air]e suerie, avec ceremonie. [to have a sweat, with ceremony]
Endeondi ...	p[ou]r ou avec, ou a l'example de q[ue]lq[u'un] [for or with or for the example of someone]
Endeonsk8a	suerie, ecorce de suerie [sweat (lodge), bark of the sweat (lodge)]
aronton8an, Atiatarihati	f[air]e suerie sans superstition [to have a sweat without superstition]
Ha8endeonsk8a₁a8i [sweat lodge smells, tastes, feels good to him] (FH1697:201)	sueur, qui aime la suerie. [sweater, one who loves the sweat lodge]

Endeon: *The Sacred Sweat*

As we have seen in the example presented above, *endeon* is typically presented in the Huron dictionaries as meaning "f[air]e suerie, avec ceremonie" (FH1697:201; c.f. FHO and FH1693:353). It would appear to have had the same meaning in seventeenth-century Mohawk, because we find the cognate *Enneon* given in separate entries as meaning both "suer, faire suerie [to sweat, to make a sweat lodge, have a sweat]" and "faire festin [to have a feast, ceremony]" (Bruyas 1970:108).

The curative aspects of the sweat lodges were pointed out in at least one dictionary entry:

la suerie est un bon remede	[the sweat lodge is as good remedy]
atetsens d'aia,₁endeon	[it cures, when one would have a sweat]
(FH1693:353)	

In the same entry, we have reference to the sacred singing that went on in the sweat lodge, using the verb root *-atonront-* (Potier 1920:200), discussed in the chapter on Huron ceremonial culture:

je chantois a la suerie.	[I would chant, sing in the sweat lodge]
e8a₁atonrontak	[I would chant, sing in such a place]
(FH1693:353)	

Endeondi contains a dative suffix, adding the sense of 'for, against, pertaining to someone.' In the example given above, we have it referring to "p[ou]r ou avec, ou a l'example de q[ue]lq[u'un] [for or with or for the example of someone]." This gives us three meanings here, each with somewhat different connotations:

(a) 'for'–suggesting that a Huron shaman might try to have a curing vision for someone by having a session in a sweat lodge;

(b) 'with'–suggesting, as does the ethnohistorical literature (Sagard 1939:197–98), that people would have a sweat together;

(c) 'for the example of someone'–possibly meaning that some people might have functioned as teachers or role models whose methods or amount of use of the sweat lodge were thought to be exemplary.

The noun derived from *endeon* takes the unusual form of adding a *-sk8a-*, probably ancient in the language, as the Mohawk cognate does likewise (Bruyas 1970:108). *Endeonsk8a* has two translations in the Huron dictionaries:

(a) "suerie [sweat lodge]" (HF59:93, HF62, FH67:184, and FH1697:201); and

(b) "ecorce de suerie [bark of a sweat lodge]" or "ecorce a faire suerie [bark for making a sweat lodge]" (FH1697:201 and FH67:184, respectively).

The only verb that I have seen incorporating this noun is *-₁a8i-* 'to taste, smell or feel good' (Potier 1920:236). The combination is used to express two slightly different ideas, one of which is the following:

sueur, qui aime la suerie [sweater, one who likes or loves having a sweat]
ha8endeonsk8a₁a8i [he finds having a sweat good] (FH1697:201)

In another dictionary, we have an entry that informs us of sweat lodge specialists, possibly the teachers or role models mentioned above:

sueur de profession [sweater by profession]
a₁a8endeonsk8a₁a8i [one who finds having a sweat good] (FH1693:353)

₍Arontonta8an *and* Atiarihati:
The Profane Sweat

When sweat lodges are referred to using terms other than *endeon* and its derivatives, the reference is not spiritual. We see this with the following two entries for *₍arontonta8an:*

₍arontonta8an	f[air]e suerie sans superstition
	[to have a sweat without superstition]
(FH1697:201)	
₍Arontonta8an	la suerie sans festins ... pas ceremonie, n'y pas superstition
	[the sweat lodge or sweat without feasts ... no ceremony, no superstition] (FHO)

This word is derived from the incorporation of the noun root *-ront-* 'stone, stones' (Potier 1920:453) into the verb *-ont-*, meaning 'to be in fire' (421). With the suffix *-a8a-*, which typically reverses or undoes the meaning of the verb root, we have a combined meaning of 'stones taken out of a fire.' This would refer to the heat source for the sweat lodge. I do not believe that this sweat lodge is physically different from the spiritual sort; it is just that the lodge was being used in a different context, one that was non-spiritual. The ethnohistorical literature (Champlain 1929:153, Sagard 1939:197–98, JR13:203, 14:65 and 26:175–77 and 245) does not present any evidence that one kind of sweat lodge involved the use of hot stones, while another did not.

The Huron word *atiatarihati* likewise refers just to a physical action. The term is composed of the verb root *-atarih-* 'to be warm' (Potier 1920:181). With the semi-reflexive prefix *-ati-*, and the causative suffix *-t-*, we get the meaning of 'one heats oneself.'

Disease

When Europeans arrived, they brought diseases that Native peoples had never encountered before and thus had not developed immunities to. The last generation of scholarship has made a good start on understanding the physical impact of these new diseases, but we still know relatively little about how Natives perceived them. In what follows, it will be suggested from ethnolinguistic evidence how the Huron may have developed a theory of smallpox and of contagion generally.

Developing a Theory of Smallpox

Judging from entries in Jesuit Huron dictionaries, I hypothesize that there were two different ways in which the Huron dealt conceptually with diseases that manifested themselves on the skin. One was to perceive them as being affairs of the skin only, spread by physical contact, much like poison-ivy rashes. The other was to see them as coming from within, an outward manifestation of an inner, spiritually related cause, possibly related to the sweat lodge. I will argue that, while the former may have been the main means through which the Huron perceived skin diseases as being passed on, they felt that smallpox was communicated through the latter method.

Skin Conditions Brought on by Physical Contact

For skin conditions brought on by physical contact, the verb root used to represent the communicability of the disorder was -o'ka- 'to spread on or coat' (Potier 1920:406).[8] This verb root was translated by Potier in the following way:

> signat proprie appliquer des couleurs a q[uelque] c[hose], l'enduire, la peindre, la mattachier, l'enjoliver, l'embellir par q[uelle] sorte de peinture (metap.) communiquer q[uelle] bonne ou mauvaise qualite a q[uelqu']un.
>
> [literally meaning to apply colours to something, to coat it, to paint it, to apply beads to it, to ornament it, to embellish it with some kind of paint or colour (metaphorically) to communicate some good or bad quality to someone] (Potier 1920:496)

The verb root's sense of 'to spread' can be more clearly seen when the causative suffix -t- is added, and noun roots denoting places are incorporated, as in the following example using the noun stem -ondech- 'country' (Potier 1920:455):

> ondecha8eti tsatondecho'kaθa, ahenhaon iesus
> repandez vous dit jesus par toute la terre
> [spread yourselves, said Jesus, all over the earth] (Potier 1920:407)

Negative qualities other than diseases said to be spread in this way are expressed using the dative suffix. Such a form could relate to ruining someone's robe by tearing it or splashing something dirty on it (Potier 1920:407).

Two skin conditions were described in the dictionaries as being spread or communicated from one person to another using -o'ka-. One was designated using the noun root -nd8st-, usually translated as "galle" (HF59,

HF62, HF65, FH67:105, FH1693:162, and FH1697:83). This seventeenth-century French word was probably the modern French "gale," meaning 'scabies, mange, itch' (Dubois 1979:340). Most Huron dictionaries refer to -nd8st- being incorporated into the verb -o'ka- (FHO, HF59, HF62, HF65:113, FH67:105, and Potier 1920:407). The following are two illustrative examples:

eskend8sto'ka	tu m'infesteras de ta galle
	[You will infest me with your skin condition] (HF65:113)
askend8sto'ka	tu m'a communique la galle, tu m'en as infecte
	[You communicated to me your skin condition, you infected me with it.] (Potier 1920:407)

Another skin condition was represented by the noun stem -tsi8ent-. It appears to be derived from a verb root presented in some dictionaries as *ₜatsi8ach*, meaning "avoir gross verole [to have large pox]" (FHO and FH1697:245); elsewhere as *ₜatsi8en*, meaning "avoir la verole [to have pox]" (HF59 and Potier 1920:370); and as *ₜats8ens*, meaning "verolé [poxed]" (HF62:131 and HF65:190). When the suffix -t- is added to the verb root, we get a noun root given as meaning "la verole [the pox]" (FHO, HF59, HF62:131, HF65:196, and Potier 1920:454). I am not sure what kind of pox this referred to, but I have never seen it translated as "petite verole" or "la picote," two French terms for smallpox. Plus, as we will see shortly, there was another Huron term that received those translations. Incorporating -tsi8ent- into the verb -o'ka-, we get examples such as the following:

ₜatsi8entoka8i ...	communique, donner la verole aux autres
	[to communicate, give the pox to others]
*ahonatsi8entoka8i	on lui a communique la verole
	[they gave him the pox]
ontatetsi8ento'ka8i	ils se sont entrecommuniques la verole
	[they gave each other the pox]

(Potier 1920:370; c.f. FHO, HF59, HF62:1341, and HF65:196)

Smallpox

Also denoting a pox is a noun root, -ndiok8-, that seems not to have been incorporated into -o'ka-. This was the term for smallpox. While in a number of dictionary entries it is translated simply as "verole [pox]" (FHO, HF62:68, HF65:109, FH67, FH1693:162, and FH1697:221), the same sources use French terms that refer specifically to smallpox: "petite verole" (Potier 1920:374, 431, and 449; HF62 and HF65) and "la picote" (HF59,

FH1697:245 and Potier 1920:374 and 449). Further, in a story entitled "The Skunks and the Smallpox," recorded by Marius Barbeau from the Wyandot of the early twentieth century, the word for 'smallpox' was a Wyandot dialect form of -ndiok8- (Barbeau 1960:96).

This association with smallpox appears early in the contact period. Using linguistic material from his own stay with the Huron in 1623–24 (in addition to the work of his predecessors), Sagard records the following, under the heading of "Maux, maladies, douleurs":

> Petite verole. *Ondyoqua.* (Sagard 1866)

Several questions come to mind. Had the Huron experienced smallpox prior to the epidemic of 1633–34 (see Trigger 1986:230)? This entry would suggest that they had, even if only indirectly through the experiences of other peoples. Was -ndiok8- a term developed just to refer to the new disease, or did it have a traditional reference? It is never presented with any other apparent meaning in the dictionaries. At this point, I can only suggest that it was a new term, quite possibly derived from the verb root -ndio- 'to sprout' (Potier 1920: 292), a verb root that typically referred to corn growing. With the addition of the instrumental suffix -k8-, which was sometimes used to turn a verb root into a noun stem e.g., with -ıentio- 'to be a matrilineal clan' (Potier 1920: 391), and -r- 'sun to rise' (324 and 452), you would get a meaning such as 'that which sprouts.'

Whether or not -ndiok8- was a new term, it referred to something different from the other skin conditions discussed above. When the spread of smallpox was referred to, a different verb was used, as we can see in the following example. The verb appears in the second word in the sentence:

> *eronhiaıeronnon eonχiendeohas d'aıaonh8a eak8atis, a8eti*
> *d'aıondiıonr8annens*
> [the sky dwellers will spread to us their beautiful bodies and their developed minds]
>
> les bienheureux nous communiquerons leur beaute et leur sagesse
> [the blessed ones will communicate to us their beauty and their wisdom]
> (Potier 1920:373; c.f. HF65)

These are more spiritual qualities than those associated with -o'ka-. The noun root -ndiıonr- 'mind, thoughts,' appearing in the last Huron word in this sentence was the term used to refer to one of the souls of Huron belief (see Steckley 1978 and chapter 1). This spirituality is reinforced by the distinct possibility that the verb used in *eonχiendeohas* could be derived from the verb root *endeon* 'to hold a sweat lodge, have a sweat with ceremony' (see the discussion above). As we have seen, this verb refers to the spiritual or sacred context of the sweat lodge. The word *eonχiendeohas* would then be adding a causative suffix *-h8-* and a dative suffix *-nd-* to the verb, giving it the additional sense of 'to cause something for someone.' This would give the combined meaning of 'to have a spiritual sweat causing something for someone.'

What Huron theory of smallpox is suggested by this? I think we get a sense that the Huron thought of smallpox as being a communicable disease, but not communicable through normal physical contact like other, more customary diseases that manifested themselves as skin conditions. Rather, the Huron seem to be saying that people spread the disease through a kind of spiritual communication, such as might have come through sorcery. The Huron executed their own "sorcerers" if they were believed to have spread smallpox and other deadly new diseases (JR13:155–57, 14:37–39, and 15:53). Perhaps they felt these individuals had used sweat lodges to spread these maladies. During the 1630s, when the Huron were suffering most severely from the new contagions, the Huron several times conjectured that the French were the cause (see, for example JR14:9, 15:19–21, and 15:33–35). These notions related to the intrusion of disease through spiritual means, through images (JR15:19 and 35) or charms made from corpses (JR15:33). I suspect that even when the putative cause appears through modern Western eyes to involve external contact, such as with French pots (JR15:211) and a poisoned cloak (JR13:147), these still could have been thought of as spiritually internal means.

Clearly, more research is necessary before conclusive statements can be made. What I hope to have established is the notion that in order to understand truly the actions of the Huron when they were confronted with new diseases, one needs to look at their language of disease.

Men: Carriers of Contagion?

The tragedy of Europeans bringing contagious diseases that killed literally millions of Aboriginal people is well known to the people themselves, and to scholars (although it often comes as a surprise to my community-college students). One question that I have long wondered about is how the Huron would have interpreted this new and foreign form of disease and death. In what follows, using the words of the Huron as my guide, I will attempt to bring to light a part of that interpretation.

In Potier's Huron dictionary of the 1740s, an entry poses some interesting questions concerning the Huron's notions of the origin of contagious disease:

ₗ*annra* ... maladie contagiuse ... pudenda viri[9]
[contagious disease ... male genitals] (Potier 1920:451)

Supporting evidence for the existence of both meanings—contagious disease and male genitals—appears in other Huron dictionaries, as we shall see.

The noun root -*nnra*-, when it occurs with the masculine singular pronominal prefix -*ha*- is used to refer to a penis:

hannra member virile [male member] (HF65:133; c.f. HF59:121, HF62:84)

In one dictionary entry, a metaphorical term was used. Whether this was of Huron origin or was a Jesuit circumlocution is difficult to say:

virga [cane, rod, graft, branch or wand] *hannra* (FH62)

There are clear cognates in several Northern Iroquoian languages: -*nr(a)*- in Cayuga (Froman et al. 2002: 530) and -*htr*- in Tuscarora (Rudes 1987:162).[10]

The other meaning for the noun root -*nnra*- is found when the feminine pronominal prefix -ₗa- was used:

ₗ*annra*	maladie contagieuse [contagious disease]
(FHO; c.f. FH62)	
ₗ*annra*	maladie (HF65:133; c.f. HF59:121)
ₗ*annra*	... contagion (HF62:84)
ₗ*annra. ahannrenha8i*	il a apporte [he brought]
[he brings contagious disease]	(FH1697:40; c.f., FH67:52)

There are clear cognates in Mohawk and Oneida: -*nhr*- (Michelson 1973:81) and -*nhl*- (Michelson and Doxtator 2002:585), but these words do not refer to male genitals in any way.

This noun root is incorporated into several verbs, with the combined meaning referring to contagious disease. The one most commonly found in the Huron dictionaries comes in the form *onnratarion*. The earliest published example is found in Brébeuf's prayer recorded in the *Relation* of 1636:

que si la contagion nous attaque derechef, detourne-la aussi
[and if contagion attacks us again, turn it aside also]

din de ongnratarrie etsesonachien, serre8a itondi
[and if contagion, he will kill us again, act it against it too] (JR10:68–72)

There is not enough evidence to read too much into the use of the masculine form (-*sona*- 'he–us') with the verb -*chia*- 'to finish' (Potier 1920:211; in this context, 'to kill') concerning contagious disease. The expression for famine also used such a form. It is more likely that the masculine pronominal prefix appeared because attacking in such a way was considered a male than a female action. The word 'again' is probably used because an epidemic had already hit the Huron in 1634.

Several Huron dictionary entries use this word *onnratarion:*

n[ou]s sommes sujets a une infinite de malades
[we are subject to an infinite number of diseases]

Te 8arati de taot onₗ8aio'θa nondratarion
[it is uncountable, all of those things that kill us, contagion] (FH1693:207)

onₗ8andrataries noun avons la contagion [we have the contagion]
(HF65:133; c.f. HF62:84)

onnratarion toute maladie contagieuse [all contagious maladies]
(Potier 1920:452)

onndratarion maladie publiq. contagieuse [(publicly) contagious maladie]
(HF59:121)

ondratarion … hotinnrataries ils ont la maladie [they have the disease]
(FH67:52)

It is difficult to analyze this noun-plus-verb combination because the verb root it would seem to take, *-(a)tari-* does not appear elsewhere. The related languages of Onondaga and Cayuga may use their noun root for 'house' to create the term for disease. In Onondaga, for example we have the following:

-nųhsodaR-/-nųhsa?tshR-   n. sickness, epidemic, disease (Woodbury 2002:729)[11]

The Onondaga noun root for house is *-nųhs-* (Woodbury 2003:726), leaving a potential verb root of *-otar-*. More convincing is the Cayuga case:

-nōhsod(a)   sickness
-nōhsōdaiyō:?   sickness, illness, epidemic (Froman et al. 2002:529)

Froman gives the Cayuga word for house as *-nōhs(a)-*, saying that the latter term adds *-iyō-*, but giving no meaning for it (Froman et al. 2002:528). If we combine that with what is left over from the word for house, we have *-ōtaiyō-*, which is virtually identical to the unidentified Huron verb.

We know the noun root is *-nnr-* and that the aspect markers *-on-*, *-e-*, and *-es-* represent the dislocative suffix in the stative, purposive, and habitual aspects respectively. This indicates that motion or travelling is involved in the meaning of the verb. Another verb root *-enha8-* 'to take, bring' uses the dislocative when combining with *-nnr-:*

n. honnrenha8in deχa [N., he brought the disease here]
n. a apporte icy la maladie [N. brought the malady here] (FH67:52; also see HF65:133)

Apparently the Huron had the notion that a person could quite literally be a "carrier" of disease.

One other verb root was used with *-nnr-*, and that is *-a₁on-* 'to be old' (Potier 1920:235). Its use points to another nuance of *-nnr-:*

₁annra	Playe [sore or wound]
onnra₁aon	vielle playe [old sore or wound]
sannra₁ao[n[sennik	tu es malade d'une vielle playe [you are sick with an old sore or wound]

(FH67:156; see also FH62, FHO:156, and FH1697:149)

The Huron–French dictionaries tend to translate this combination as "maladie" (HF59:121, HF62:84, and HF65:133). Having "playe" and "maladie" referred to with the same noun root in this way suggest that the diseases referred to with *-nnr-* were ones in which sores developed.

Summary

Like the Huron themselves, their word *-ren-* is very familiar to scholars, often referred to in the ethnohistorical literature, usually as *orenda*. Again, this familiarity is deceptive. Tuscarora scholar J. N. B. Hewitt wrote about *orenda* early in the twentieth century, making it an often-repeated (but seldom contextualized) part of comparative religion. As far as I know, the only previous attempt to study the term with some sense of context is Wallace Chafe's "Linguistic Evidence for the Relative Age of Iroquois Religious Practices" (1964), and his purpose was more to engage in the historical linguistics of the Seneca than to set the term in a particular historical and cultural context. I hope that the discussion presented in this chapter, which outlines all the uses of the word in the seventeenth century (and later), will cause a rethinking of how this familiar term is used.

Sweat lodges are a familiar part of contemporary Aboriginal culture in Canada. It is important that we study their past. This chapter showed that sweat lodges could be either sacred or profane, and that a terminology existed to reflect this.

Concerning the Wendat terminology for contagious diseases, we have asked how it came to be that—uniquely among Iroquoian people—the

Huron apparently had the same noun root meaning 'penis' and 'contagious disease (with sores).' To me, this suggests that syphilis may have been the first contagious malady that the Huron encountered. French males would have introduced it to the Huron. Those coming over as carriers would have had old scars from the disease. The time period is certainly right. It was first written about in the mid-1490s, after the French army of Charles VIII took Naples (hence its early names as the French or Italian pox, or the disease of Naples). By the early 1500s it had spread throughout much of Europe, later hitting the Americas. The Huron referred to syphilis using a word that had spiritual as well as phallic connotations, suggesting that they thought of it as different in nature from other skin afflictions.

Notes

1 For a good overview of the Midewiwin, see *Preserving the Sacred: Historical Perspectives on the Ojibwa Midewiwin*, by Michael Angel (2002).
2 For a look at the nature of the False Face Society and other Iroquois medicine societies of the 1930s and 1940s, see Frank Speck's *Midwinter Rites of the Cayuga Long House*, 1995.
3 The word represented as *issa* is the second person ('you') particle pronoun.
4 The *s* is used here to indicate that the subject of the verb is represented by the patient. This letter is used as the second person singular forms typically begin with an *-s-*.
5 The verb root *-atrondrak8-* means 'to gain, profit' (Potier 1920:198).
6 This may just mean that he checked with someone whether this form was right, or whether the form was in fact used at Lorette.
7 This is a word that Brébeuf made up. He took a noun-plus-verb combination meaning 'to save' (lit. 'to get hand out'), added the nominalizer *-ch-* and then a verb, the meaning of which is not clear. He dropped this kind of linguistic concoction once he became more fluent in Huron.
8 The cognate in Cayuga is translated as 'coat, clean (something)' (Froman et al. 2002:537), while the Onondaga cognate is translated as 'spread on, coat' (Woodbury 2003:753).
9 As we have seen before (chapter 7), the Jesuits used a Latin rather than French word to translate a word they considered sexual or dirty.
10 It should be noted here that *-n-* in Huron and other Northern Iroquoian languages typically corresponds to *-t-* in Tuscarora.
11 The *-R-* here refers to an *-r-* phoneme that is realized in several forms.

10 The Jesuits and the Huron

What can the language tell us about the relationship between the Huron and the Jesuits? As we learned in the kinship chapter, the Huron would often address the Jesuits (and other Frenchmen) as 'my sister's son,' referring to the fact that there is a mentor–mentored, teacher–student, possibly patron–client relationship between mother's brothers and sister's sons, who always belonging to the same clan.

Unfortunately, we cannot learn much from the term that the Huron used to refer to the French. Récollet Brother Gabriel Sagard wrote in the 1630s that the Huron called the French "*Agnonha*, c'est-a-dire gens de fer, en leur langue [that is to say, the iron people, in their language]" (Sagard 1990:148). Unfortunately, Sagard was wrong. As we have seen in the material culture chapter, the Wendat word for iron came from the noun root *-8hist-*. The word that Sagard was trying to write out, recorded by the Jesuits as *ɿannionɿenhak* (Potier 1920:451) or *hatinnionɿenhak* (with the masculine plural agent; Toupin 1996:232), does not have this element in it. Now, while we can identify the *-hak-* as either an element that means 'people of' or as the habitual aspect plus past suffix, meaning 'used to' (as used in the name for the Cord nation), the rest of the word has defied my analysis. I suspect that it is a term borrowed from another Northern Iroquoian language, perhaps one of the languages or dialects of the St. Lawrence Iroquoians.

Huron Names for the Jesuits

Who Are These People Called Charcoal?

How did the Huron name the Jesuits? First off, they did not call the them 'Black Robe' exactly. They referred to the missionaries as *hatitsihenstaatsi* 'they are called charcoal.' Not surprisingly, this was the Huron term for 'black,' a good number of Huron colour terms being created with the verb root *-as-* 'to name, be called' (Potier 1920:208). In contrast, the Récollets were called *hochita₍on*, meaning 'he has bare feet' (see *achita*, the noun for feet, in Potier 1920:445, and the verb root *-a₍on-* 'to be pure, empty' (163)), based on their practice of wearing sandals.

More significant are the personal names that the Huron gave the Jesuits. Names were sacred to the Huron. The noun root *-chien-* meaning 'name' (446) was an important source of metaphor in their language. To 'put' (*-en-*) or 'make' (*-on(n/d)i-*) someone's name was to praise that person. The act of assigning a name to a new owner after the previous owner died was referred to as 'washing a name' (Potier 1920:404, with the verb root *-ohare-* 'to wash'), in part, no doubt, from the grave in which it had been buried.[1] French military officers were called *hochiend8annen* 'large name' (Toupin 1996:262 and 265).

It was important that names of the recently deceased, particularly those of leading figures were resuscitated or brought back to life (the latter a literal translation of the Huron verb form *onsa8-atonnhonti* (Potier 1920:415)) by an eligible candidate. The names and the individuals that held them had duties and shared characteristics that were vital to the functioning of the society.

In his *Relation* of 1642, Jesuit Father Jerome Lalemant described this process as follows:

> [I]t is arranged that, if possible, no name is ever lost; on the contrary, when one of the family [clan or lineage] dies all the relatives assemble, and consult together as to which among them shall bear the name of the deceased; giving his[2] own to some other relative. He who takes a new name also assumes the duties connected with it, and thus he becomes a captain [leader] if the deceased has been one. This done, they dry their tears and cease to weep for the deceased [a Huron expression]. In this manner, they place him among the number of the living, saying that he is resuscitated, and has come to life in the person of him who has received his name. (JR23:165)

If the name was an especially esteemed one, the appropriateness of its new bearer had to be publicly demonstrated, as described in the following passage from the *Relation* of 1636:

[T]he one who resuscitates him—after a magnificent feast to the whole country, that he may make himself known under this name—makes a levy of the resolute young men and goes away on a war expedition, to perform some daring exploit that shall make it evident to the whole country that he has inherited not only the name, but also the virtues and courage of the deceased. (JR10:275–77)

Other Iroquoian peoples, such as the seventeenth-century Neutral (Sagard 1939:209–10) and the Iroquois to this day (Tooker 1978a:424–29), possess similar customs and beliefs regarding names. With the latter, the name "Condolence Ceremony" is attached if the name momentarily lost to death is that of one of the fifty sachems (i.e., chiefs) of the Confederacy.[3]

Naturalizing the Outsiders

In order to be placed in Huron and Iroquois society, the Jesuit missionaries had to be named and adopted into a clan. The "naturalization" process involved in incorporating outsiders was well described by Cadwallader Colden in the eighteenth century, concerning his being named and thereby placed in Mohawk society:

This [naturalization] is not done by any general act of the nation, but every single person has a right to it, by a kind of adoption. The first time I was among the Mohawk, I had this compliment from one of their old sachems, which he did, by giving his own name *Cayenderongue*. He had been a notable warrior, and he told me, that now I had a right to assume to myself all the acts of valour he had performed, and that now my name would echo from hill to hill all over the Five Nations. As for my part I thought no more of it at that time,… but when about ten or twelve years afterwards, my business led me again among them, I directed the interpreter to say something from me to the sachems; he was for some time at a loss to understand their answer, till he had found that I was really known to them by that name, and that the old sachem, from the time he had given me his name, had assumed another of himself. I was adopted, at that time, into the tribe [clan] of the Bear, and, for that reason, I often afterwards had the kind compliment of Brother Bear. (Colden 1972:10–11)

The names given to the Jesuit missionaries by the Huron and Iroquois can be placed into four categories:

1. attempts at pronunciation that continued as names;
2. attempts at pronunciation that did not continue as names;
3. names with meaning that continued as names;
4. names with meaning that did not continue as names.

Attempts at Pronunciation That Continued as Names

Father Jerome Lalemant wrote in 1639 that the Huron

> not being ordinarily able to pronounce our names or our surnames—as
> they do not have in their language several consonants[4] that are found
> therein—get as near to them as they can; but if they cannot succeed, they
> seek instead words used in their own country, which they can readily pro-
> nounce, and which have some connection either with our names or with their
> meaning.[5] (JR16:239–41)

That year, when the Jesuit missionary community of Sainte-Marie-
Among-the-Hurons was established, the *Relation* contained a list of eleven
Huron names for the resident missionaries (JR16:239). Four were based
on Huron pronunciations of the Jesuits' French names:

HURON NAME	FRENCH NAME
Hechon	Jean de Brébeuf
Anwennen	Antoine Daniel
Chauose	Joseph Le Mercier
Wane	Simon Le Moyne

It seems that the preferred naming strategy of the Huron was to adapt
the first name of the Frenchman, as in three out of the four cases above.
It was also true earlier of the Huron name given to Sagard, whom they
called *Auiel* (Sagard 1939:73), as the Huron language has no -*b*- or initial
-*g*-.[6] The first two continued as names that were resuscitated after the death
of the original owner. I believe that this was possible as both names acquired
meaning, the first through association with characteristics of the first owner,
the second through being reshaped into components with meaning in
Huron.

Hechon

This name was first recorded in 1635 (JR8:93, 97, and 99), and was an
attempt to pronounce the 'Jean' of Brébeuf's name. The -*ch*- (as in Chicago)
replaced the ž sound of -*j*- as the latter did not exist in Huron. The -*h*- was
added at the beginning of the word to give the name the sound of a man's
name. Initial -*h*- in Huron is the point of difference in some pronominal prefixes that distinguishes male from female (e.g., *hahiatonk* 'he writes' versus *ɩahiatonk* 'she writes;' and *hatihiatonk* 'they (masculine) write' versus
atihiatonk 'they (feminine) write').

After Brébeuf's death in 1649, the name Hechon seems to have taken
on the associated meaning of 'outsider who is gifted in the Huron language.' Brébeuf had been the first Jesuit to speak Huron fluently and had
given the study of the language an impressive start. Both the next two

Hechons lived a long time with the Huron and became well known for their ability to express themselves in the language. Father Pierre Joseph-Marie Chaumonot was the next Hechon, probably receiving the name a short time after Brébeuf died. From that time to his death in 1693, Chaumonot was almost constantly with the Huron, working with the language, writing Huron dictionaries and translating Huron speeches (JR44:221; 53:101; 55:257; 57:57, 61, 65, and 297).

Father Daniel Richer, the third Hechon, lived with the Huron from 1715 t01760, and composed written works in the language (Potier 1920:xvii and 152). It was also my honour, after studying the Huron language for more than twenty years, to be given the name myself by members of the Huron community of Lorette in Quebec.

Anwennen

Anwennen, which carries no meaning, was an attempt to pronounce Father Antoine Daniel's first name (there is no *-tw-* in Huron). By at least the early 1670s, it appears to have been altered to become *Aronto₁ennen* (Potier 1920:661), meaning 'under the tree' (405 and 453). This name appears in various forms in 1697 (JR65:39–41). In one instance it is presented as "P. Garontoguennen" (JR65:41), the 'P' tending to be a standard symbol for 'Pere,' this may refer to a priest who had this name.

Attempts at Pronunciation That Did Not Continue as Names

Chauose (JR16:239) was the Huron pronunciation of Father Joseph Le Mercier's first name. As we have seen above with *Hechon*, the Huron replaced the ñ sound represented by the French *-j-* with the closest sound in their language, the š sound of the French *-ch-*. The *-f-* sound of the *-ph-* did not exist in Huron, so it was simply dropped from the word. This name did not last long; it was replaced by a more meaningful name that was probably given to Le Mercier when he began his work with the Onondaga (see below).

Wane would appear to be a Huron rendering of the last name of Father Simon Le Moyne, with the Huron replacing the 'm' that did not then exist in their language (see discussion on the letter 'm') with a 'w.' This was also done in the Huron word for Marie (JR31:181). As we will see later, Father Le Moyne later resuscitated the name *Ondesonk*.

Names with Meaning That Continued

This is by far the largest category of names. It can be subdivided into three sections:

1. names that became exclusively Jesuit missionary names;
2. names that were predominantly Jesuit names;
3. names that were predominantly Huron names.

Names that became essentially missionary names seemed to have done so because, like *Hechon*, they developed an associated meaning or title status after the death or disappearance from Huronia of the first owner. The most obvious such case is *Hachiendase* 'he has a new name' (Potier 1920:174), the new name being a new position of authority.

In 1639, Father Jerome Lalemant bore the name *achiendase* (JR16:239; also JR22:151 and 24:109), probably a bad recording of *hachiendase*. He was the Superior of the Jesuit order in New France at that time, and the name came to be associated with that position (JR41:121; 43:163, 169, 173, 185, and 277; 44:107 and 113; and FH1693:241).[7]

Governors encountered by the Huron and the Iroquois also bore an Iroquoian title. The governors of New France were named *Onnontio* 'large or great mountain' (Potier 1920:396 and 451), a translation of Governor Montmagny's surname (JR20:221 and 227; 21:39, 47–53, and 61; and passim JR27, 28, 31, 35, 36, 41, 43, 45, 47, 51, 53, 54, 62, and 66). The Iroquois called the governor of New York *Corlaer* after a prominent early Dutch official (Colden 1972:xv–xvi and 31–32), of Virginia *Assarigoa* (Colden 1972:49 and 140) and of Pennsylvania *Onas* (Colden 1972:90 fn).

Following the powerful Bishop Laval, the Bishop of New France was called *harih8a8a$_l$i* (JR45:41–43; 49:89; FH1697:71), meaning 'he holds matters of importance in his hands' (based on the noun root *-rih8-* 'matter, affair') (Potier 1920:453) and *-8a$_l$-* 'to hold in one's hands' (223)). There is one exception to this in the ethnohistorical record, however, as it was also given as the name for a young Wyandot girl of the mid-eighteenth century (Toupin 1996:248).

A missionary name that does not seem to have had any particular title aspect or significant meaning is *Horonhia$_l$e'te* 'he bears the sky' (Potier 1920:250 and 453). While this could be a traditional name existing prior to the coming of the Jesuits to Huronia (many names Huron and Iroquoian generallycontain the noun root *-ronhi-* 'sky') it is possible that it refers to the holder being a missionary, thereby bearing heaven to the Huron. The first time this name was recorded was as *Oronhiaguehre* (the *-r-* before the final *-e-* was a typographical error for *-t-*). It was presented as the Neutral name for Chaumonot (JR18:41) in 1640. Strangely, the first Huron name given for Chaumonot was the slightly different *Aronhiatiri* (JR33:169–71), which meant 'he supports the sky,' containing the verb root *-atiri-* 'to support' (Potier 1920:191). This particular configuration does not appear again as a Jesuit name.[8]

Since Chaumonot probably gave up the name for the more significant *Hechon* a short time after 1649, *Horonhia₁e'te* may have gone without resuscitation from then until 1677, when the next known bearer, Father Claude Chauchetiere, came to the Huron community of Lorette (FH1693:241 and Jaenen 1969b:139–40). After his death in 1709, there appears to have been another long hiatus (perhaps a sign of the lack of significance of the name) until at least 1743, when Father Pierre Potier came to New France. The name probably died with him in 1781.

Another missionary name/title containing the noun root *-ronhi-* was *Te haronhia₁ann'rak* 'he looks at the sky,' with the verb root *-₁annra-* 'to look at' (Potier 1920:235). It seems to have developed an associated meaning of 'missionary to the Iroquois.' The first recorded bearer of the name, Father Joseph Le Mercier (who, as we have seen, was termed *Chauose* by the Huron in 1639), may have obtained it and/or started its association sometime around 1656, when he first went to Onondaga territory (JR8:291 fn11; 55:297; and Campeau 1966:458–60). It probably would not have stayed long with Le Mercier, because he become Superior of the Jesuit order in New France in 1665, thus obtaining the name *Hachiendase*.

Father Pierre Millet, the next to have the name, probably received it as soon as he went to the Onondaga in 1668 (JR56:43). He relinquished it, to his benefit, when he was captured by the Oneida in 1689. The Christian Oneida saw to it that he received the highly prestigious name of *Odatsighta*, one of the fifty great names of the sachems of the Iroquois Confederacy (Tooker 1978:424). This enabled him to have a say in the highest councils of the Iroquois (Campeau 1969b:473–74).

Father Sebastian Rale came to New France that same year, and probably became *Te haronhia₁ann'rak* shortly after Millet became *Odatsighta*. While most of Rale's missionary work was done among the Algonquian-speaking Abenaki, he may have retained his name for Iroquois speakers until his death in 1724 (Charland 1969b:542–45).

The name was next resuscitated by Father Jean Baptiste Tournenois, who came to New France in 1741, going immediately to live with the Christian Mohawk at Kahnawake, near Montreal. Midway through the eighteenth century it was given to another missionary to the Iroquois, Father Pierre René Floquet (Toupin 1996:236). In the nineteenth century, another Kahnawake priest, Father Joseph Marcoux, bore the name (Shea 1973:345).

Shared Names

Ondesonk

Three names borne by Jesuit missionaries were also held by at least one Huron or Iroquois, even though the name was held by more than one priest. One such name was *Ondesonk* 'hawk' (FHO:232). The first references to this are with respect to its being the name for the leader of the "Petite Nation" Algonquin in 1637 (JR13:211–12), and for a Huron war leader in 1638 (JR15:25).

Father Isaac Jogues was recorded as bearing the name in 1639 (JR16:239). After Jogues died in 1646, it seems to have taken on the associated meaning of 'missionary to the Mohawk,' the nation into which Jogues had been adopted in 1642. The next *Ondesonk* was Father Simon Le Moyne, who also worked with the Mohawk. He probably acquired the name in 1654, and kept it until his death in 1665 (JR41:89, 96, 109, and 117; Pouliot 1966b:460–62). It was quickly resuscitated by Father Thierry Beschefer (JR50:171 and Campeau 1969b:61–62) in 1666. He left Mohawk (and Iroquois) territory in 1670–71, so it is not too surprising that the name was recorded as being held by someone else, a man named Joseph, in 1671 (JR55:45). The ethnic identity of this man is not clear. He may not have been called *Ondesonk* very long, because the next person recorded as having the name, Father Jacques de Lamberville, entered the Iroquois mission in 1674. He probably revived the name shortly after his entry into the mission, keeping it until his death in 1711.

In 1729, a Wyandot with the Christian name of Pierre took on the name (Toupin 1996:822).

Haondeche'te

A second name resuscitated by more than one Jesuit missionary but also held by a Huron or Iroquois is *Haondeche'te* 'he bears or carries the country' (Potier 1920:250 and 455). It would have been an appellation replete with meaning, for *-ondech-* was metaphorically rich (see Steckley 1990). We see one aspect of this meaning in the following passage written in the early 1670s. It describes Father Paul Ragueneau's attempt to link the Bear tribe of the Huron with the Onondaga after the dispersal of the Huron. As country-bearer he is spoken of as carrying the Bear:

> *haondechete ontahondechenha8i d'atinnia8enten aherhonsk eskat a8o ahondarat onnonta₍eronnon ₍ato₍en ethontinda₍eren d'atinnia8enten hotirih8iosti de hontrendaen*

> [Country-bearer wanted to carry the country of the Bear to be one with the Onondaga so that the Onondaga would imitate the Christian Bear when they (the Bear) pray] (Potier 1920:660)

Father Paul Ragueneau was the first person recorded as having the name (JR16:239). He bore the name from at least 1639 until he left New France in 1662. It appears to have remained dead for four years until it was resuscitated by Father Etienne de Carheil sometime after his arrival in New France in 1666 (JR50:19).

While it would seem reasonable to believe that Carheil retained the name until his death in 1726, there is a reference in 1675 to a Huron named Pierre who bore the name at that time (JR60:89).

Ta‚orhenche

Ta‚orhenche is a commonly found Iroquoian name.[9] Among the Huron, it was first written as the appellation for an old man (JR17:145). The next person to bear it, we only know from a reference to his widow in 1721 (JR67:69). Then there was a Pierre Taorhenchre among the Wyandot in 1747 (Toupin 1996:856). Eventually it became associated with the Picard family at Huron Lorette. Written typically as Tahourenche, it was held by Francois-Xavier Picard, chief from 1879 to 1883 (Tehariolina 1984:82), by Alphonse T. Picard, chief from 1954 to 1964 (87), and more recently by Elphege Picard (381).

It may have been as an Onondaga name that it was first resuscitated by a Jesuit missionary. When Father Jean de Lamberville was first recorded as bearing the name, it was as Teiorhensere, a non-Huron form (NYCD3:453). The Onondaga were the first people with whom Lamberville lived as a missionary, probably giving him the name in 1669. He died in 1716. It was apparently resuscitated shortly afterwards, as Father Jacques La Bretonniere, the next Ta‚orhensere, was a missionary at Kahnawake from 1721 to 1754 (Potier 1920:152 and Cote 1974:329).

Primarily Huron Names Held by One Priest

Four names appear to have been primarily the possession of the Huron, with only one missionary recorded as having the honour of bearing the name.

Hatironta

Hatironta was an important Huron name that probably meant 'he pulls, attracts, draws it along' (Potier 1920:192), possibly metaphorically referring to a leader drawing his people behind him. It was originally recorded in the 1620s as being the appellation of the foremost figure among the Arenda‚eronnon or Rock nation of the Huron. His name represented or signified that nation when it was spoken in council (Sagard 1939:91 and Champlain 1929:81).

In 1642, that man's brother, Jean-Baptiste, received the name in a resus-citation ceremony witnessed and recorded by the Jesuits (JR23:159 and 167). It was not to be his for very long (JR28:147–55, 159 and 171; 29:163; and 33:121 and 133). He died in 1650 (JR35:203), but may not have kept the name until his death. Father Gabriel Lalemant arrived in Huron late in 1648, and became *Hatironta* before his death in March 1649 (JR34:157). Jean-Baptiste was a Christian and spent much of his last few years near the French settlements. He may have given his name to Lalemant as a ges-ture of goodwill, much as the Mohawk leader would give his to Colden a century later.

The next time we read of this name is with the death of a Christian leader of the Huron near Quebec, reported in 1672 (JR57:37).

The name later had significance for the mid-eighteenth-century Wyan-dot. *Hatironta* appears to have been a Deer clan name of some note at that time, with the bearer, Jacques, being the nephew of a Deer clan female elder, Marie *Nendaentons* (Toupin 1996:225) and the husband of a Wolf clan elder Marie-Joseph *Nenditaχon* (221). Interestingly *Nendaentons* is recorded as being the sister of Jesuit Father Armande de la Richardie (Toupin 1996:258), Potier's predecessor as missionary to the Wyandot, perhaps a continuation of a close Jesuit–Huron family connection.

Shorenhes

The name *Shorenhes* incorporates the noun root -*renh*- 'treetops, branches' (Potier 1920:452) into the verb root -*es*- 'to be long, tall' (385), to mean 'tall treetops, trees.' It was recorded as the name of a prominent Huron trader, who died in 1636 (JR8:151).

In the mid-1740s, it was held both by a missionary, Father Nicholas de Gonnor (Potier 1920:152) and an eight-year-old Wyandot (149).

Totiri

The name *Totiri* was held by an influential Huron of the Cord nation dur-ing the 1640s (JR22:285; 23:135, 145, and 241; 26:259, 283, and 291; and 27:21). In the 1690s, a "frere bouffet," a lay brother, was recorded as hav-ing the name *totiri hatetsens* (FH1693:241), the latter word meaning 'he cures, is a doctor' (Potier 1920:369).

Tentenha8iθa

The Huron name by which Father Jacques Bruyas was known in the 1690s, *Tentenha8iθa* [he brings something to or from a field] (Potier 1920:248 and 455), may earlier have been used by a Huron or another missionary. While Bruyas did not come to New France until 1666 (Jaenen 1969a:106–8), this name first appeared in 1651 (JR36:149), without a clear reference as to whom it referred.

Names with Meaning That Did Not Continue

There are a few names with meanings that seem to have lasted only a short time. Father Charles Garnier was referred to as *Ouracha* (JR16:239; 22:151; 33:111; and Potier 1920:661). One possible meaning is 'cloud' (Potier 1920:452). He was killed in 1649. In a list of missionary names recorded in the 1690s, his Huron name was presented opposite "P[ere] garnier" (FH1693:241). Although there was a Father Julian Garnier who came to New France in 1662 and stayed there until his death in 1730 (Pouliot 1969:237), this name probably refers to Charles.

It is not easy to know exactly what *Arioo*, the name given to Father Pierre Chastelain (JR16:239) was intended to be. Was it an attempt to pronounce 'Pierre,' there being no -*p*- in Huron? More likely it was a translation of the French word 'pierre' into *ₗari8'ta*, one of the Huron terms for 'rock' (Potier 1920:453).

Father Pierre Cholenec, who came to New France in 1674, and did his missionary work with the Huron at Lorette, and the Christian Mohawk in New France (Bechand 1969:144–5), was called *onnon'k8ahi8ten* (FH1693:241). As the name means 'one has a gentle or pleasant nature' (Potier 1920:262), it possibly described the missionary himself.

The term *annonchira* appears twice with reference to Father Francois Du Peron (JR15:189 and 16:239). There is no apparent translation of this name.

Jesuit Names Summary

The Jesuit missionaries to the Huron and Iroquois were given names as part of their adoption into Iroquoian society. In the early years of the Huron mission, some of the names were merely attempts to pronounce the French names of the Jesuits. But it seems that it was important that the names 'have meaning,' so these early appellations were either replaced by meaningful substitutes, or were themselves given meaning through association with the characteristics of the initial bearer.

Names having meaning could be exclusively Jesuit names or could be shared with the Huron or Iroquois. Where they were exclusively Jesuit, a status or title-like quality went along with them.

Names that were predominantly Jesuit may also have had such status, but with the exception of *Ondesonk*, which possibly had the status of missionary to the Mohawk, these details are not yet known. Where names were recorded as being held by only one Jesuit, these appear to be either significant traditional names assigned to special individuals or temporary appellations for people who may not have made a lasting impression on the people.

Notes

1 See the similar expression involving longhouses and scaffolds in the material culture chapter.
2 The patriarchal bias of the Jesuits should be noted here. Of 301 Huron names that appear in the *Jesuit Relations*, only thirty-four are female names. As I have argued in an unpublished paper on the Wyandot descendant group and their elders council, the names and statuses of leading women were also important to the people.
3 For an account of the Condolence Ceremony, see William Fenton's *The Great Law and the Longhouse*, 1998.
4 The sounds he was talking about were primarily the labials m, p, b, f, and v. Of course, the Huron could say that same thing about the Jesuit inability to hear or pronounce initial -h- or final glottal stops. We can see in the discussion below of the name *Hechon* that, from a Huron perspective, that French inability could cause some important mistakes.
5 A non-Jesuit example would be Guillaume Couture, a lay helper of the Jesuit missionaries at Sainte-Marie-Among-the-Hurons. He was called *ihandich* (JR28:183; also see JR14:49), literally 'he sews' (Potier 1920:292), which was a Huron translation of his surname.
6 They had no -*l*- either, but for some reason it was included in Sagard's name.
7 The name *hachiendase* appears in a mission record among the Wyandot in 1770, but it is not clear whether the reference is to a Jesuit or a Wyandot (Toupin 1996:973).
8 It appears in 1770, as *ₗaronhiatiri* as the name of a baptized child's godfather (Toupin 1996:893).
9 In the eighteenth century we find *Tiorhensere* recorded as a Seneca name (NYCD4:655) and *Tahorheusere* and *Tyeransera* as different versions of a Mohawk name (NYCD6:315 and NYCD8:137).

11 After-Words

My immodest goal in first engaging in the research that resulted in this work was to, in some significant sense, "rewrite the book on the seventeenth-century Huron." I wanted to make a contribution using anthropological linguistics, which I interpret as the study of language with a constant eye to what that study says about the culture and history of its speakers, that would equal the outstanding efforts over the years of the archaeologists and historians who have written about the Huron. This was the opportunity I first saw more than thirty years ago, when I was looking for research that would engage both my mind and my heart. I have never regretted the decision to see where that research path would take me, although those around me at the time must have questioned it as a career move.

I have long said that the Wendat language has been my best teacher. It has taught me far more than I could have imagined. I cannot even speculate as to what it might still have to teach me. All the material written in and about the language is a virtual gold mine of information waiting for the researcher. Perhaps a more culturally appropriate metaphor would be that it is a field filled with ripe corn, beans and squash yet to be harvested. The only parallels I can think of are of the writings of the ancient Egyptians, before the Rosetta Stone was discovered, or of the syllabic stone texts of the Classic Mayans of Mexico, before the mystery of their writing was finally solved.

With all this material available, I can only hope that other anthropological linguists become involved, bringing their unique approaches, gifts, and insights. Although I love my job teaching at a community college, I regret that I do not have graduate students to assist in their own investigations into this subject. However, there are the descendants of the seventeenth-century speakers of Wendat, in their communities in Quebec, Kansas, and Oklahoma, and as individuals spread across the continent. Many are working to learn whatever they can of their ancestral language. That is inspiring. They would all understand the effect Ojibwa elder and language teacher Fred Wheatley's words had on me, when he spoke of his grandmother greeting him, on his return from living in the city, with the simple sentence, "I hear you have lost your tongue."

What have I learned that I have tried to express in this book? Fundamentally, I have learned eight things that I have tried to communicate. One teaching comes from the relationship between the grammar or structure of the Wendat verb and the practices and thoughts of Huron culture. The Jesuits saw something of this in their own studies. Even with their broad previous experience with the Indo-European languages such as French, Latin, and Greek, and Semitic languages such as Hebrew and Arabic, the structure of the Wendat came as something of a surprise to the Jesuits, but it was surprise accompanied by respect. In Brébeuf's description of Wendat in the language chapter of his 1636 report, he used words such as "La merueille ['the wonder'], p118 "plus remarquable ['most remarkable'],'' "plus rare" (JR10:118, 120, and 122 respectively) in speaking of features that impressed him. Clearly, as a linguist trying to interpret the thinking of the Huron, the original *Hechon* felt, like the current one (me), that there were unique links forged between the ways of Huron language structure and culture that joined somewhere in the minds of the people. We can see Brébeuf trying to work out those connections when he speculated (with a great deal of projection from an ideal female type of his own European culture) about the relationship between Wendat pronominal prefixes and gender roles. It is ironic that what he was writing about here was a linguistic feature (a feminine pronoun) not found in the language of most of the Aboriginal people of what is now Canada.

> What I find most extraordinary is that there is a feminine conjugation, at least in the third person both of the singular and of the plural; for we have not discovered more of it, or very little. Here is an example of it: *ihaton*, he says; *iwaton*, she says; *ihonton*, they [ils] say [masculine]; *ionton*, they [elles] say [feminine]. The principal distinction of this feminine conjugation from the masculine is the lack of the letter H, in which the masculine abounds— perhaps to give the women to understand that there ought to be nothing rough or coarse in their words or in their manners, but that the grace and law of gentleness ought to be upon their tongues. (JR10:123)

My discovery of the matched dualism of prefix (the dualic -te-) and culture is one of the main points of this book. I strongly suspect that there are other links, perhaps of the Huron notion of 'oneness' and the repetitive prefix, yet to be found.

A second lesson comes from how extensive the Huron's use of metaphor was. Brébeuf noticed early that Huron speech-making was loaded with metaphors. In 1636, for example, he wrote that:

> It is true that their speeches are at first very difficult to understand, on account of an infinity of Metaphors, of various circumlocutions, and other rhetorical methods: for example, speaking of the Nation of the Bear they will say, "the Bear has said has done so and so; the Bear is cunning, is bad; the hands of the Bear are dangerous." When they speak of him who conducts the feast of the Dead, they say "he who eats souls;"... (JR10:257)

One of my greatest challenges in translating the Jesuit religious text *De Religione* from Huron to English was in taking what I knew about the literal meanings of words and trying to determine what their metaphorical meaning could be. As I stressed in my article "The Warrior and the Lineage: Jesuit Use of Iroquoian Images to Communicate Christianity"(1992), metaphors of war and of family were extensively used by the Jesuits, clearly following Huron tradition. In this book, I have added to that collection with discussions of mats of war and peace as part of Huron dualism, of longhouses as full or empty, the washing of objects and of names, and expressions using words for pots and axes.

Third, there is the ethnic evidence of dialects, which I suspect will someday be connected not only with archaeological sites in seventeenth-century Huronia and Petunia (land of the Petun, not just a flower) but also with pre-contact, pre-Huron more southern settlements. In this study and in earlier works, I have grouped the dialects of the Southern Bear, the Cord, and whichever Petun dialect later became Wyandot, in opposition to the separately distinctive dialects of the Northern Bear, Rock, Deer, and maybe even the Bog. Particularly dear to my heart is the Southern Bear and Northern Bear distinction, as it was my first dialect discovery. Highest placed on my archaeological wish list is for the diggers to find "stones-and-bones" evidence to support my hypothesis that the Northern Bear were the result of two peoples coming together, one Huron-speaking, the other speaking a dialect that is more like the languages of the Iroquois nations (i.e., having a -g- where Huron has a -y-). I am heartened by finds in sites in the Greater Toronto Area, such as Seed-Barker in Vaughan, and the Mantle site near Stouffville, where there are artifacts identifiable as coming from

Iroquois country mixed in with the more typical Ontario Iroquoian finds. Now if they can only trace some of these artifacts to the Penetang peninsula in the north of Bear territory.

Fourth comes my discovery of the "clan-logic" of the Huron. Of course, simply identifying the eight clans of the Huron as Bear, Deer, Turtle, Beaver, Loon-Sturgeon, Hawk, Wolf and Fox was gratifying. This opened the longhouse door to even more intriguing finds. The Turtle clan connection between the Southern Bear capital of Ossossane and the adopted refugees of the turtle-named Wenro let me look through that door, but did not, unfortunately, let me walk right in and see other such linkages (as in the Wolf and Hawk clans) as clearly. And then there is the mysterious dualic of the seventeenth-century Huron Loon/Sturgeon clan that would extend to the similar duality of the eighteenth-century Wyandot Loon/Aataentsik [she is old; the name for the first woman to come to earth] clan. Second on my archaeological wish list is for discovery of a stone pipe bowl with a loon and a sturgeon on it, or some other manifestation of the linkage between the (to my clanless mind) unlikely pair.

Fifth is the knowledge learned from kin terms, which has helped me in the classroom When I first took an anthropology course, I found kinship terminology both uninteresting and unenlightening. So, no doubt, did the students of my first anthropology class at Humber College, when I dwelled for some time on the subject, the only time I ever did. It was only when I began to investigate the vast array of Huron kinship terms that I started to see the tremendous potential the words provided in learning more about the people. The mandatory grammatical respect for age (having the older relative always the subject of the verb expressing the relationship, the younger relative always the object) has been a great tool for me to teach my students some small part of the traditional respect for elders in Aboriginal society. It resonates with the kinship term experiences of Asian, African, and even some European students in my classroom and shows their North America peers that there is an alternative casting of age in other cultures. When I do class visits to grade-six classes, I never fail to teach them that the Huron called the French "my nephew(s)." The students never fail to respond correctly when I ask them why that is. It is a clear illustration of the point that there was a lot that the Huron had to teach the newcomers, before these persistent visitors could know how to live well in this land. It also makes a good segue into Huron humour, with stories that begin with "There was a mother's brother and a sister's son" (their equivalent of "Two guys walked into a bar …"), with nephews consistently interpreting too literally the metaphors of their uncles (e.g., "Present your face to the tall trees" as a way of saying invite the chiefs to the feast). For my older students the mother-in-law avoidance makes a similar connection.

The sixth area of teaching is in Huron ethnobiology. It is well recorded in the anthropological literature that the indigenous peoples of the world have tremendous knowledge of the botany and biology of the plant and animal species that surround them. I think that many anthropologists in other areas of study are a little envious of the discoveries of Canadian anthropologist Wade Davis in his ethnobotanical work. It was on that account important for me to find one stellar example of the seventeenth-century Huron's knowledge of their environment: their discovery of the nutritional value of the liver of the burbot or freshwater cod. I wonder whether Huron children had to go through the "eat it, it's good for you" that I did when I took cod liver oil. Even though I know that what is considered good-tasting is culturally relative, I find it hard to believe that burbot's liver was ever considered a "treat" by anyone. Archaeological evidence of when and where this was discovered should eventually be forthcoming. The scales of the burbot are larger than those of most fish. Even when archeologists are forced by constraints of time and budget to use wide mesh in their labour-intensive work of sifting through the earth that has been dug up, the scales would be more easily caught in the mesh.

The matching of archaeological sites with seventeenth-century Huron communities has not achieved a great deal of success. Perhaps the tree-focused names of so many of these communities might provide some assistance. Using pollen samples on sites named after a particular tree or collection of trees might prove useful in this regard.

Seventh is the Huron use of song. One aspect of traditional Aboriginal culture in Canada that I believe is constantly underestimated is the significant extent to which song played an important role. A meaningful by-product of my study of Huron ceremonies for this book was uncovering a rich vocabulary differentiating the kinds and functions of songs that the seventeenth-century Huron had. There is a tremendous potential in the ethnomusicological study of the Huron. I have walked a few steps down this path in translating the Huron Carol into English, with words much different from those created by J. E. Middleton ("'Twas in the Moon of Winter-time"—which winter moon was that?), and in looking at that popular piece in terms of the cultural collaboration of its initial creation by Brébeuf (with possible assistance from the musically gifted Father Antoine Daniel) and his Huron language teachers. There are many more Christian songs composed in Huron that bear further analysis, in terms of both cultures and languages from which they sprang.

An eighth teaching relates to how the Huron perceived the French and the materials and diseases that they brought with them. We have too easily and too often looked at this perception from the point of view literally illustrated by a painting by C. W. Jeffries, a Canadian painter whose works found their way into a good number of history textbooks in elementary and secondary grades. There is a Jesuit holding up a cross and teaching a dumb brute-faced Aboriginal person who looks upon him with awe. It is one in a series of such paintings I have seen in which the European stands taller and more majestic than the Aboriginal. I hope that in this book, the reader has seen through the Huron perceptions of smallpox and other communicable diseases, of the new *08hista* materials, of guns, and of the French as sister's sons, that there is greater complexity and knowledge in Huron perception of the newcomers than was earlier expressed in European writing. It is a perception of equality. If this alternative vision is to have a physical artistic manifestation, then what comes to my mind is a pair of bronze statues that stand at the southeast corner or Major Mackenzie and Islington, in Vaughan, just north of Toronto. They are of Jean de Brébeuf and Joseph Chihoatenhwa, a Christian Huron who taught Brébeuf about the language and culture of the Huron. The statues were created by religious artist Antonio Caruso, and unveiled on May 15, 2005. The European is reading, and the Aboriginal person is giving directions. Both stand equally tall.

References

Unpublished

Barbeau, Charles Marius. n.d. *Wyandot language card file*, MS.

Bruté, T. 1800. *Dictionnaire Huron Portif.*

FHO. c. 1656. Dictionnaire Huron et hiroquois onontaheronon, MS, Archive Séminaire de Québec.

FH62. c. 1656 French–Wendat section, MS 62 (as cited in Victor Hanzeli, 1969. *Missionary Linguistics in New France.* The Hague, Mouton), Archive Séminaire de Québec.

FH67. n.d. French–Wendat dictionary, MS 67 (as cited in Hanzeli), Archive Séminaire de Québec.

FH1693. c. 1693 French–Wendat dictionary, MS, Archive Séminaire de Québec

FH1697. c. 1697 French–Wendat dictionary, MS, John Carter Brown Library, Brown University, Providence, Rhode Island.

HF59. n.d. Wendat–French dictionary, MS 59 (as cited in Hanzeli), Archive Séminaire de Québec.

HF62. n.d. Wendat–French section, MS 62 (as cited in Hanzeli), Archive Séminaire de Québec.

HF65. n.d. Wendat–French dictionary, MS 65 (as cited in Hanzeli), Archive Séminaire de Québec.

Warrick, Gary. 1990. *A Population History of the Huron-Petun, A.D. 900–1650.* Phd dissertation, Department of Anthropology, McGill University.

Published

Angel, Michael. 2005. *Preserving the Sacred: Historical Perspectives on the Ojibwa Midewiwin.* Winnipeg: University of Manitoba Press.

Arnold, Phyllis A., and Betty Gibbs. 1999. *Canada Revisited: Aboriginal Peoples and European Explorers.* Edmonton, AB: Arnold Publishing.

Barbeau, Charles Marius. 1915. *Huron and Wyandot Mythology.* Memoir 80. Ottawa: Dept. of Mines, Geological Survey.

———. 1917. Iroquoian Clans and Phratries. *American Anthropologist* 19:392–402.

———. 1960. *Huron-Wyandot Traditional Narratives in Translation and Native Texts.* Bulletin 105. Ottawa: National Museum of Canada.

———. 1961. The Language of Canada in the Voyages of Jacques Cartier (1534–1538). Bulletin 173, 108–229. Ottawa: National Museum of Canada.

Bonvillain, Nancy. 1973. *A Grammar of Akwesasne Mohawk.* Ottawa: National Museum of Man.

Brébeuf, Jean de. 1830. Doctrine Chrestienne, dv R. P. Ledesme de la Compagnie de Iesvs. In *Voyages*, Samuel de Champlain, vols. 1–3. Paris.

Brown, R., and A. Gilman. 1960. The pronouns of power and solidarity. In *Style in Language*, ed. T. A. Sebeok, 253–76. Cambridge, MA: MIT Press.

Bruyas, Jacques. 1970. *Radices Verborum Iroquaerum.* Ed. J. G. Shea (originally published 1860–64). New York: AMS Press.

Chafe, Wallace. 1964. Linguistic Evidence for the Relative Age of Iroquois Religious Practices. *Southwestern Journal of Anthropology* 20: 278–285.

———. 1967. *Seneca Morphology and Dictionary.* Washington, DC: Smithsonian Press.

Champlain, Samuel de. 1929. *The Works of Samuel de Champlain*, Vol. 3. Ed. H. P. Biggar. Toronto: Champlain Society.

Charland, Thomas. 1969a. Entry for Bigot, Vincent. *The Dictionary of Canadian Biography*, Vol. 2, 64–68.

———. 1969b. Entry for Rale, Sebastien. *The Dictionary of Canadian Biography*, Vol. 2, 542–45.

Clarke, Peter D. 1870. *Origin and Traditional History of the Wyandotts.* Toronto: Hunter, Rose.

Colden, Cadwallader. 1972. *The History of the Five Nations of Canada* (originally published in 1747). Toronto: Coles Publishing.

Connelly, William. 1900. The Wyandots. *Annual Archaeological Report.* Appendix to the Report of the Minister of Education of Ontario for 1899. 92–123.

Cuoq, Jean-André. 1966. *Etudes Philogiques sur quelques Langues Sauvages de l'Amerique* (originally published in 1866). New York: Johnson Reprint.

Curnoe, Greg. 1996. *Deeds/Nations.* Ontario Archaeological Society Occasional Publications #4. London, ON. OAS.

Dodd, Christine. 1984. *Ontario Iroquois Tradition Longhouses.* Mercury Series, Archaeological Survey 124. Ottawa: National Museum of Man, 181–437.

Driver, H. E. 1970. *Indians of North America.* Chicago: University of Chicago Press.

Eggan, Fred. 1971. Respect and Joking Relationships among the Cheyenne and Arapaho. In *Readings in Kinship and Social Structure*, ed. Nelson Graburn, 141–44. New York: Harper & Row.

Ember, Carol, and Melvin. 1990. *Anthropology*, 6th ed. New Jersey: Prentice Hall.

Fenton, William N. 1951. Locality as a Basic Factor in the Development of Iroquois Social Structure. In *Symposium on Local Diversity in Iroquois Culture*, ed. William N. Fenton, 35–54. Washington, DC: Smithsonian Institution.

Fenton 1974. See entry under Lafitau.

———. 1998. *The Great Law and the Longhouse.* Norman: University of Oklahoma Press.

Finley, James. 1840. *History of the Wyandot Mission at Upper Sandusky, Ohio.* Cincinnati.

Froman, Francis, Alfred Keye, Lottie Keye, and Carrie Dyck. 2002. *English–Cayuga/Cayuga–English Dictionary.* Toronto: University of Toronto Press.

Goddard, Ives. 1984. Agreskwe, A Northern Iroquoian Deity. In *Extending the Rafters*, ed. M. K. Foster, J. Campisi, and M. Mithun, 229–35. Albany: State University of New York Press.

Hanzeli, Victor. 1969. *Missionary Linguistics in New France.* The Hague: Mouton.

Havard, Gilles. 2001. *The Great Peace of Montreal of 1701: French–Native Diplomacy in the Seventeenth Century*, trans. Phyllis Aronoff and Howard Scott. Montreal: McGill-Queen's University Press.

Heidenreich, Conrad. 1971. *Huronia: A History and Geography of the Huron Indians 1600–1650.* Toronto: McClelland & Stewart.

Hodge, Frederick Webb. 1971. *Handbook of Indians of Canada* (originally published in 1913). Toronto: Coles Publishing.

Hudson, R. A. 1980. *Sociolinguistics.* Cambridge: Cambridge University Press.

Illich, Ivan. 1976. *De-Schooling Society.* Harmondsworth: Penguin Education.

Jones, Arthur E. Rev. 1908. *"8endake Ehen" or "Old Huronia."* Ontario Bureau of Archives, Fifth Report. Toronto.

JR. See under Thwaites.

Kinietz, W. Vernon. 1965. *The Indians of the Western Great Lakes, 1615–1760.* Ann Arbor: University of Michigan Press.

Knight, Dean, and J. Melbye. 1983. Burial Patterns of the Ball Site. *Ontario Archaeology* 40:37–48.

Kottak, Conrad Phillip. 1987. *Cultural Anthropology*, 4th ed. New York: Random House.

Lafitau, Joseph. 1974–77. *Customs of the American Indians Compared with the Customs of Primitive Times.* 2 vols. Ed. William Fenton. Toronto: Champlain Society.

Lagarde, Pierrette. 1980. *Le Verbe Huron: Étude Morphologique d'après une description grammaticale de la seconde moitié du XVIIe siècle.* Paris: éditions l'Harmatton.

Latta, Martha A. 1985. Iroquoian House Ends: Semantic Considerations. *Arch Notes* 5:5–6.

Le Moine, J. M. 1882. *Picturesque Quebec.* Montreal: Dawson Bros.

Lounsbury, Floyd. 1953. *Oneida Verb Morphology.* New Haven: Yale University Press.

———. 1971. The Structural Analysis of Kinship Semantics. In *Readings in Kinship and Social Structure*, ed. N. Graburn, 258–71. New York: Harper & Row.

Marshall, Joyce (ed. and trans.). 1967. *Word from New France: The Selected Letters of Marie de l'Incarnation*. Toronto: Oxford University Press.

Melbye, Jerry. 1983. Burial Patterns at the Ball Site. *Ontario Archaeology* 40:37–48.

Michelson, Gunther. 1973. *A Thousand Words of Mohawk*. National Museum of Man, Ethnology Division, Mercury Series, Paper No. 5. Ottawa: National Museum of Man.

———. 1991. Iroquoian Terms for Wampum. *International Journal of American Linguistics* 57:108–16.

Michelson, Karin, and Mercy Doxtator. 2002. *Oneida–English/English–Oneida Dictionary*. Toronto: University of Toronto Press.

Mithun, Marianne. 1984. The Proto- Iroquoians. In *Extending the Rafters*, ed. M. Foster, J. Campisi, and M. Mithun, 259–82. Albany: State University of New York Press.

Morgan, Lewis Henry. 1966 (originally published in 1871). *Systems of Consanguinity and Affinity of the Human Family*. In Smithsonian Contributions to Knowledge, vol. 17. Washington: Smithsonian.

Nanda, Serena. 1987. *Cultural Anthropology*, 3rd ed. Belmont, CA: Wadsworth Publishing.

NYCD. See under O'Callaghan.

O'Callaghan, Edmund. 1853–87. *Documents Relative to the Colonial History of New York*, 15 vols. Albany, NY: Weed, Parsons.

Potier, Pierre. 1920. *Fifteenth Report of the Bureau of Archives for the Province of Ontario*. Toronto: C. W. James.

Pouliot. Leon. 1966a. Entry for Daniel, Antoine. In *The Dictionary of Canadian Biography*, vol. 1, 246–47.

———. 1966b. Entry for Le Moyne, Simon. In *The Dictionary of Canadian Biography*, vol. 1, 460–62.

Powell, J. W. 1881. Wyandot Government. *Bureau of American Ethnology*, 1st Annual Report, 57–69. Washington, DC.

Richards, Cara. 1967. Huron and Iroquois Residence Patterns 1600–1650. In *Iroquois Culture History and Prehistory*, ed. E. Tooker, 51–56. Albany: State University of New York Press.

Rudes, Blair. 1987. *Tuscarora Roots, Stems and Particles: Towards a Dictionary of Tuscarora*. Memoir 3. Winnipeg, MB: Algonquian and Iroquoian Linguistics.

Sagard, Gabriel. 1866. *Histoire du Canada,… avec un dictionnaire de la language huronne*. Paris: Edwin Tross.

———. 1939. *The Long Journey to the Country of the Hurons*. Toronto: Champlain Society.

Schulz, Emily A., and Robert H. Lavenda. 2005. *Cultural Anthropology: A Perspective on the Human Condition*. New York: Oxford University Press.

Shea, John. 1970. *A French–Onondaga Dictionary* (originally from a seventeenth-century manuscript). New York: Cramoisy Press.

———. 1973. *History of the Catholic Missions among the Indian Tribes of the United States 1529–1854* (orig. 1855). New York: AMS Press.

Steckley, John. 1978. Brebeuf's Presentation of Catholicism in the Huron Language. *University of Ottawa Quarterly* 48(1–2):93–115.

———. 1982a. Huron Clans and Phratries. *Ontario Archaeology* (OA) 37:29–34.

———. 1982b. The Cord Tribe of the Huron. *Arch Notes* (AN):3–15.

———. 1983. The Huron Calendar. AN 1:11–12.

———. 1985a. An Ethnolinguistic Analysis of Tobacco among the Huron. AN 2:13–17.

———. 1985b. What Made the Wenro Turn Turtle? AN 3:17–19.

———. 1986a. Adopting the Priests. *Onomastica Canadiana* 68:39–50.

———. 1986b. Were Burbot Important to the Huron? AN 1:19–23.

———. 1986c. Raccoons and Black Squirrels. AN 2 (1986d): 23–25.

———. 1986d. Ataronchronnon: The Linguistic Evidence. AN 3:47–48.

———. 1986e. Whose Child Is This? AN 5:23–25.

———. 1987a. Toanche: Not Where Champlain Landed. AN 2:29–33.

———. 1987b. Linguistic Identification of French-influenced Huron Village Construction. AN 3:13–14.

———. 1987c. Huron Bead Ethnolinguistics. AN 4:13–15.

———. 1987d. Huron Armour. AN 5:7–11.

———. 1988a. An Ethnolinguistic Look at the Huron Longhouse. OA 47:19–32.

———. 1988b. Enditenhwaen. AN 2:9–10.

———. 1989a. Huron Sweat Lodges: The Linguistic Evidence. AN 1:7–8.

———. 1989b. Men: Carriers of Contagion? AN 2:26–29.

———. 1989c. Owhista. AN 4:31–34.

———. 1989d. The Huron Mat of War. AN 6:5–11.

———. 1990a. The Early Map "Novvelle France." OA 51:17–29.

———. 1990b. Developing a Theory of Smallpox. AN 1:17–20.

———. 1990c. Reciprocal Burial: The Aiheonde Relationship. AN 5:9–14.

———. 1990d. One Bear or Two? AN 6:29–33.

———. 1991a. One Bear or Two Too. AN 1:12 and 14–15.

———. 1991b. The Mysterious M. AN 2:14–20 and 25.

———. 1991c. The First Huron–French Dictionary? AN 3:17–23.

———. 1991d. Rock and Southern Bear: Another Feature Shared. AN 4:12–15.

———. 1991e. From Your Place to Mine: Huron Marriage Gifts. AN 5:20–21.

———. 1991f. Southern Bear's -chr-: How Can a Sound Be Like a Bat's Wing?" AN 6:11–14.

———. 1992a. Pieces of -8-: Another Southern Bear Feature. AN 1:5–9.

———. 1992b. The Warrior and the Lineage: Jesuit Use of Iroquoian Images to Communicate Christianity. *Ethnohistory* 39(4):478–509.

———. 192c. The Wendat: Were They Islanders? AN 5:23–26.

———. 1992d. Tying the Cord with the Southern Bear. AN 2:12–16.

———. 1993a. Huron Kinship Terminology. OA 55:35–59.

———. 1993b. Who Are the Cord? AN 1:10–11.

———. 1993c. Linguistically Linking the Petun with the Southern Bear. AN 2:20–26.

———. 1993d. Scanonaenrat. AN 5:28–30.

———. 1993e. Guns and Angelica. AN 6:23–24.

———. 1994. Tsa8enhohi: The Vulture Seen through Huron Eyes. AN 1:31–32.

———. 1995a. Hatindia8enten: They of the Bear People. AN 1:21–28.

———. 1995b. A Unique Feature of the Cord Dialect? AN 6:22–26.

———. 1997. Wendat Dialects and the Development of the Huron Alliance. *Northeast Anthropology* 54:23–36.

———. 2004. *De Religione: Seventeenth-Century Jesuits Telling Their Story in Huron to the Iroquois.* Tulsa: University of Oklahoma Press.

Tanner, Adrian. 1979. *Bringing Home Animals: Religious Ideology and Mode of Production of the Mistassini Cree Hunters.* New York: St. Martin's Press.

Tehariolina, Marguerite Vincent. 1984. *La Nation Huronne: Son histoire, sa culture, son esprit.* Quebec: Editions du Pélican.

Thwaites, Reuben G. 1959. *The Jesuit Relations and Allied Documents.* New York: Pageant.

Tooker, Elisabeth. 1970. Northern Iroquoian Sociopolitical Organization. *American Anthropologist* 72:90–97.

———. 1971. Clans and Moieties in North America. *Current Anthropology* 12(3):357–76.

———. 1978a. The League of the Iroquois: Its History, Politics, and Ritual. In *Handbook of North American Indians*, vol. 15: *Northeast*, ed. Bruce Trigger, 398–406. Washington: Smithsonian Institute.

———. 1978b. Iroquois since 1820. In vol. 15: *Northeast*, 449–65.

———. 1978c. Wyandot. In vol. 15: *Northeast*, 398–406.

Toupin, Robert, s.j. 1996. *Les Écrits de Pierre Potier.* Ottawa: Les Presses de l'Université d'Ottawa.

Trigger, Bruce. 1969. *Huron: Farmers of the North.* New York: Holt, Rinehart and Winston.

———. 1976. *The Children of Aataentsic.* 2 vols. Montreal: McGill-Queen's University Press.

Trudgill, Bruce. 1974. *Sociolinguistics.* New York: Viking Penguin.

Vincent, Marguerite Tehariolina. 1984. *La Nation Huronne.* Quebec: Editions du Pélican.

White, Marian. 1978. Neutral and Wenro. In *Handbook of North American Indians*, vol. 15: *Northeast*, ed. Bruce Trigger, 407–11. Washington: Smithsonian Institute.

Williamson, Ronald, and Debbie Steiss. 2003. A History of Iroquoian Burial Practice. In *Bones of the Ancestors: The Archaeology and Osteobiography of the Moatfield Ossuary*, Mercury Series, Archaeology Paper 163, ed. Ronald Williamson and Susan Pfeiffer, 89–132. Ottawa: Canadian Museum of Civilization.

Woodbury, Hanni. 2003. *Onondaga–English/English–Onondaga Dictionary.* Toronto: University of Toronto Press.

Index

257